# MEEKRAKER

# MEEKRAKER
## *BEGINNINGS...*

J. Bartholomew Walker
*and*
Emma B. Quadrakoff

Quadrakoff Publications Group, LLC
Wilmington, Delaware
USA

Copyright © 2016 Quadrakoff Publications Group, LLC All rights reserved.

Except as noted, All NASB scriptures taken from The New American Standard Bible® Copyright © 1960, 1962, 1963, 1968, 1971, 1972, 1973, 1975, 1977, 1995 by the Lockman Foundation, LaHabra, CA.

Special thanks to the Lockman Foundation for the finest Bible version available; as well as for their permission to use the same. All Scripture passages taken from The Holy Bible, King James Version, are as noted.

ISBN: 978-0-9886945-6-9

All rights reserved. No part of this publication may be reproduced, stored in a retrieval system or transmitted, in any form, or by any means, electronic, mechanical, recorded, photocopied, or otherwise, without the prior written permission of both the copyright owner and the above publisher of this book, except by a reviewer who may quote brief passages in a review.

The scanning, uploading, and distribution of this book via the Internet or via any other means without the permission of the publisher is illegal and punishable by law. Please purchase only authorized electronic editions and do not participate in or encourage electronic piracy of copyrightable materials. Your support of the author's rights is appreciated.

Printed in the United States of America.

Any and all characters appearing that are not in any of the versions of the Bible are fictional. Any resemblance to any living person is strictly coincidental.

*Dedicated to the Father. We ask that you do with it according to your will.*


*Also for Lucy, Bonnie, Gracie and Ann.*

*"Contradictions do not exist. Whenever you think you are facing a contradiction, check your premises. You will find that one of them is wrong."*

Ayn Rand

*"Once you eliminate the impossible, whatever remains, no matter how improbable, must be the truth."*

Arthur Conan Doyle

MeekRaker Monograph 601 "SHÂMAR TO SHARIA: *Biblical Roots and Mechanisms of Islamic Radicalization*" is also available in print and electronic formats:

> "There is a worldwide malignancy "out there" known as Islamic Radicalism. Claiming to be engaging in the work of God, these seemingly insane individuals are "on the march," metastasizing to every location inhabitable by man. Are they merely insane, or is something much more than mere insanity involved? Or is it even a certainty that they are in fact in any way insane?"
> From "SHÂMAR TO SHARIA"

Also available MeekRaker Monograph 603 "Donald Trump Candidacy According to Matthew?" *A Monograph Analyzing the Donald Trump Candidacy from a Biblical Non-Political Perspective* in print and electronic formats:

> "No matter which aspect of his candidacy is examined; he seems to have broken, and continues to break essentially all of the known rules of politics. Is there any rational explanation for this phenomenon? Does the Bible provide any guidance as to how this could be? The process is not new, and not unique to Donald Trump. It is just that it has been long forgotten. Find the explanation; understand the mechanisms; and see if the process can work for you."
> From "Donald Trump Candidacy According to Matthew?"

# *Contents*

**Preface** ---------------------------------------------------------------------- i

**Introduction** ----------------------------------------------------------------- v

**Chapter 1**
*In the Beginning... The Creation* ---------------------------------------- 1

**Chapter 2**
*The Formation* ------------------------------------------------------------ 13

**Chapter 3**
*Emergence of the Breath of Life* ----------------------------------------- 29

**1st Intermission**
*Life and Death - Material and Immaterial* -------------------------------- 51

**Chapter 4**
*You the Man!* -------------------------------------------------------------- 61

**Chapter 5**
*Thoughts, Ideas, and Suggestions* ---------------------------------------- 81

**Chapter 6**
*CJHG   C=J+M  ∴ J=C-M* ------------------------------------------------- 109

**2nd Intermission**
*Laws of Compensatory Blessing-Saying and Sowing* -------------------- 121

**Chapter 7**
*You're a Dead Man!* ------------------------------------------------------------135

**Chapter 8**
*The Case for Adultery* --------------------------------------------------- 149

**Chapter 9**
*Job's Predicament* ------------------------------------------------------ 159

**3rd Intermission**
*Antennas Work* ---------------------------------------------------------- 181

**Chapter 10**
*The Slanderer* ----------------------------------------------------------- 191

**Chapter 11**
*Pericalvaric Apocrypha* ------------------------------------------------- 219

**Chapter 12**
*Reprise* ----------------------------------------------------------------- 247

**About the Title** ------------------------------------------------------- 265

**Glossary** -------------------------------------------------------------- 269

**Bibliography** ---------------------------------------------------------- 279

# PREFACE

For the record, we (yours truly) are not "know it alls." No human is; some just think they are; we don't. To some who read this tome, this may be the impression that could be left, but is simply not so. Admittedly, we (the authors) are not perfect. We have endeavored to present God's truth to the best of our abilities. We have tried to take other's views into consideration, both for wisdom and guidance. Nevertheless, the ultimate test must necessarily be what God said. There is an old expression, reputedly from the Italians, which states: "When you don't know, that is bad, when you don't know you don't know, that is worse." No claims of omniscience are stated or implied anywhere herein.

We suppose that these writings will ultimately get us in a lot of trouble with a lot of people, but that is really not the issue. Our goal is not to offend anyone. The sole concern is truth. We are not trying to do anything other than to provide an unbiased read of the Word of God.

James Abraham Garfield, our 20th president is credited with having said: "The truth will set you free, but first it will make you miserable." I (I/we will interchange singular and plural from here on.) think it is fair to say that the beauty of this is that we each set our own level of misery, thus we each have control over the same. Why? Because we each can and in reality do decide which has a higher priority, that of being "right" or that of being correct, and we each determine the precise emotional costs involved in this transition.

Thus I might add, that an inverse relationship exists between the avoidance of misery and the acquisition of truth; and a direct relationship exists between the acquisition of truth and the acquisition of freedom. So decisions must be made regarding priorities; feeling good about ourselves; or knowing the truth and being set or made free. Again we ourselves individually determine the cost. Without a doubt, some will determine that the cost is simply too great.

Science and the Word of God are very often in conflict, at least that is the common belief. How old is the world? How long has man been on the earth? Evolution or intelligent design? When encountering these questions, one must usually be forced to choose between science and the Word of God. One must choose between being a "man of science" or a "believer," because they are generally considered to be mutually exclusive. If one agrees that words mean things, then an unbiased fair read of God's Word presents no such paradox. But one must read what God actually said, not merely what one thinks He said, what one was told He said, what one wished He said, or would rather He had said.

This effort by no means represents any type of attempt to come up with crazy notions that endeavor in any way to impeach the Word of God, in order to make a best selling book or movie. In fact, the reverse is true. This is all about the literal "Word of God;" about understanding God's Word as it is actually written.

There is the old "saw" about the tree falling in the woods, and whether or not there is any sound, if there is no one who is able to hear it. The answer of course depends upon one's definition of "sound." If sound were to be defined as the movement of air within the frequency range of an audio spectrum, then of course the sound exists without regard to any biological apparatus capable of detection being present. Surely a rock, which is perched on a precipice; and then is somehow caused to move slightly and then release its potential energy from the effects of that sound; would prove the existence of *something* by its fall.

If on the other hand, as many dictionaries define sound, it is the sensation produced in a hearing apparatus which constitutes and is in fact a prerequisite for sound, then the answer would clearly be no, as it would then be the *perception* of the vibrations that defines sound, rather than the *existence* of the vibratory energy.

Should it be the case that a group of individuals were all in the woods at the time of the fall, any of those who were deaf could quite truthfully argue that there was no sound, as the more common definition requires the perception of the observer. Others could quite truthfully argue that there was a sound because they heard it. So both would be correct. We have a situation where two mutually exclusive and contradictory statements exist simultaneously and are both true. By definition, there was a sound according to those who heard it, and there was no sound to those who did not. Yet the physical phenomenon that precipitated the discussion either existed or it did not.

The reason for this; is because the truth or falsity of the existence of a "sound" according to the second and more common definition, is based solely upon reality; irrespective of actuality. Reality being defined as what is perceived, actuality being defined as what in fact exists. (Solipsism reserved for a future discussions; if possible.)

Although defining a phenomenon based upon reality might be a very good tool for analyzing an individual, (as in a Rorschach test), it falls far short for an objective analysis of a phenomenon. As a phenomenon, whatever it is, if it exists, clearly exists independently of its recognition, acceptance or belief. One can truthfully state that there was no sound because he or she did not hear it. But to state that the tree did not fall, or that there was no disturbance in the air that could have produced a "sound" had the person been closer, had more acute hearing, been in an environment with less background noise, or been paying closer attention, is clearly false and can be very dangerous if objective truth (actuality) is what is being sought.

If you can temporarily set aside any preconceived notions about what it is generally believed what it is that God said, and look at what He actually did say, then come with us and judge for yourself.

MEEKRAKER *Beginnings...*

# INTRODUCTION

The Bible is a book about redemption. Although it contains a certain level of historical factual information, it is by no means a historical reference book. Neither does the order of appearance of the books necessarily correlate to either the dates they were written, or the dates when the events occurred. When these chronological discrepancies appear, we will document the evidence as best as we can to illustrate this.

For the record, there is no complete agreement about the number of books, or even which books should be included in the standard "Bible." We will concern ourselves solely with those 66 books which contemporary consensus generally believes constitute the "Word of God," as contained in versions such as the KJV, NASB, Amplified KJV, NIV etc. This is not to say that some of the "Apocrypha" (hidden things) writings are not or should not be a part of the "Word," but only that we will not be considering them at this time. I suspect that there are more than an ample supply of ideas contained in this text to create sufficient controversy among many scriptural scholars.

This work is based solely on the writings which are generally accepted as the Word of God; without introducing any additional writings whose authenticity would also be a matter of controversy. Thus the "Prime Directive," in this effort is or was to use only these generally accepted books.

This approach represents a kind of "two edged sword." On the one hand, information which is likely completely accurate and quite revealing, is purposely omitted because its source is not considered as completely reliable or authentic. Unfortunately, this can result in the deliberate omission of what very likely represent additional Divine truth. On the other hand, since all the sources used generally are all agreed as authentic, they are unimpeachable.

A distinction should be made between the use of the terms translation and version. A translation should be precisely that. Two individuals who spoke entirely different languages witnessing any particular event, should result in the same version of the recollection of said event upon translation. Translators for foreign dignitaries should be able to translate the words of the dignitary, so that the listener knows in their own language, precisely what it is or was that the dignitary said in theirs. If successful, this is an accurate translation; or perhaps better stated; to the extent it is successful, the translation is accurate.

But language can be a slippery thing. Often times no words exist in another language which convey the precise meaning of the original. This generally will result in additional words being used to describe the idea or phenomenon. How would a television be described to George Washington? However this would be done, it would undoubtedly begin with "It is like," as no words for this device existed in the language of Washington's time. Once again, to the extent that an adequate description is provided; irrespective of the number of words required, the "translation" would be equally accurate.

It would be much easier to for us to understand the phenomena of Washington's time then the reverse, because if one is willing to do the research, much of that information already exists historically. But the reverse would be much more difficult, since it is likely that the word "internet" did not exist in Washington's time; neither would he be able to research the available materials of his time and obtain an understanding of it.

Thus, even assuming 100% accuracy in translation is desired, there still exits an inherent inescapable tendency for translations to become versions. The truth is altered simply because no perfect translation is possible 100% of the time.

Unfortunately, "versions" can also occur deliberately. When something in the Bible disagrees with what the bible scholar or scholars believes or believe; it is the Bible that must be "wrong," the easiest culprit of course being the translation. So a word that will better describe and is more consistent with what the scholar believes the Bible means, as opposed to what it actually states, is substituted for what would otherwise be the best available translation.

It is believed that the Bible was originally written in continuous form without punctuation chapters or verses.  Although the addition of these devices is often convenient and usually makes reading and "understanding" easier, they can and do sometimes result in misunderstanding. The same is true with the addition of titles and subtitles to the original manuscripts.  Often these added titles and subtitles can and will result in the misinterpretation of the meaning.  Again, we will do our best to present the evidence as best we can for clarity of meaning.

With respect to the original terminology, we will also do our best to represent the exact meanings(s) of the original.  Not being fluent in Hebrew or Greek, and particularly the Hebrew used at that time, this is by no means an easy task.  As stated, different words can have subtle different meanings, which can result in huge differences when applied to the Scriptures. This can at first appear almost silly, and those that actually are, are not included herein. But others, which may at first seem silly; at least until the implications are realized, can provide immense understanding of the subject matter.

It must be noted that the information provided about the meanings of some of the original terminology may appear excessive to some. This was done purposely in order to provide all available evidence to the reader.  Although it would have been easier to provide more brief definitions; deliberately including only those definitions which were believed to be consistent with a particular interpretation, our view was that this would have been intellectually dishonest.

Most Freemasons define Freemasonry as a system of morality, veiled in allegory, and illustrated by symbols.  Here the use of allegory is by design, in order to "veil" this system of morality, because of many years of persecution.  Some Freemasons forget this veiling, and take quite literally, things that are allegorical by design; many things which often times could not possibly be true. Here, the allegory is erroneously considered to be the literal truth.

In the case of the Bible, the opposite is often the case. Many things in the Bible are literally true, but today are considered at best allegory by many, because it does not seem that they could possibly be literally true. This is not to say that allegory does not exist anywhere in the Bible. But rather, that all that is seemingly untrue or does not seem to make sense, is not necessarily allegorical, but rather is often merely misunderstood; and there exists a plethora of reasons for these misunderstandings.

Finally, we are not experienced or professional writers. I state this not because this is not obvious to the reader, but because we want it known that we are also aware of this fact.

.

# Chapter 1

## In the Beginning…
## The Creation

*"1: In the beginning God created the heavens and the earth.
2: The earth was formless and void and darkness was over the surface (face) of the deep, and the Spirit of God was moving over the surface (face) of the waters."*[1.1]

The year was circa 4000 BC; approximately 6 thousand years ago—at least that is what is generally believed to be so.

There is however, a minor problem with this belief; said problem seeming to stem from the fact that nowhere does any indication whatsoever of this timeframe appear. There is no Scriptural reference as to when any of this actually occurred. For some reason, most people generally believe that God created the world and all of its forms in about a week, and sometime during or shortly after that week Adam hit the scene, lost a rib maybe at breakfast, sinned at either lunch or dinner, and was ejected on or about that very same day. Thus, because of this belief; the actual age of the earth necessarily must be about one week or older than when the clock started running after Adam became "persona non grata."

The truth is that one might as well assign any particular year of their choosing to this event or these events, as not so much as a clue is provided therein. As long as one chooses a date that is at least 6 thousand years ago or more, any year one might choose would then necessarily be equally not inconsistent Scripturally, since there is no reference whatsoever at this point. Four thousand five hundred million years, as science states or used to state; or 6 thousand years, as many believe; have equal Scriptural validity. Some tend to use the terminology of four thousand five hundred million years, rather than four and one half billion, because of certain geology professors who insisted upon this nomenclature, and old habits are tough to break.

But the Bible is not a history book. Neither is it a scientific text, a biological text; nor is it an anthropology text. Historical and other "scientific" types of information contained in the Bible, are generally provided as required, for understanding the lessons and other information contained therein. Thus, the Bible is incomplete as a historical reference by design. This in no way detracts from its credibility; secular arguments notwithstanding. The Bible is concerned with redemption and salvation; essentially being a handbook in this regard. It is also an excellent guide as to how to live one's life while maximizing profits; although not by the methods normally and usually employed.

Thus, given the overwhelming scientific evidence that more than suggests that earth is much older than 6 thousand years; it simply seems prudent to side with science, as science has substantial and arguably irrefutable evidence of something about which Genesis is entirely silent.

As of the time of this writing, news stories are on the Internet about a surprising discovery concerning the climate in which humans were able to live over 900 thousand years ago. Of course this presents a double problem; in that it not only establishes scientifically that the earth is at least 900 thousand years old; but also that in their view, humans were living on the earth at that time. But this current "discovery," whether true or not, in no way contradicts the "rightly divided" Word of God in this regard as it is written. One might find that the 6 thousand year viewpoint is reasonably Scripturally contradicted later, but that is getting ahead of things.

Other than presuming the date that this event of creation occurred, all else seems pretty self-evident. The only *reasonable* explanation for the creation of the heavens and the earth is intelligent design; and Genesis 1:1 tells us precisely "Who," although providing not a clue therein as to precisely *when* it was that He actually did so.

But from here on, things becomes somewhat problematic. In the very first two verses of the very first book, something else of great significance seems to have happened. As it reads, God no sooner created the earth and it appears that the earth was "formless and void," "and darkness was over the surface of the deep, and the Spirit of God was moving over the surface of the waters."

Some may refer to this as "The Genesis Gap." This is a bit of a misnomer though, as it implies that there is only one. Various explanations exist as to why this gap does not exist. Some believe that for this gap to exist, this would require God to be less than omnipotent.[1,2]

But by this very same reasoning, there then should be no war, no famine, no crime and no sin. Can it then likewise be said that the existence of any or all of these would also mean that God is not omnipotent?

Clearly God now has, and at that time had, the *power* to stop it all. Yet, He does and did not. The issue is not one of capabilities, but rather is one of free will. Simply because God chooses to allow us to have free will with respect to making decisions; some of which are evil and/or wicked; in no way implies that He is weak. The fact that He *chooses* to permit these things to happen is completely unrelated to his *power* to stop them. And as we will see, He did in fact intervene; although perhaps not at the time when many believe that He should have.

There are several possible interpretations of this "formless (some translations are "without form") and void." The easiest being that this refers to the contents of or on the earth. The earth was created, but there was nothing on the earth that was created. It was completely void, *and* formless. Void meaning containing nothing (no-thing); and formless meaning essentially the same thing; "less any forms." This may seem reasonable, although perhaps a bit redundant. Another interpretation of course being; that this means that the earth was somehow without form, in the sense of not being the oblate spheroid it is today, or any other recognizable shape.

Many, if not most, believe that this state (without form and void) of the earth represents a transitional state between nothingness and the creation of the earth; as though for some reason, an omnipotent God had to create the earth in stages. The state of the earth at this time is often referred to as "chaos." The Message Bible states: "First this: God created the Heavens and Earth – all you see, all you don't see. Earth was a soup of nothingness, a bottomless emptiness, and inky blackness."[1.3]

This theory seems to be stating that "the earth" which was created, was in fact not earth at all; but rather some sort of "pre-earth mass," (authors' terminology) which for some reason is simply referred to as "earth" in the beginning of Genesis; but the actual earth not being created until afterwards. This theory also then necessarily requires that God would be the author or the creator of chaos.

Earth, Mars, Venus etc. are all planets. In order to be considered a planet, certain criteria must be met; criteria which in the opinion of some, the former planet Pluto, as of this writing, no longer satisfies. Pluto is thus no longer considered a planet. The term "planet" means wanderer, as that is how they appeared to move in the sky with respect to the stars that appeared relatively fixed in their individual movements. When we have planets, we call them planets, and usually by name. When we have asteroid belts, comets, stars, or black holes; we call them such, because they are not planets, but something else. In our solar system, the asteroid belt is called such, because a belt of space debris is not considered a planet.

Neither do we need, nor did we need to know the nature of the surface of a planet; nor what forms might exist upon it, to call it a planet. But to be considered a planet, which earth clearly is, it must have form, and thus cannot be without form. Whether or not any forms exist *on* said planet, or what the same may be, is irrelevant in general with respect to the planet designation; and is irrelevant specifically with respect to the earth.

Now one might ask why God would create chaos, when He was trying to create the earth; and His Word clearly states that He succeeded? There is also a second question that necessarily arises: If God had created the earth in stages, why would it be necessary for us to know that the earth was created in stages? It would have been one thing if God merely created the earth this way, but it is an entirely different thing for Him to make sure that we *knew* that the earth was created this way.

Everything in the Bible is there for a reason. Isaiah 40:8 tells us: "The grass withers, the flower fades, But the word of our God stands forever."[1.4] Thus, including this description of events was done with purpose; and the understanding that it would be of value for all generations and ages. This is especially important; if it is remembered that the primary purpose of the Bible is redemption; it being an instruction manual relating to the same.

Obviously, no one actually witnessed these creative events, because no one had been created at the time. That would not have helped much anyway, because it seems that there was not yet any light with which to see these events. Thus there is a clear purpose for the inclusion of this seemingly two staged event—so that we could *later* interpret the significance of the same.

It seems reasonable; that in the beginning, God created the heavens and the earth just as the book states, and not chaos or a deep or a pre-earth mass. Then something happened which made the earth without form (or formless) and void; that after all being the way it reads. Most translations and versions do not actually state *"and then,"* but that is the only explanation that seems to make any degree of sense. Although it must be stated, that the *Interlinear* version on *Scripture4all.org* does include in their translation: "she (the earth) became."[1.5]

As we will see, there is also the issue of the water(s). No explanation is provided as to the origin of these water(s). Water has no form. It will take the form of any container in which it is placed. Water will seek its own level. Water is non-compressible, and is generally necessary for almost, if not all, forms of life as we know them. Water also has an unusual characteristic; in that it's maximum density is achieved at about four degrees Celsius, and as it further cools, crystals are formed and thus it's density decreases. This is very important for life; because it causes ice to float; something that is crucial for aquatic life forms.

At this time, this "pre-earth mass" appears to have been either covered in water, or included substantial amounts of water; water which the Spirit of God was moving or hovering over the surface of. Since the earth of today is covered approximately two thirds by water; would it not be reasonable to assume that the earth which was created in verse 1, became formless and void and was ultimately covered with water; covered with this same water that had already existed on and as part of the earth; hence requiring no separate reference to the water's creation?

Moses is generally believed to be the "author" of Genesis; and so of course, he could not also have been present during creation of the earth. How then did he know what to write? Generally the Scriptural prophets are considered to be individuals who some how have knowledge of the future; as exemplified by prophets such as Isaiah, Daniel, Ezekiel, and of course the Apocalypsa; (revealed things) which is now often called the "Book of Revelation." The assumption here being that prophesy is always concerned with an unknown future; after all what possible value would there be to a prophesy that is merely recollecting the past?

Nevertheless, the Mosaic authorship of Genesis proves there is tremendous value in recollecting the past; when mankind does not have this information, and said information is pertinent to redemption; which again, is what the main purpose of the Bible is believed to be. Even if one believes that Moses did not write Genesis; someone most certainly did, so the same still holds. In contradistinction to prophesy; which is concerned with unknown future events, this phenomenon, which we could here call *"retrophesy;"* (authors' terminology) is concerned with revealing unknown events that happened in the past.

Without digressing too much, a fair argument can be made that the Book of Revelation contains some information about some events that had already happened. Again, the original title of The Apocalypse or Apocalypsa, meaning "revealed things," does not necessarily discriminate with respect to the timeframe of the occurrence of these "revealed things." Just assuming this is true for a moment to illustrate a point; we could only know if these events were "retrosophical" or "retrospohetic" events; meaning that they had already occurred; if and when we had other reasonable evidence that these events had in fact already happened.

If any part of John's prophesy contained in the Book of Revelation; (not really prophesy in the usual sense of revelation by divine inspiration, but rather in this case, recollection by actual witnessing; at least from Chapter 4 onward) concerned any historical events; but we have or had no evidence these events had already occurred; we would probably erroneously assume they had not yet happened. Thus, we would be assuming quite erroneously; that John is speaking prophesy, when he in fact is engaging in retrophesy; irrespective of the method by which the information provided to him was obtained by him. In the case of the recollection of creation contained in Genesis, assuming we believe the Word; we have no choice but to know this must necessarily be retrophesy; as it is a recollection of events that had already happened, as the earth is here and so are we.

Jeremiah is generally considered a prophet. Prophets of course generally engage in prophesy; loosely translated as "speak before." Jeremiah or "Yirmeyah or Yirmeyahuw" literally means, "Jah will rise;" Jah meaning "the Lord" or Yehovah.[1.6]

In Jeremiah 4:23-28, we are told:

> *"I looked on the earth, and behold, it was formless and void; And to the heavens, and they had no light. I looked on the mountains, and behold, they were quaking,*
> *And all the hills moved to and fro. I looked, and behold, there was no man,*
> *And all the birds of the heavens had fled.*
> *I looked, and behold, the fruitful land was a wilderness,*
> *And all its cities were pulled down Before the LORD, before His fierce anger.*
> *For thus says the LORD, "The whole land shall be a desolation, Yet I will not execute a complete destruction. "For this the earth shall mourn And the heavens above be dark, Because I have spoken, I have purposed, And I will not change My mind, nor will I turn from it."*[1.7]

One can find no historical or Scriptural account of this ever happening after Genesis 1:2; particularly given the seeming absence (not mere geocentric darkening) of the luminaries. It does state regarding the heavens, that "they had no light." It is also interesting that it appears that it is Jeremiah speaking in verses 23-26; and it is God that is speaking in verses 27 and 28; and that Jeremiah is speaking in past tense; and with respect to the earth, it is God speaking in future tense.

God speaks of not executing a "complete destruction." But whether the pre-earth mass represents a transitional state from nothingness to creation, as many believe; or represents a residual formless and void chaos because of the destruction of the original earth referenced in Genesis 1:1; the result would be the same.

Either of these would represent something, and not nothing; and thus must necessarily be less than complete destruction.

Although Jeremiah states that the mountains were "quaking" and "all the hills moved to and fro;" it is also true he does not actually say that the mountains were "pulled down," as he stated were all the cities. And again, God does say that the destruction would *not* be complete. Whether this merely means incomplete because the mountains, unlike *all* the cities, did not actually fall; or because it was the case that the earth was left "without form and void" ie: the "pre-earth mass;" one cannot say with certainty based upon this passage. It is also worth posing the question of whether all the cities being pulled down; and the mountaintops, even if still remaining; would in any way preclude the use of the term without form and void?

In addition, God does not say that the *earth* below will be darkened, as in the case of an eclipse; but rather the "heavens above be dark." God's first three proclamations have to do with the earth; but the dark, refers to the heavens; and not to the earth. Of course if the heavens above are (be) dark; barring the presence of any other light source; the earth would necessarily be dark. But if the earth becomes dark; it does not necessarily imply that the heavens are also dark. If it was just the earth that became dark, it is fair to suspect that God would have said this; but He did not.

Here in Jeremiah, either there were no longer any luminaries; or the light from the luminaries was somehow completely blocked; not just with respect to the earth; but also in the heavens above. This likely did not happen before there was any light; because there would be no need for the statement about darkness had there never been any light. There is usually a belief that the luminaries referenced in Genesis were the very first. But a valid argument exists that this is not so. Thus it seems that some type of luminaries; or some other source of light, may very well have existed prior to the luminaries referenced in Genesis.

It appears Jeremiah is recollecting what he had seen in a vision, yet as stated; no evidence whatsoever can be found that it had happened during Jeremiah's time. Furthermore, no clear

Scriptural reference (other than Jeremiah) can be found that indicates this will ever happen in the future; whether again or otherwise. Even the most pessimistic reading of the Book of Revelation does not fit this description very well at all.

Revelation 8:12 tells us:

> *"The fourth angel sounded, and a third of the sun and a third of the moon and a third of the stars were struck, so that a third of them would be darkened and the day would not shine for a third of it, and the night in the same way."*[1.8]

This is far different. And the other New Testament corroborations of Revelation 8:12, such as contained in the various versions of Mark and Matthew, clearly refer to, and actually state, post tribulation; which clearly occurs near the end of time, and not near the beginning.

Jeremiah speaks of no forms, void, no light, no man, no birds, (assuming birds is literal, rather than the bird which symbolizes Ba, the Egyptian soul entity) wilderness, of mountains and hills rocking; and all the cities were pulled down. This is clearly a pretty grim picture. Either way you read formless; either an earth without form or containing no forms; there appears to be no one left; nothing left. If this particular passage of Jeremiah is prophesy and not retrophesy; and barring God intervening for the earth yet again; this being something for which there is no Scriptural evidence; Jesus would be then necessarily returning to nothingness; if the timing of this was anytime in the future, i.e. between now and the return of Jesus.

Revelation 19:19 tells us:

> *"and I saw the beast and the kings of the earth and their armies assembled to make war against Him who sat on the horse and against His army."*[1.9]

Clearly this in no way represents the conditions "on the ground," as described by Jeremiah.

The second half of the very next verse, Jeremiah 4:29, in fact states: "Every city is forsaken, And no man dwells in them."[1.10] The key word here is forsaken.

It is a fair question to ask if Jeremiah's description necessarily must represent prophesy; or could the same also be said if it were retrophesy? It must be either prophesy, retrophesy, current events or nonsense. There seems to be no record that this event took place circa Jeremiah's time; neither is there credible Scriptural evidence that it will ever take place. Thus, this leaves either retrophesy or nonsense.

It is also fair to ask if this could have also been similar to what Moses experienced when he wrote of things long before his time? Both Jeremiah and Moses received revelation directly from God. There seems to be no reason to preclude Moses experiencing a similar event for his retrosophical revelations.

Looking through *St. Joseph New Catholic Edition Bible*, (1962) an interesting footnote to Genesis 1:1 can be found. "1. <u>Created</u> both the Hebrew word and the context show that a real creation, i.e. a <u>making out of nothing</u>, is meant. This Hebrew word is used only in reference to God in the Old Testament."[1.11] (emphasis added)

The actual word for "created" referenced therein is "*bara.*" "1254 bara, a prim. root; (absol.) to create; (qualified) to cut down (a wood), select, feed (as formative processes): - choose, create (creator), cut down, dispatch, do, make (fat)."[1.12] "The verb expresses creation out of nothing..."[1.13]

Clearly, this word is reserved for Divine acts of bringing something into existence from nothing.

Based upon this, there is a "two pronged" test for whether or not the bringing into existence of something qualifies as bara. Firstly; it must be God that either directly or indirectly causes the manifestation to come into being. Secondly; said manifestation cannot in any way be the result of the use of anything that currently exists in the material realm at the time of the creating. There can be no raw materials utilized; neither can it involve the transformation of anything material.

Words mean things, and perfect synonyms are difficult,

especially in translations. Actually, it is not certain that there are any perfect synonyms within the same language. In the beginning, it was the heavens and the earth that was created. In fact, the terms "created" or "creature," do not appear again in Genesis until verses 21 and 20 respectively.

Thus it was the earth that God created, i.e. made out of nothing. If one believes that our actual earth was made slowly or in stages, for whatever reason(s); then one must also believe that it was only this "pre earth-mass" which was actually created, (bara) and not the final product of the earth as it was/is when it was completed. This is because these subsequent changes clearly do not qualify as creation (bara); and Genesis does not in any way state or imply otherwise.

In order for this piecemeal approach to be true, then the finished product (earth) *was not* what was created in the beginning; even though Genesis tells us precisely that it was in fact the earth that *was* created in the beginning.

It then also must be believed that the transformation from whatever was created in the beginning; this pre-earth mass into the final product; earth; somehow constitutes bara. This by definition cannot be; as transformation requires that something be made from something; and bara requires that something be made from nothing.

It is both fair and Scripturally consistent to believe that earth means earth, as we commonly believe it to be. It was first created, and *then* earth became without form and void. The incomplete destruction of the created earth; as per the Jeremiac retrophesy; resulted in the land being totally or almost totally covered by the already existing water. As will be seen in the next chapters, it is or was this "chaos" that the Spirit of God hovered or moved over slowly, but not as commonly believed. What He instituted at that juncture were changes, and not creation. As previously stated, the word "created" does not appear again in Genesis until verse 21.

# Chapter 2

## The Formation

The remainder of Genesis 1:2, and 1:3-5 tells us:

*"...and darkness was over the surface (face) of the deep, and the Spirit of God was moving over the surface (face) of the waters"*
*"Then God said,"*
*Let there be light"; and there was light. God saw that the light was good; and God separated the light from the darkness. God called the light day, and the darkness He called night And there was evening and there was morning, one day."*[2.1]

This is very interesting phrasing. "Darkness was over the surface," as opposed to the surface was dark, or a dark surface. As written; there is an implication of "darkness" which is different than that which we usually consider darkness to be; which of course is merely the absence of light. Light is not the absence of darkness, but rather the presence of light. Light is the entity. When it is present, there is light, the default being darkness. One need do nothing for darkness, but light requires some type of energy. The implication here by the use of darkness as both a noun and the subject of the sentence, is that darkness *is* some type of entity, rather than the usual default condition of merely the absence of its opposite. "Darkness *was*," as opposed to "was dark."

The actual Hebrew word used which is translated as darkness, is "2822 choshek, from 2821; the *dark;* hence (lit.) *darkness;* fig. *misery, destruction, death, ignorance, sorrow, wickedness:* - dark (-ness), night, obscurity."[2.2]

But if we look to John 1: 3-5 it states:

> *"All things came into being through Him, and apart from Him nothing came into being that has come into being. In Him was life, and the life was the Light of men. The Light shines in the darkness, and the darkness did not comprehend it."*[2.3]

Here John is speaking about Messiah. "He" was present from "the beginning" and onward. Thus the essence of what was ultimately to become Messiah, was present when creation began; as all that was created came through Him. It does not say *by* Him; thus the use of "through" implying at least three entities: that which created, that which was created, and that which creation was through. This is likely one of the reasons for the use of the plural in later passages of Genesis.

The use of "comprehend" regarding the darkness, clearly provides characteristics not generally attributed to normal darkness. An interesting note, is that the Interlinear Bible translates this word "comprehend" as "overtake."[2.4]

The original Greek word used by John for darkness is "4652 skoteinos, from 4655 opaque, i.e. (fig.) benighted; - dark, full of darkness."[2.5] The root of this word also is utilized in the formation of other words describing a cover, such as skene; which means a tent.[2.6]

There is a slight problem with the concept in John of a cover, a tent or darkness not being able to comprehend or overtake the light. Would it be reasonable to think this possible, based upon the above definitions only? How would it be the case that darkness could be comprehending anything? This would require intellect of some type; this being something which the mere absence of light most certainly does not have. If the word overtake is used, again the same question arises. How is it that literal darkness could overtake light? A diminishment in the level of light in essence could do this, but the active party would then be the light and not the darkness. If the concept of a covering is the true meaning; which it appears to be here; then if God is not directing this covering to overtake the light, some other entity must be. Thus there is necessarily an implication in John, of some "force" capable of comprehending or causing a physical cover to overtake the light. This then by definition, is the force of darkness.

Thus the two original words that are used for darkness; "skoteinos" and "choshek;" define darkness as: darkness as the mere absence of light; darkness as a physical covering literally; and necessarily an implication of substantial wickedness or evil, respectively. There are strong implications in the meaning of the first word, that the lack of any light was perhaps only a secondary and an indirect result of this covering or tent; rather than merely the absence of light due to the absence of any source of light. This concept of a covering or tent; as opposed to merely the resultant lack of light; gives an entirely different conception as to precisely what was likely going on at this time. It would likely be a mistake to assume that this "darkness" was merely because of the absence of the luminaries; and it is in fact arguable that had the luminaries been present, this would have little or no effect upon the existence of this cover. Furthermore, at least with respect to whatever was under the cover, the same logically would be largely or completely unaffected by these light sources.

This is further evident, because this darkness or cover was not *on* the deep; such as "darkness has fallen on us; but rather *over* the surface (face) of the deep. This suggests that some type of physical gap may have existed between the "darkness" or "covering," and the surface of the deep; but no further information about this is provided therein.

The word "surface" does not seem to appear anywhere in Strong's Concordance or Vine's Complete Expository Dictionary. Thus, the word face, is most likely the better translation.

"Face" (Strong 6440) is the word *"paneh."* [2.7] Paneh seems to be a rather complex word with many, and sometimes mutually exclusive meanings; thus unfortunately, provides no clear revelation. Thus it is probably fair to assume it just means face.

This darkness was over the face of the "deep." Most readers of the Scriptures probably have no idea what "the deep" is, other than whatever it is or was, must certainly have been quite deep. (The authors for many years did not.)

The original word translated as deep is "8415 Tehowm or Tehom from 1949; an *abyss* (as a *surging* mass of water), espec. the *deep* (the *main* sea or the subterranean *wate- supply*): - deep (place), depth." "1949 huwm a prim. root {comp. 2000}; to *make an uproar*, or *agitate* greatly: - destroy, move, make a noise, put, ring again."[2.8]

Thus this "deep" then likely represents a surging mass of water, perhaps a very large mass of water or subterranean water supply. ("Waters" definition to follow.) This is the same water of which the Scriptures make no clear or direct reference with respect to its origins.

This likely was very similar to what planet Earth would look like if all of the dry land were somehow leveled or destroyed; say by earthquakes or some other massive destructive force(s). Or to put it another way; the conditions that would result if the land elevations became less than the height of the water level. Islands are in reality merely mountains whose elevations are greater than the height of the surrounding water levels. The Hawaiian Islands are or were believed to be the tallest mountains in the world, if their elevation is measured from the ocean floor.

So it is both fair and Scripturally accurate to translate this part of Genesis 1:2 into English as: "A covering, probably wicked in origin or representing wickedness; was over, but not on, the face or surface of a large sea, subterranean water supply or surging water supply."

At some point, the *"Spirit (breath) of God was (gently) moving over the face of the waters."* Whether immediately or 1,000 million or more years later is neither stated nor implied. Was it these same waters of unknown origin over which existed this "cover?" If not, than what or which waters was it?

The original word for "waters" here is actually "4225 Machbereth from 2266; a *junction*, ie. seam or sewed piece; - coupling." 2266 "chabar a prim. root; to *join* (lit. or fig.); spec. (by means of spells) to *fascinate:* - charm-(er), be compact, couple (together), have fellowship with, heap up, join (self, together), league."[2.9]

Thus it appears that the Spirit of God was gently moving not over water as we use the term today; but rather over the face of some sort of a joining, coupling, junction, seam or sewed piece; specifically created by fascination or charm. Often the word fascinate is used to mean awe or amazement, but that is not accurate. There is a sense in the meaning of this word of gaining one's attention to the point where all else is disregarded; as resulting in a truly captivated audience. The most immediate questions of course being: What and where was this seam or joint; and who or what was it that did the fascinating or charming, not to mention why?

There were only three physical or quasi-physical things that Scripturally we know existed at that time germane to this. The actual water supply or sea (the deep) under the cover, the covering (darkness), and whatever was outside the covering (the original heavens).

Based upon the nature of water, it does not seem likely that this seam or joint would be water to water, as water sort of does that automatically without any fascination. The covering was actually over the water and not on the water, so it does not seem likely that the cover was seamed to the water. The covering could have been seamed to itself, but that would imply that there were at least two coverings, or some sort of a gap(s) in the cover; a proposition for which there is no Scriptural evidence or suggestion. It seems most likely that this seam or joint represented a junction between the outer part of the cover, and the original heavens that were outside the cover. Today we might call this an "interface" between the cover and the heavens.

It is also important to remember that the root of this word for seam, (chabar) has a specific meaning related to the causation of the seam by fascination or charming. This necessarily implies the existence of some type of entity capable of successfully engaging in fascinating or charming. It is also important to remember the figurative use of the word darkness to mean wickedness or evil. It simply does not seem to make any sense that God would put this covering over the waters; thus creating a seam or interface between the covering and the heavens by fascination or charming; and then move gently over it in order to remove it.

It seems reasonable; perhaps even certain; that another entity was involved. An entity that could fascinate or charm, and prefers darkness to light.

Genesis 1:3 tells us:

> *"Then God said, "Let there be light"; and there was light."*[2.10]

No reference to the word "let" can be found prior to Genesis 24:14. Thus we are forced to use the term as to permit or to command.

It is very important to remember that this "light" does not refer to the "creation" of the luminaries; as that did not happen until later. Depending on how it is read, the luminaries were not made until either the third or fourth "day." How did God "create" this light? He spoke the light into existence—sort of. Regarding these very matters, Psalms 33:9 states: "For He spoke, and it was done; He commanded, and it stood fast."[2.11]

It is interesting to note, that there is no evidence that in any way even suggests this particular "light" was created (bara) by God at that time; but rather that the light manifested solely by His command and/or His permission. Let the light shine, "Lazarus come forth." The implication being that the "latent" light was present and was merely released upon His command.

Alternatively, "Let light be"[2.12] is the translation that is closest to the original. This can of course be interpreted in a completely different way. Given the context, it seems quite possible that there may have been a specific intended recipient to this command; i.e. the entity which caused the darkness/cover; and caused the seam by a spell or charm. Today, if an older sibling is bullying a younger sibling, we might say to the older sibling: "Leave him/her alone," or "Let him/her be." Thus "leave the light alone," or "let (the) light be," is perhaps another reasonable interpretation of these events.

God did not merely state His intentions, then engage in some additional activity, and then there was light. The very act of Him speaking caused the light to manifest, and according to Psalms 33:9, it held. Irrespective of how it cursorily may read, this seems to represent nothing less than the beginning of a major battle; said battle being between God and the forces of darkness. It also should be remembered that since there is a figurative meaning or interpretation of wickedness associated with or related to the darkness; thus logically, there then should be a figurative meaning or interpretation of goodness associated with or related to the meaning of the light.

An argument could be made that this seam; "Machbereth/chabar," represents the junction between the acquired domain of the charmer or fascinator, and the rightful domain of God. Thus God moved gently; in order that He remain in His rightful domain while engaging in battle with the enemy.

Genesis 1:4-5 tells us:

> *"God saw that the light was good; and God separated the light from the darkness.*
> *God called the light day, and the darkness He called night And there was evening and there was morning, one day."*[2.13]

A note about the use of the term "day:"

Common usage of the word "day," usually refers to the period of daylight; or a period of 24 hours; or a period of activity. The first two are generally presumed to be the case when analyzing a "day" referenced in Genesis. Thus, the reasonable conclusion being that the entire process took less than one week. This is problematic for several reasons. The luminary from which we derive the use of the 24 hour day and the day/night cycles did not exist until later. One could argue that the later creation of this luminary was to create in relative perpetuity; a means of continuing the periods of time that was either required or chosen by God to complete His work. That of course then necessarily implies that an omnipotent God either could not do it any faster; or for whatever reason(s) did not wish to.

And among the many possible definitions of the word "day," the actual word used here in verse 5 is: "3117 Yowm, from an unused root mean. To be hot: a day (as the warm hours) whether lit. (from sunrise to sunset, or from one sunset to the next), or fig. (a space of time defined by an associated term) -age,… season…"[2.14]

Here we see that the definition of "day;" cannot exclusively be considered to consist of a 24 hour period. It is interesting that this meaning of hot; is essentially still in use today as an indication that someone is in the middle of an activity, and experiencing a considerable degree of success. Whether it is the case the dice are "hot;" or when someone states: "Leave me alone I'm hot;" the meaning is the same. They are in a process and wish to continue it until completion, because things are going well. A still somewhat current slang version would be *"smokin."*

Thus this term translated as day, Yowm, (sometimes spelled *Yom*), can easily refer to a period or "season" or "age" relating to activity, and can refer to a rather long period of time, based upon either activity or lack of activity; which is precisely what Genesis is describing. Without getting too much into the differences between time as *"Chiros"* (Chiro - hand as in chiropractor - chiro -hand, practica practical, easily done by hand) and *"Kronos;"* (as in chronometer) there is nonetheless a difference. The use of the term

"Day" as any measurement of time (chiros) can be based upon events, (hand of God) rather than the rotation of the earth or the movement of the "hands" (interesting) of a clock (Kronos/Chronos).

Some might say "back in my day we used to...." This usage does not refer to one day as normally understood as a measurement of duration; but rather represents the measurement of a period of time, which is defined by some type of circumstances or events.

This is very important, because the common belief about the Scriptural age of the earth; and the time of the emergence of life, and ultimately man; is based upon the understanding that these seven days in Genesis comprise a "regular" week. Since actual recorded Bible history is believed to have begun about 4,000 BC; (let's assume even 5,000 BC) and both the earth and man were made within one week; then the earth cannot be any older than about 7,000 years. But if we do not know the actual period of duration of these "days," but rather only the events, there is no way to say.

If "a day is like 1000 years to the Lord,"[2.15] or as Moses stated " For a thousand years in Your sight are like yesterday when it passes by, or as a watch in the night,"[2.16] then the actual age of the earth would be 14,000 years (roughly 1,000 years per day of creation plus 7,000 years since then) if taken literally, so we would then be off by 7,000 years. But these are not supposed to be taken literally, but rather they are similes. Peter or Moses could have used a 100,000,000 years for these similes and made the same point.

Thus the use of the term *"one day,"* could easily refer to a period of activity, followed by a period of inactivity, constituting a period of unknown duration; but rather a period measured by events.

Genesis 1:6-8 tells us:

> "Then God said, "Let there be an expanse in the midst of the waters, and let it separate the waters from the waters." God made the expanse, and separated the waters which were below    the expanse from the

> *waters which were above the expanse; and it was so. God called the expanse heaven. And there was evening and there was morning, a second day."*[2.17]

Following is the original terminology:

Expanse: "7549 raqiya from 7554; prop. an *expanse*, i.e. the *firmament* or (apparently) visible arch of the sky:- firmament." 7554 "raqa; a prim. root; to *pound* the earth (as a sign of passion); by analogy to *expand* (by hammering); by impl. to *overlay* (with thin sheets of metal);- beat, make broad, spread abroad (forth, over, out, into plates), stamp, stretch."[2.18]

Midst: "8432 tavek from an unused root mean. to *sever;* a *bisection, ...*"[2.19]

Waters: "4325 mayim dual of a prim. noun (but used in a sing. sense); *water...* "[2.20]

Made: "6213 asha ..accomplish, advance, appoint..."[2.21]

The only easy thing about understanding these verses; (6-8) is that this time, "waters" (mayim) actually means water, and a fair definition of "made," (asha) is that it means accomplish(ed).

It appears that this "expanse" or "firmament" was made in the midst or middle of the water. This "midst" or *tavek* does not mean middle as in "the boat was stranded in the middle of the lake;" but from the context necessarily meaning middle; as in actually submerged beneath the water. This is more like a submarine located somewhere under the surface, and severing or bisecting the water. This does not mean with water all around, as the stranded boat, but actually severing or bisecting the waters. Thus both necessarily and by definition, would result in water being both above and below this firmament.

This may seem like a digression, but movies are often copyrighted MMXI, at least in 2011. Precisely how would one add MMXI and MMXI? The easiest way would be to convert these Roman numerals into our usual Arabic numerical system; then add them together, and then reconvert them back into Roman numerals—but of course that is not quite the same thing. Most people have no experience in adding Roman numerals directly; and thus would have no other way of actually accomplishing this. The process is unfamiliar, and thus the conversion to something of familiarity would be necessary.

Likewise, and most often commonly attributed to The Book of Revelation, prophetic visions are described using terms that were commonly understood; but really do not in any way suffice as complete descriptions. The reader has never seen or experienced these things, and thus necessarily has to rely upon the imperfect descriptions; as no other words exist to describe these phenomena. It is doubtful that John had ever seen anything similar to what he witnessed; so when writing the Book of Revelation, even *he* did not know the precise words that could describe what he saw. And even if he had, it seems unlikely that anyone else would have understood such terms.

As previously referenced, we know that this Expanse is the word "raqiya" from "raqa" and translates as "an *expanse*, the *firmament* or visible arch of the sky:- firmament." and is derived from "raqa" which means "to *pound* the earth (as a sign of passion)" and by analogy to "*expand* (by hammering); by implication to *overlay* (with thin sheets of metal);- beat, make broad, spread abroad (forth, over, out, into plates), stamp, stretch."

This firmament or expanse is the visible arch of the sky, and is related to passionately pounding the earth. Was it the previous cover and seam from which God established the firmament? This firmament was not actually created; (bara) but rather by the use of the term "let," it was commanded or permitted. Thus its prior material existence in some form is at least implied, and arguably required.

This firmament or expanse is difficult if not impossible to comprehend. Also, we have no information whatsoever as to what happened to the waters that were on top of it at the time of the bisecting or severing of the waters; nor at any time thereafter.

Genesis 1:9-10 tells us:

> *"Then God said, "Let the waters below the heavens be gathered into one place, and let the dry land appear"; and it was so. God called the dry land earth, and the gathering of the waters He called seas; and God saw that it was good."*[2.22]

This seems pretty straightforward. God permitted or commanded the gathering of the waters into one place; (Psalms 33:7 "He gathers the waters of the sea together as a heap; He lays up the deeps in storehouses.")[2.23] and He commanded or permitted the dry land to appear. Again, there is no suggestion of any creation (bara) for this event; because it was that He *gathered* the waters, and *commanded* the dry land to "appear." The waters existed but were scattered; and it follows logically that the dry land must have been hidden. It seems reasonable that the mechanism was likely the raising of the land upwards, with the result being hills and mountains; and the waters gathering downward. He did not command the non-dry, or wet lands to do anything, because they were under the waters. This also lends some Scriptural credence to the secular theory that at one time all the land of the earth was one land mass. One interesting note are the words "sea," and "seas;" as opposed to the use of the term "one place" The original word is: "3220 Yam from an unused root mean. to *roar;* a *sea* (as breaking in *noisy* surf)"[2.24] Thus it seems that this characterization was based upon sounds rather than appearances; perhaps from the waters rolling down the newly raised land.

Genesis 1:11-13 tells us:

> *"Then God said, "Let the earth sprout vegetation, plants yielding seed, and fruit trees on the earth bearing fruit after their kind with seed in them"; and it was so. The earth brought forth vegetation, plants yielding seed after their kind, and trees bearing fruit with seed in them, after their kind; and God saw that it was good. There was evening and there was morning, a third day."*[2.25]

In the prior verses 9-10, again, we are aware of the existence of water, and at least arguably the existence of land under the water, by the use of the word *appear*. His commands thus related to physical entities that we either know existed or can reasonably infer existed. Otherwise the land would have necessarily had to appear out of nowhere; as there is no place or entity referenced where it could have been at that time, except under the water.

In verses 11-13 however, God is issuing permission or a command directly or indirectly to the earth to sprout things to which there are no previous Scriptural references. The word sprout is: "1876 "dasha a prim. root; to *sprout*- bring forth, spring,"[2.26] and seems clear in this regard. Again it appears that this does not in anyway represent any type of creation; (bara) but rather permitting or commanding something that must have already been there, at least latently; and was ultimately capable of manifestation. There is no evidence of God doing anything here other than commanding or permitting.

Unless of course one wishes to suggest that there was also an earth god who received this command; and is also capable of creating; (*bara*), there is no reasonable alternative other than the potential for this vegetation must have already been in or on the earth. All life was created by God; but clearly He was not creating life in 11-13; neither is there any evidence that He created it anywhere prior to these verses. Thus, the question of course becomes; then when did He create it? The only reasonable alternative being back, perhaps even way way back in verse 1?

If this is interpreted as the command being directed to the forces of darkness to release the potential of the vegetation to sprout; one is still left with the inescapable conclusion that the vegetation and/or the potential for the same, must have been created before the forces of darkness obtained control over them.

It is difficult to imagine the level or intensity of this darkness or cover. It is fair to say that none of us have ever experienced anything like this; nor would we ever wish to. Nothing was alive. In this type of situation, seeds could not sprout, they could not even rot, as all life forces likely were blocked by this darkness or cover; including even the bacteria that would cause them to rot. Genesis 1:14-19 tells us:

> *"Then God said, "Let there be lights in the expanse of the heavens to separate the day from the night, and let them be for signs and for seasons and for days and years; and let them be for lights in the expanse of the heavens to give light on the earth"; and it was so. God made the two great lights, the greater light to govern the day, and the lesser light to govern the night; He made the stars also. God placed them in the expanse of the heavens to give light on the earth, and to govern the day and the night, and to separate the light from the darkness; and God saw that it was good. There was evening and there was morning, a fourth day."*[2.27]

Here we have a situation in a very real sense, that similar to the vegetation or the firmament; but now this is with respect to the luminaries. The original word here for "made" is the same word as in making the firmament. "Made" here is: "6213 asha, Accomplish, advance, appoint..."[2.28]

This clearly is not bara. A fair word for "placed" seems to actually be "set;"[2.29] as the original word is: "5414 Nathan a prim. root; to *give,* used with greatest latitude of application (*put, make,* etc.)"[2.30]

Thus as it is written, it appears that God made or accomplished the lights without creating them from nothing. If they were not made from nothing, then they must have been made from something. This may sound a bit strange but nevertheless, that is what it states. Information with respect to what raw materials may have been used; or what type of conversion may have taken place; is not provided.

These verses seem to consist of three sections: God stating what his intentions were; God stating what he did and why; bridged together by the phrase "and it was so." It is also noted that these luminaries were first made, and then placed.

There are 10 reasons listed for the illumination.

1. Separation of day from night.
2. Signs
3. Seasons
4. Days
5. Years
6. Lights in the expanse
7. Light on earth
8. Govern day
9. Govern night
10. Separate light from darkness.

Most of the rest of these are self-explanatory. It is interesting to note that there is a distinction made between separation of the day from night; and the separation of the light and darkness. It is also the use of the word "signs" which is also intriguing. Signs: "226 owth prob. from 225 (in the sense of *appearing*); a *signal* (lit. or fig.), as a *flag, beacon, monument, omen, prodigy, evidence,* etc.: - mark, miracle, (en-) sign, token."[2.31]

These signs may refer to what many believe will be signs in the sky in the end times. The problem with that view, is that this passage and the use of "signs" seems to only refer to what was made then; and not what might be made sometime in the future; the future being from then and not today. Meaning: that the signs such as those which guided the wise men, were not made at this time. What is clear however; is that it was God's intention that one purpose for the luminaries was to provide "owth." According to Chambers, prodigy; which is included as one of the definitions of "owth;" means "marvel, wonder. Before 1470 *prodige* extraordinary sign, portent, omen."[2.32]

There seems to be no reasonable conclusion other than the luminaries were by His intention, designed in part, to provide information about future events.

MEEKRAKER *Beginnings...*

# Chapter 3

## Emergence of the Breath of Life

While assiduously analyzing the portions of the Book of Genesis which relate to the emergence of life; particularly that of man; what immediately and repeatedly comes to mind is a quote by Mark Twain, when self describing his efforts in writing Huckleberry Finn. Twain stated: "In this book a number of dialects are used, to wit: … The shadings have not been done in a haphazard fashion, or by guesswork; but painstakingly, and with the trustworthy guidance and support of personal familiarity with these several forms of speech. I make this explanation for the reason that without it many readers would suppose that all these characters were trying to talk alike and not succeeding."[3.1] No disrespect is meant here. Whatever Twain wrote clearly was inspired by God. Why this similarity comes to mind will become evident.

Everyone knows the story of the emergence of man. God created Adam, put him in the garden, saw it was not good for Adam to be alone, took Adam's rib and created Eve, Eve bought the lie, conned Adam, he ate the apple, sin was born and he was thrown out and we all suffered for it. Heck, the term Adam's apple is believed to have originated when that very apple somehow got stuck in his throat. There are problems with this story however, as much of this is in no way Scripturally accurate. On the lighter side, the fact is that nowhere does the Word state it was an apple; and nowhere is there any evidence whatsoever that whatever it was; apple or otherwise; it or anything else ever became lodged in his throat.

But first, let's take a look at what happened prior to the creation of man.

Genesis 1:20 tells us:

> "Then God said, "Let the waters (4325 Waters "mayim dual of a prim. noun (but used in a sing. sense); water...") [3.2] teem with swarms of living creatures, and let birds fly above the earth in the open expanse of the heavens."[3.3]

The *Interlinear Bible* uses the term "soul of life" instead of "living."[3.4]

Here in verse 20; we again see God announcing his intentions, ultimately resulting (as stated in verse 21) in the fruits of His creation. (bara) Or rather, merely by Him speaking, creation was the result. Ergo, He made them from nothing. The next verse will be the first time we see the use of the term "create" (bara) since Genesis 1:1. It is important to distinguish God's command here in verse 20, from his previous command to the earth to bring forth the sprouting. Here He is describing His desire for the resultant condition of the water being inhabited by swimming creatures, as well as the birds that fly in heavens. He is not commanding the water to produce or bring them forth. It is God Himself who creates these life forms as described in the very next verse. This is the very same mechanism with which He created the heavens and the earth and only the second time this mechanism appears in Genesis thus far.

Genesis 1:21 tells us:

> *"God created (bara) the great sea monsters and every living creature that moves, with which the waters swarmed after their kind, and every winged bird after its kind; and God saw that it was good."*[3.5]

The word "after" seems to be a bit slippery. The *Interlinear Bible* translates this as "according to," and again uses "having a living soul" as the translation for "living."[3.6]

There are two key points:

Firstly, at this time, God created only the creatures which inhabit the water, and the birds. The passage may seem to imply that every moving creature was created at this time, but this is not so. That phrase is qualified to indicate only those in the water and the birds with wings.

Secondly, there is the matter of the use of the terms "after its kind" or "according to its kind." A cursory read of this seems to make perfect sense. A logical explanation would be one of design. Meaning that the sea creatures would swarm the water as designed or according to its or their design. Likewise the birds would fly according to their design or kind. Perhaps this is so; but the question then arises as to where one might expect sea creatures and birds to swim and fly, and so why the need for these statements? To be fair, there is also however, an implied distinction between winged birds and "unwinged" birds.

This also represents completion of a particular "phase" of creation; in that "God saw that it was good" phrase appears as an indication of this completion or conclusion.

Another explanation of this "after its kind" or "according to its kind" would be that these creations would be able to reproduce themselves. And given the instruction in verse 22, this makes some degree of sense.

Genesis 1:22 tells us:

*"God blessed them, saying, "Be fruitful and multiply, and fill the waters in the seas, and let birds multiply on the earth."*[3.7]

The problem with this interpretation; is that it would seem that God would be saying the exact thing twice in two different ways; in two consecutive but different verses; and at three different times. A similar type of repetition does happen in verse 26, but the reason for this repetition in verse 26 will become apparent.

"According" to Strong's, the word "according" does not appear in the Bible until Genesis 18:10.[3.8] Thus it would seem likely that "after" would be the more correct translation.

There are two sets of related terms for the original phrase that is translated into "after its kind."

Strong's references "after its kind" as: "4327 *miyn* from an unused root mean. to *portion* out; a *sort*, i.e. *species*: - kind. Comp. 4480."[3.9] "4480 min or minniy, or minney, prop. a part of; hence (prep.), from or out of in many senses (as follows): - above, after, among, at, because of by (reason of), from (among), in, x neither, x nor, x (out) of, over, since, x then, through, x whether, with."[3.10]

In the "*Strongest Strong's*;" the definition of 4480 includes: "marker of a source or extension from a source."[3.11]

If the meaning of "kind" is limited to the "species" or "sort" definitions, then the answer is obvious. The air and the water is to teem or swarm with the same "species" or "sort" as those which were created. Taxonomic classification begins with Kingdom, and runs through Phylum, Class, Order, Family, Genus, Species and Variety. By the time Species is reached, this represents a relatively limited area. For example: the classification of microorganisms is usually expressed as Genus and Species. Legionella Pneumophila is of the Genus Legionella; named from the American Legion in Philadelphia; and the Species Pneumophila; (air lover) because it is or was found in the air conditioning ductwork. Species in this example would be limited to only the varieties of Pneumophila; excluding all other microorganisms, including all other possible species of Legionella. (Just as a matter of seemingly unrelated trivia, Leigonaires Disease was originally termed "Philadelphia Fever," but this term was allegedly changed because of political pressure.)

If however, the "marker of a source," or "extension from a source," and/or "because of" and "reason of" definitions are employed for the word "kind;" or rather, the meaning of the original single word for which the phrase "after its kind;" which was previously considered the best translation; then an entirely different significance becomes apparent.

This significance concerns all those various life forms which represent an extension from the source; or those who claim the original created source as their marker; (or after the marker of their source), rather than just those who are a mere replication of the original source. Over time, these would necessarily become all of the subsequent life forms which "swarmed" or had wings. These subsequent life forms; although quite different than the original *created* life forms; came into being "because of" or "by reason of" the originals.

The phrase "with which the waters swarmed after their kind" could also possibly refer to those life forms that would come later; those "extensions from the source," and neither the original created life forms or their direct offspring. The after "their or it's kind" meaning *when* it would be that these new and different life forms; or all of those those extensions; would be swarming. They would be swarming chronologically *after* the originals.

It is also interesting to note that neither of the types of creatures created at this time were designed to live directly on the land, but rather in the water, in the air, or generally animals whose abode is in or on structures distant from the ground. The likely reasons for this is will be discussed later.

Thus, depending on how this is read, one must necessarily take one of the two following positions:

Any and all created (bara) species that ever existed, or

were to ever exist, were created at this time and in this manner; thus precluding the addition of any other created species. This would be so, at least with respect to those life forms that reside in the water or are winged birds. Some forms may have become extinct, but all current existing forms which were ever created, must have been created at this time. No new created sea creatures or winged birds could have been introduced later.

or

The original created species were created with the understanding by God, that they would somehow *evolve* (not bara) into other life forms; again; at least with respect to those life forms that reside in the water or are winged birds. The created sea and air species represented the "source" of all of the various life forms which would later swarm and fly, and represent the "extensions" of these original "marker" species, and these *evolved* forms came into existence "because of," "by reason of" and "through" the originals.

This is necessarily so, because there is no Scriptural evidence that God ever again created (bara) these type of life forms. (sea life and winged birds)

Genesis 1:23 tells us:

> "There was evening and there was morning, a fifth day."[3.12]

This represents the closing of another period of time based upon events (chiros). How long after the creation of the heavens and the earth did this occur? How long was this day in terms of measured time (chronos)? How long before the next "day" began? The Scriptures provide no information, at least in Genesis, with respect to answering these questions.

Genesis 1:24-25 tells us:

> "Then God said, "Let the earth bring forth living creatures after their kind: cattle and creeping things and beasts of the earth after their kind"; and it was so. God

> made the beasts of the earth after their kind, and the cattle after their kind, and everything that creeps on the ground after its kind; and God saw that it was good."3.13

The word "create" does not appear with respect to the "cattle and creeping things and beasts of the earth;" nor does this word appear anywhere else in these two verses.

The phrase "bring forth" is the word: "3318 yatsa a prim. root; to *go* (causat. *bring) out,* in a great variety of applications, lit. and fig., direct and proxim.: - x after, appear x assuredly, bear out…"3.14

This bringing forth, (*yatsa*) is not bara; and thus does not in any way refer to creation; which again is to make something out of nothing. Ergo, they were necessarily made out of something rather than nothing. The permission or command was directed at the earth, and the word "made" here as attributed to God we see again as: "6213 asha… accomplish, advance, appoint…,"3.15 which is not a substitute for create, but rather signifies accomplishment.

Permit the earth to bear out or bring out the creatures, (the word creature here is not as the result of bara, i.e. a creation resulting from actual creating at that time), but instead is a translation of: "5315 nephesh from 5314; prop. a *breathing* creature" "5314 Naphash a prim. root; to *breathe*; pass., to *be breathed* upon, i.e. (fig.) *refreshed* (as if by a current of air): - (be) refresh selves (-ed)."3.16

The use of "creature," thus means those with the soul of life with respect to cattle, creeping things, and beasts of the earth; rather than their existence being the direct result of bara. These "creatures" are entirely separate and distinct from the previously created (bara) beasts of the water or the air.

This represents a similar situation of the creation of the sea beasts and the winged birds in terms of result; but is entirely different in terms of causation. We know that plants, sea animals and winged birds already existed at this time. We also know that these earth beasts, unlike the sea beasts and birds, were not made out of nothing.

The most reasonable explanation being that these earth beasts actually *evolved* from either the winged birds, or from the beasts of the sea, the latter being something which science has been proclaiming for many years. If the same rationale is used for the "after its kind" statements, it is likely that these evolved creatures continued to evolve into other life forms over very long periods of time. Many became extinct, and many others continue to exist today.

Thus it seems more then reasonable to believe that it is the very *process* of evolution which the Bible is describing in these verses. First God created or bara; and *then* there was the evolution of these life forms.

Irrespective of what one wishes to believe about this process; what *is* unreasonable to believe is that creation and evolution are in any way mutually exclusive. On the contrary; evolution *requires* or *required* creation; and thus cannot preclude it. First there was creation; and *then* there was evolution. In order for evolution to proceed, creation was first required. Creation did not exclude evolution, but was in fact the prerequisite for evolution. Creation happened before evolution and did not require evolution; but evolution could *not* have happened without creation.

It is not revealed Scripturally precisely how far this evolution was to proceed, nor do we have any idea how long it took.

What we do know Scripturally however, and the Scriptures are quite clear on this, is that it was not any type of evolution which was the source of human beings.

Genesis 1:26 tells us:

> "Then God said, "Let Us make man in Our image, according to Our likeness; and let them rule over the fish of the sea and over the birds of the sky and over the cattle and over all the earth, and over every creeping thing that creeps on the earth".

And then Genesis 1:-27 tells us:

> *"God created man in His own image, in the image of God He created him; male and female He created them."*³·¹⁷

"God created (bara) man in His own image, in the image of God He created him; male and female He created them." Again, He stated His intentions, to "make man in Our image, according to Our likeness," and then He did it. How did He make man? "He created man." Thus man was a creation or a creature, here not merely because man had the breath of life; (i.e. *nephesh*), but because he was created by the Creator.

In Genesis 1:27, the word "created" appears three times in the same sentence. It seems fair to say that God wanted to be certain; certain that we knew for certain; that man was created; (bara, made out of nothing; *no-thing*) lest we come up with some other explanation; as many have tried to do. It is clear that man was made "out of," or "from," nothing, (no-thing), by God. There is no suggestion here of any raw materials involved, no "pre-man mass." There is no suggestion of forming man out of anything else; as the use of any raw materials is precluded by the use of the term bara. There is no suggestion of any intermediate state; neither is there any other process other than as described. In addition, there is no suggestion of evolution of any sort.

Thus it seems certain that the "missing link" for which scientists have been searching simply does not exist. There may be discovered something very close at some point; something which may fit this transition within certain parameters; but the same will ultimately be disproved.

How then did God create man and all else that He created? He created solely by speaking his intention, and was then clearly pleased with the results. Arguably, by the time He finished speaking *"Let Us make man in Our image, according to Our likeness;"* (present tense) it was already done; a "done deal" as we might say today. The later statement that "God created man in His own image, in the image of God He created him; male and female He created them." (past tense) describe the results; and although provides illumination about the process, it does not explain the process in detail, but does confirm to us that He was successful; after the fact.

Genesis 1:26 states that man was made *"In Our image, according to Our likeness;"*

Regarding an image: *"ymage* statue, effigy; *image,* from Latin *imago* (genitive imagines) copy, likeness, statue, picture, thought, idea, semblance, appearance, shadow; related to *imitare* copy, IMITATE."[3.18]

Regarding likeness: *"licnesse;* later *liknesse* an analogy, something similar; appearance, guise, shape; developed from Old English *gelidness,* from *gelic* like, similar + *-ness.* "[3.19] (An gelic?)

Strong's provides two original Hebrew words for likeness: "1823 d<sup>e</sup>muwth from 1819; *resemblance*; coner, *model, shape*; adv. *like*: - fashion, like (-ness, as), manner, similitude." "1819 damah a prim. root; to compare; by impl. to resemble, liken, consider: - compare, devise, (be) like (-n), mean, think, use similitudes." Strong's also indicates that Genesis 1:26 is the first time the word *likeness* appears in the Bible.[3.20]

Since it is often said that "God is a Spirit;"[3.21] the term spirit being used a bit loosely here, (more about this later) in essentially meaning not material; then it stands to reason that the use of the terms image and likeness do not refer to the material which God is not; but rather to the immaterial; which God is. Even Moses was not permitted to see the face of God; so even when God chose to take on *material* form, his image was not known. This is to be distinguished from God taking *human* form as Messiah.

Thus it would seem pointless to indicate that man was created to materially look like God when God is immaterial; and no one, even Moses, ever knew, or likely ever would know what God (The Father), would actually look like if and when He ever appeared materially. Consequently, if interpreted as physical image and likeness; then the best conclusion one could draw would be that God must physically look like us. But that is not what is actually stated. The image and likeness then necessarily must refer to our spiritual composition.

How many people in their thoughts or actions are in any way similar to or in any way like God? The term "walk with God" does not refer to a stroll. Walk, used in this sense, refers to one's lifestyle. Obeying the commandments out of fear of the repercussions of disobedience, is not walking with God. Self-centeredness, or selfishness is not like God. Refusing to believe the truth because of pride, is not like God. God's love is "agape," roughly meaning: that He will continue to love us no matter and despite what we do to Him. If that is the way we were created, but not the way we "walk;" then the presence of some intervening entity contrary to God would be necessary in order for this to be so. And this is just about our thinking and behavior. The power part will be addressed later.

Genesis 1:28 tells us:

> *"God blessed them; and God said to them, "Be fruitful and multiply, and fill the earth, and subdue it; and rule over the fish of the sea and over the birds of the sky and over every living thing that moves on the earth."*[3.22]

God's commanded us multiply, bear fruit, and fill the earth. This requires that the earth was at least somewhat empty; at least with respect to man. It is His desire that we subdue the earth and rule over all the other life forms. This means man was designed to be kings of the earth and all the life forms on it. This is where the often misunderstood "King of kings" term came from. Messiah is the King of the kings, or man; based upon God's intentional design. Why don't most of us ever feel like kings? Because; since we do not operate fully according to our design; we thus do not reap fully the rewards of this design. To the extent we do, we do; to the extent that we do not, we do not.

Genesis 1:29-31 tells us:

> *"Then God said, "Behold, I have given you every plant yielding seed that is on the surface of all the earth, and every tree which has fruit yielding seed; it shall be food for you; 30 and to every beast of the earth*

> *and to every bird of the sky and to every thing that moves on the earth which has life, I have given every green plant for food"; and it was so.*
> *God saw all that He had made, and behold, it was very good. And there was evening and there was morning, the sixth day.* "[3.23]

    This tells us that man was *given* a source, or actually sources, of food by God. How does one earn a gift? The answer is that one does not. This passage neither states nor implies that if you work the fields, then you will have food to eat. It states that "*every,...shall*" be food for you. It does not state some. It does not state might or may be food. There are no preconditions for these to be used as food. There is no indication that lying around all day and all night in green pastures by the water, (see 23rd Psalm) would in any way decrease the amount of available things to eat. Probably the most similar thing would be the later provision of manna. Manna literally means: "What is that?"[3.24] It must not have looked like anything ever known to exist, or it would have had a different name. All one had to do with manna was pick it up and consume it. And it would not keep overnight.

    God did not just see what He had made here. This is the first time that God saw not what He made, but rather *all* that He had made. Thus there is a clear implication of completion or finality. This is also the first time God uses the term *"very good"* to describe what He made.

    The original word translated as "very," is Strong's: "3966 m$^e$od.... prop. *vehemence,* i.e. (with or without prep.) *vehemently;* by impl. w*holly, speedily,* etc...."[3.25] Wholly meaning whole or complete. And of course speedily necessarily implies completion.

    Also, we have what appears to be the completion of the sixth day. One must take the position that the use of the "sixth day," means that the sixth day either began or ended at that time. If it began at that time, then we have no idea what if anything happened on that sixth day, as no later or further reference is made to the sixth day; but rather only to the seventh. In our society, is dawn the beginning of the daylight or the end of the night? Is midnight the end of the previous calendar day, or the beginning of the next? It is true that we use conventions such as 12:01 AM or one second after midnight, but at that cusp precisely when the ball hits the ground in Times Square, which day is it? It seems likely that the reference to the sixth day, refers to the end of the sixth day; as in the sixth day was now complete. This rather than meaning the beginning of the sixth day; as no further information would then be provided as to what, if anything, actually happened on the sixth day.

Genesis 2:1 is perfectly consistent with this idea of completion:

> *"Thus the heavens and the earth were completed, and all their hosts."*[3.26]

Genesis 2:1 seems straightforward enough until you get to the word "hosts." This is not in terms of a statement of completion; but rather with respect to the meaning of the terminology. Host, hosts, hostess; meaning: the person having the party, the person who leads you to the table, the person who introduces guests, etc.

There is also a usage in the sense of a parasitic organism's target or the life form in which it resides or intends to reside. Theologically, host can refer to a willing participant, or the wafer used in Catholicism. Somehow, none of these; with perhaps the willing participant usages or meanings, seem to make any particular sense with respect to Gen 2:1. Although it is fair to say; that all of these have an air of some type of authority; one way or another; that is at least suggested.

Precisely from where is this term host derived? "Host: large number, multitude. (year) 1265 *host* multitude of armed men. Borrowed from Old French *ost, oost, host,* from Medieval Latin *hostis* army, warlike expedition, from Latin *hostis* enemy, stranger; …"[3.27] This *"hostis"* is likely the root for words such as hostile or hostage.

The actual Hebrew word for "hosts" here is "6635 tsaba or ts$^e$ba'ah from 6633; a *mass* of persons (or fig. things), espec. reg. organized for war (an *army*); by impl. a *campaign,* lit. or fig.

(spec. *hardship, worship):* - appointed time, (+) army, (+) battle, company, host, service, soldiers, waiting upon, war (-fare). 6633 tsaba a prim. root; to *mass* (an army or servants): - assemble, fight, perform, muster, wait upon, war."[3.28]

In today's age, the understanding of the actual definition of "host" in this regard has been lost. In 1952, Isaac Asimov wrote a story called *"The Monkey's Finger."* Asimov wrote: "Shakespeare *did* write "sea." But you see that's a mixed metaphor. You don't fight a sea with arms. You fight a host or army with arms."[3.29]

Thus, one extremely important answer is provided to the age-old question of "Why are we here?" This answer of course being that we are here to fight in a war. Unfortunately; as often happens; obtaining an answer to a question can lead to even more questions; questions which can be even more difficult to answer.

What kind of war are we to fight? Is this war a war within, or a war without, or both?

Man was created in the image and likeness of God. Thus, unless God wars with himself; we, by design, were clearly not created to engage in any inner wars. This not to say that we do not; or at times should not do this; but merely that this was not by intention or design. This will be explored a bit more shortly.

If war is to be waged, then at least two parties are necessary in order to wage said war. It does not seem likely; nor is there any evidence to suggest; that God enjoys causing or watching war for sport. Therefore, whatever creatures he created were not created to wage war with each other.

It does not seem likely, nor is there any evidence to suggest that God created creatures to wage war with Him; as though He needs or needed something to occupy his time. Therefore, as stated, this war is not supposed to be between any of the hosts; neither is this war to be between the hosts and God.

If we go back to the "cover" and "darkness" in Genesis 1:2; as well as the seam or joint created by fascination or charm; we can find our enemy in this war. In Job 26:10; Job is rebuking his friends. Later, in chapter 42; God also rebukes them. In fact God essentially threatens to kill them, but that is another matter. In Job's rebuke, he states the following:

Job 26:10-14 tells us:

> "He has inscribed a circle on the surface of the waters At the boundary of light and darkness. The pillars of heaven tremble
> And are amazed at His rebuke. He quieted the sea with His power, And by His understanding He shattered Rahab. By His breath the heavens are cleared; His hand has pierced the fleeing serpent. "Behold, these are the fringes of His ways; and how faint a word we hear of Him!
> But His mighty thunder, who can understand?"[3.30]

Rahab is "7293 rahab from 7292, *bluster (-er):* - proud, strength.[3.31]

Pierced is "2342 chuwl or chiyla a prim. root; prop; to *twist* or *whirl* (in a circular or spiral manner), i.e. (spec.) to *dance*, to *writhe* in pain (espec. of parturition) or fear;…"[3.32]

Serpent is "5175 nachash from 5172; a *snake* (from its *hiss*); - serpent." 5172 nachash a prim. root; prop. to *hiss,* i.e. *whisper* a (magic) spell; gen. to *prognosticate*: - x certainly, divine, enchanter, (use) x enchantment, learn by experience, x indeed, diligently observe."[3.33]

This retrosophic passage from Job, provides a better idea of the circumstances surrounding some of the previous portions of Genesis. Although *Genesis* does not state this; here clearly the enemy was involved in whatever transpired that resulted in the "without form and void" condition; this being the condition that the earth was in at the time of God's intervention. One other translation of the word "Rahab," as used in this passage, which means pride, can also be translated as "chaos."[3.34]

The term "serpent" does not actually mean snake; but rather, as will be later seen, seems to represent a snake simply because of the "hiss." More importantly here also is the "magic," or "enchantment" component that seems to be related to the existence of the "skoteinos" or "cover." In addition, Genesis does not describe the twisting or whirling or writhing in pain or fear of the enemy, as the transition occurs from the dark "without form and void" state to light.

Note the references to the inscribing the circle, the light and dark boundaries, the clearing of the heavens.

In the following passage: Ezekiel 28:16-17, we see the reference to the enemy, and God casting him to the ground so that the kings may see him. It seems as though this must necessarily be retrophesy rather than prophesy, as clearly the enemy has been with the earth for quite some time; as certainly he was present long before the time of Ezekiel. But this strictly "retrosophical" conclusion is quite incorrect. Although the following seems to present some interesting background as to the circumstances surrounding his fall; it must be read very carefully as these passages refer to separate events.

Ezekiel 28:16-17 tells us:

> *"By the abundance of your trade You were internally filled with violence, And you sinned;*
> *Therefore I have cast you as profane From the mountain of God. And I have destroyed you, O covering cherub,*
> *From the midst of the stones of fire. Your heart was lifted up because of your beauty; You corrupted your wisdom by reason of your splendor.*
> *I cast you to the ground; I put you before kings, That they may see you."*[3.35]

There is a point of transition between retrophesy and prophesy which occurs between the words "God" and "And;" translators choice of tense notwithstanding. How do we factually know this? Because we know that Satan has already been thrown down to earth; and we also know that Satan has yet to be destroyed. We also know this, because it was not for the reason that men or kings would see Satan that he was originally cast down; but rather because there was no place for him in heaven. Thus the original "thrown down" because of there being no place for him, is an entirely separate event; an event which has already happened. Thus, this part of the passages represents retrophesy.

All that which occurs after the word "And" until the "see you" has yet to happen, and thus represents prophesy. This prophesy is consistent with Isaiah; as well as John's Book of Revelation. The time period in between these two events; the original throwing down, and this later destruction and casting down to the ground; represents the duration of the war which is currently being fought by the "hosts." This war began with the throwing down, and will conclude with the casting down and ultimate destruction.

It is in the interest of contextual integrity, that they are provided here together. In a subsequent chapter, their significance will be examined more closely and in greater detail.

Therefore, our war is necessarily with this enemy, this "covering cherub." It would be fair to ask at this juncture: Precisely what is a covering cherub? It seems that God is perhaps being a bit sarcastic towards Satan. It is believed that Satan is or was an archangel; thus referring to him as a cherub is deliberately demeaning. It is the "covering" part which provides the link back to early Genesis; as no other explanation makes any degree of sense.

Understandably, there is much ado these days with the Muslim term of "Jihad." Some Muslims profess that it refers to a war within. Others, the radical Muslim sects, believe it is a war without.

The first believe that this is an inner war, which of course we all have; albeit not by design; but rather because of the influence or attempted influence of the enemy. When this influence is successful, we have corrupted soldiers; said level of corruption being proportional to the extent to which the enemy's influence succeeds.

But even corrupted soldiers are not the real enemy. To the extent we listen to and act upon the enemy's ramblings, we have trouble; and to the extent we ignore him, we do not. Jihad in this sense seems to be more of a war of self-cleansing or purification. This "dirt" is present not by design; but rather as the result of succumbing to evil influences.

The radical Muslims believe it is an outer war. Their jihad or war is not against the actual enemy; but rather is against anyone whom these radicals merely *believe* is the enemy. This being simply because these proclaimed "enemies" dare to disagree with them, and their radical, and out of the mainstream Muslim viewpoints. These radicals are actually waging war against the very "hosts" created by God to wage war against the real enemy. This is why western civilizations and leaders are often referred to as the great, or agents, of Satan. This is merely pride, and we have seen the fruits of pride.

Looking back at the text of Job 26:12, ("And by His understanding He shattered Rahab") and the two possible translations for "Rahab" (pride and chaos), by this there is a clear implication of a relationship between pride and chaos. Chaos distinguished here as the result of destruction, rather than the process of destruction. This gives a different insight into Proverbs 16:18 "Pride *goes* before destruction, And a haughty spirit before stumbling."[3.36] Haughty meaning arrogant; a-rogare being from the negation of the Latin "*rogare;*" *rogare* meaning to question; "a" being the negation of rogare, or to question; taken together actually literally meaning "*not* to question."

Genesis 2:2-3 tells us:

> "By the seventh day God completed His work which He had done, and He rested on the seventh day from all His work which He had done.
> Then God blessed the seventh day and sanctified it, because in it He rested from all His work which God had created and made."[3.37]

This is where the interpretation of "the sixth day" seems to show that it must mean the end of the sixth day, rather than "morning" of the sixth day; as we are now on day seven, with no mention whatsoever of day six. Also, there is a clear distinction made between what God *created* and what He *made*. This can be interpreted as that which He both "created and made" or, as those things which He "created," as well as those things He "made." Since, not surprisingly, the actual words used here are "bara" and "asha"[3.38] respectively; the latter interpretation; those things which He "created," as well as those things He "made," appears to be the correct one.

God resting does not mean sleep. It means ceasing from activity. This is probably the origin of the seemingly popular "deism." Simply put: this is the belief that God acted for a limited time, and then He just sat or sits back, and He just watched or watches, and continues to do so.

Genesis 2: 4 tells us:

> *"This is the account of the heavens and the earth when they were created, in the day that the LORD God made earth and heaven."*[3.39]

The actual word for account is: "8435 towl$^e$dah or tol$^e$dah from 3205; (plur. only) *descent*, i.e. *family*; (fig.) *history*: - birth, generations."[3.40] Thus, some translations use the word generations instead of account.

This is a key verse and must be read very very carefully. Once again the word created is "bara" and the word made is "asha."[3.41] Rephrased a bit, this is the generations or history of the birth of the heavens and the earth when they were "bara", or uniquely created by God out of nothing; said historical account being *given* in the day when God "asha" or made them.

This clearly makes a time distinction between creation and making. It simply makes no sense to phrase it this way if it was the same event, or even if they occurred simultaneously. And Genesis clearly shows a process, which negates the possibility of any simultaneity with respect to the final product; which is what Genesis 2: 1-4 is all about.

Genesis 2:5 tells us:

*"Now no shrub of the field was yet in the earth, and no plant of the field had yet sprouted, for the* LORD *God had not sent rain upon the earth, and there was no man to cultivate the ground."*[3.42]

There are three important words here: "cultivate, field and yet." It should be noted that the word translated as cultivate, actually is: "5647 abad a prim. Root; to *work* (in any sense); by impl. To *serve, till,* (caus.) *enslave,* etc.: - x be, keep in bondage..."[3.43] It should also be noted that another name for Satan is Abaddon, a term which is generally considered to mean destroyer.

It seems it was not very long ago (Gen.1: 29 in fact) that God had *given* every plant and tree for food. So God has essentially just given every plant and tree for food; and for some reason or reasons we are now being told that there is no man to work, serve, till, to be caused to be enslaved by or to be kept in bondage by the ground. This does not sound like revelation, but rather what not too many years ago would probably have been described as a "no-brainer."

This can only mean one of three things: First, this could mean that there was no man, no man to cultivate the ground, or to do anything else for that matter. But we just read that all the hosts were completed, and also; to whom then would God have given the gift of food?

The second possibility being that there was not yet any earth or ground to cultivate. But this verse clearly speaks of fields, earth, ground, and rain; the rain being an entity which of course did not yet exist; or at least had never been sent; according to this passage.

The third possibility being that there was both man and ground but because, food was a gift, there was no need for man to work, serve, till, or caused to be enslaved by or to be kept in bondage by the ground. A fair read is that even the animals ate for free.

Why then is this revelation? Because it would not remain this way, and in fact by the time Moses wrote this, no one could even imagine obtaining any substantial amount of food from the ground without having to work for it.

As evidenced by previous verses, clearly there were shrubs and plants. But there were no fields. That is why it was written the way it was. *"no shrub of the field was yet in the earth, and no plant of the field"* There was no need to create a field, to clear an area of all unwanted things, and labor constantly to keep it clear, because food was a gift, it was free. There was harmony.

Yet the Word indicates that there was a change that was coming or came, depending upon one's perspective. This change resulting in the need for fields, and rain, and the need to work the ground.

Genesis 2: 6 tells us:

*"But a mist used to rise from the earth and water the whole surface of the ground."*[3.44]

This is a description of a condition; actually descriptions of two conditions. The description of which was written in the past; but it was about a condition that existed in an even more distant past. At the time this passage was written; it was a time when the mist no longer rose, as it is described as "used to rise." The word "but" can reasonably be translated here as "because;" as it is offered as an explanation as to how the plants were watered without rain, as indicated in the previous verse.

So when the mist was rising, there was no need for rain. But at the time of its writing, it seems there was no more rising mist; but nowhere is it actually stated as to what replaced the mist. You have to jump back and forth in time to get the meaning.

Back when the mist was rising, there was no need for rain. But the "no rain" was before the "used to" or rather when the mist "still was." So when the rain was not yet; then the mist necessarily still was. Once the status of the mist became "used to;" (no more mist) then either the rain or something else had to water the ground. Since there is no reference to any way of watering the ground other than mist and rain; and since the mist was no more; it is most likely that rain began; at some point, the "yet" being fulfilled. This is clearly an indication that time had passed and circumstances had changed.

Genesis does not tell us what happened. Since we have rain today; we have plants in fields today; we have to till and work the fields today; it is likely that this same change remains with us today.

# 1st Intermission

## Life and Death—Material and Immaterial

What is life? This is of course by no means a new question. The answer however, necessarily depends on the context in which this question is asked. This "Intermission" is not about near death experiences or séances, nor any communication(s) with any departed souls or spirits.

From the standpoint of the Scriptures, life in no way means existence. Meaning: that the existence of anything that was ever alive continues long after the "life" is gone. When so called "death" occurs; both the vessel, and the previous contents of the vessel, continue their existence, but separately. Whatever "remains" here continues to exist; and will undergo changes as time goes on, but it does not cease to exist. But the truth is: that vessel was undergoing changes since it's very beginning at fertilization.

An ovum is a relatively large "cellular" structure. Because of the surface area to volume ratio; as well as in order to fulfill its purpose; as soon as it becomes activated by fertilization, it begins to change by division, ultimately becoming a human being. After birth, it changes constantly while maturing and is always undergoing changes while it is alive. These changes continue as it becomes older; and changes, although different types of changes; even continue after so-called "death;" but this death does not make it cease to exist.

The immaterial portion of this life form also does not cease to exist. When this "passes on," it goes *some*where; but clearly it does not cease to exist. If it ceased to exist, then there would be no heaven or hell. There would be no eternal life or eternal damnation possible, unless it existed eternally. Most if not all religions recognize this; because otherwise; outside of some matters such as moral living; there really would not be all that much to talk about.

This distinction between material existence and life is often blurred. Although funerary practices differ greatly between cultures and religions, there is often an assumption made that the corpse, or the "remains," represent more than they actually do. Although this may prove psychologically or emotionally beneficial for the living, it has no basis in fact.

In a word, life simply means connected. If something is alive, it is connected. If it is dead, it is disconnected. When we refer to an electrical circuit, we consider it as "live" when connected to a power source; when disconnected, it suddenly becomes "dead." A "dead end" street is a street that has no connection at one end.

So then what does physical life mean? All living beings must be connected to the life source in order to be alive. This life source first enters the body with the first breath, and exits with the last. As long as the being is connected, the being is alive. These are the life forms with the "breath of life" as referenced in the scriptures. Even Noah received some instructions based upon this nomenclature.

It could be reasonably argued, that the body or vessel is of one polarity; usually considered negative. Whatever the entity is that enters the body at birth; this entity being of the opposite, or "positive" polarity; it is attracted to the negative vessel or body, and will remain with it until the "negativity" of this vessel diminishes beyond a certain threshold; and the immaterial portion will then depart. We have become so accustomed to this "dual" existence, that we fail to truly appreciate how unusual it is. We pay no mind to the fact that something departs from a living entity, and just consider it "normal." When in fact; nowhere is there any known evidence that would support the contention; at least in our solar system; that this duality is not unique to earth; at least as of this writing.

Thus we have two worlds here: the physical or material world in which we live; and another world or realm of the non-physical or immaterial.

The material physical world exists solely because of the immaterial. Whatever God created in the material, he created from the immaterial. It could not be otherwise. So anything that exists in the material, had to exist in the immaterial first. If it did or does not exist in the immaterial, then in cannot ever exist in the material.

Whenever discussing the immaterial, one will eventually get into trouble, because the use of precise terminology can become extremely difficult. This is because as a general rule, it simply does not exist. What usually happens is that words used for the physical realm are used to describe the immaterial; and they will only work so far. Ultimately, the word "like" or "as" or both are incorporated; not as a simile; but used literally—because those words, and their combinations most closely describe a phenomenon for which no precise descriptions exist. Often; this description will then later be confused with or rather mistaken for a simile; this being done by those who do not believe the literal description could possibly be taken literally. Or sometimes: similes are mistaken for literal meanings; this by those who simply want to believe something else does or does not exist. And on it goes.

A few distinctions should be made here regarding terminology that is often used. Previously the "God is a spirit" statement was cited. This term "spirit" can be a very slippery one. Spirit comes from the Latin "spiritus" which literally means breath. But in actuality, God is not merely a "breath." What this then actually means: is that God is Spiritlike; or "like" a breath; in the sense of meaning non-material.

Technically, spirit is that quantity or entity emitted from God which gave or gives matter its very existence in the material realm. A rock has spirit; the earth has spirit; and a deceased person has spirit. Anything that exists in the material has spirit. None of which of course is necessarily alive. True, this *is* a connection; but this is merely the connection that is required for physical existence; which is an entirely different matter with respect to life. (no pun intended here)

There are essentially two categories of physical life. Those life forms that do not have the breath of life, such as plants; but these are not the subject of this "intermission;" and those that do, such as animals; which are the subject here. This breath of life or what could even be literally translated as "spirit of life," is usually referred to as soul. Soul is often defined as "the emotions, will and intellect;" but that is really an erroneously and incomplete definition, as it is much more. It is that breath of life that God places in us and it is that which ultimately either returns to him, or does not. This soul also contains the vital life force, which is what keeps us all physically alive. Now some may believe that this is an over simplification, and perhaps that is so. Nevertheless, it represents a fair working model. The subject of the term "nous" being reserved for another time; other than perhaps to say that this vital life force portion of soul was the basis for the original development of the science of chiropractic. Chiropractic however, does not refer to the VLF as such, but rather as "innate intelligence."

Thus, any life form that contains the breath of life has a soul. To all of those that believe that only humans have this soul, they are quite incorrect. Dogs and cats, and certainly any animal that has a developed respiratory system, has soul. Just because they were not created in the spiritual image and likeness of God; (and even this is not actually certain) this does not mean that they do not have a soul.

Obviously, any material life form that can be physically detected as such; must also have spirit. Just because it has spirit, does not necessarily mean we can physically detect it; but if we can detect it, then it must have spirit. Thus, life forms that have the breath of life, have both spirit and soul. When this soul is not contained in a physical body, it is known as a ghost. This is why it is so misleading to use the term "Holy Spirit;" rather than "Holy Ghost;" likely because of entertainment originated pressure. The Holy Ghost wants to reside in us, by design. The use of the term Holy Spirit as Its substitute; is thus inadequate, misleading, erroneous, and is also quite dangerous.

What do we know about the material realm? Not really very much. The reason for this is that we are usually trying to determine "actuality," which can loosely be defined as what exists, by our "reality" which is only what we perceive. Just run the vacuum cleaner by the dog, and you will see. A dog can hear the higher frequencies that the vacuum emits that we humans cannot hear. All that extra money to obtain a quiet vacuum, and it is very quiet; unless of course you happen to be a canine. Then those frequencies we did not and still do not know were even there, come through loud and clear. Their (canines) reality is quite different. Otherwise, why is he/she running around in circles and attacking the hose? The actuality is the high frequencies the canine hears that we do not; as well as the frequencies we do hear; and who know what else; in fact (in actuality), constitute a very noisy machine. But the reality to us is a very expensive and quiet vacuum; quite possibly missing a usable hose.

We know even less about the immaterial realm. What is fair to say, is that it is likely that whatever the material realm is, the immaterial realm is not. Specifically, the existence of time and distance. In the immaterial realm there is no time and there is no distance. These are quantities that exist only in our physical realm. (There may exist other unknown physical realms, with other rules; so discretion is advised here.) This is one of the reasons why reading from Chapter 4 onward in Revelation can be so confusing, as John was permitted into *a* realm or perhaps *the* realm with no time. Separating the prophesy, the retrophesy and the current events of John's time can be difficult. He saw things with no reference as to when they actually happened; as the time and distance factors do not and did not exist in the immaterial. Based upon this, there is no argument possible as to whether God is omnipresent, as there would be nowhere else He could be. And with no time factor, He had to always be and He could have neither any beginning, nor any end.

In the beginning the earth was created. The precise purpose for this is unknown. We do know that the earth was created from nothing; likely God spoke it into existence as he did with other created things. This represents *bara* in its absolute true sense—as there was no known material existence from which anything could be otherwise brought into existence. It seems it was a slowing down of the immaterial into the material; at the same time creating time and space. Not space in the sense of nothingness; but rather dimensions, and the requirements of length, height, width and time; a four dimensional realm, created from the immaterial.

It is important to realize that we exist in at least a four dimensional realm. Often times this may seem absurd; but nevertheless it is so. If one has an appointment which is intended to be kept, usually only three of these four dimensions are necessary. Specific latitude and longitude values exist for anywhere on the planet, and with a high degree of precision. Anywhere can be located using these dimensions. The only thing left of course would be the factor of time. Get all three right and you succeed. Unless of course, the appointment happens to be in a "high rise" building; particularly if one did not know this; at which point the vertical dimension becomes a serious factor. Now, four dimensions would be required in order to not miss the appointment. No problem, just look at the directory. This is not the point, but rather that this fact remains; you still would need four dimensions in order to keep the appointment.

Everything in the material realm is vibratory in its ultimate nature. If it were possible to look down at an orbiting electron, one could graph the motions of an electron around a nucleus. The result would be similar to a sine type wave with the electron's location as the vertical axis while using time as the horizontal axis. Unless absolute zero is obtained; which as of this writing not only has never been done, but is also considered to be impossible; it is a fact that atoms, molecules and sub-atomic particles are all and always vibrating or moving, and this requires time.

Thus we are faced with time and motion everywhere in the material realm.

It seems that part of this phenomenon appears in Einstein's relativity equations concerning velocity and time. As the velocity of matter or a mass increases, times slows, one dimension decreases, and mass increases. At the speed of light, or "C," time becomes zero, one dimension becomes zero and mass becomes infinite. Which is why any mass reaching the speed of light is considered to be unattainable, as there simply is no way to obtain sufficient power to accelerate an infinite or even an almost infinite mass. Mass would somehow have to be negated in order to accomplish this. Theoretically, it is not stated therein what would actually happen if the speed of light is exceeded, as there is no such thing as the square root of -1; science fiction notwithstanding.

Thus one could argue, and perhaps many have, that at least speculatively it could be concluded that matter is essentially the "slowing down of light energy;" and there is no reason to limit the definition of light energy to only those wavelengths visible to humans. Therefore time was created in order to permit or facilitate this slowing down, and space was necessary because no two material objects can occupy the same space at the same time. The conclusion of course being, that the act of actually creating matter (or creating material actuality) is actually in essence this "slowing" process; from the immaterial existence, into material existence. God did it by speaking His intentions. One of the many things we know for sure, is that God did not actually say: "Let us make man..." We know this because there is no evidence whatsoever that the English language existed at that time. So whatever He actually did say, we know it was not that. Yet nevertheless, since it obviously succeeded; this could not have been because of the actual words He spoke. It was His intention expressed as vibration; which of course by definition requires time; that produced the results. This concept will be discussed a bit further in another "Intermission."

A short personal anecdote here: A few years ago, I had a discussion with a highly educated friend about astral projection. I told him that my view was you could both do it and not do it. He told me that made no sense; either you could do it or you could not. I asked him if he agreed that if one were to astral project, that this occurred strictly in the immaterial realm. He indicated that it in fact did. I then asked him if the immaterial realm had any type of space or distance constraints. He stated that it did not. So I then asked him; given those two agreed upon conditions; if you astral projected to your friend house across the street, where did you actually go? To this day he has never answered that question.

But back to the issues of life and death. Life means being connected, not existing. For those that believe in Jesus, and even for those who believe He has yet to come, He brings eternal life. If that meant eternal existence, it would then have been a waste of time; as we already had or have that. If it meant eternal physical life here on earth, then He failed at that one. In fact, it is believed by many, that physical death is Scripturally referred to as the "final enemy." It was this eternal connection to God that He brought, and that is the eternal life.

When one is required to take a series of tests, once one mistake is made, an average of one hundred percent is then impossible. And no mater how many additional tests are used to average the score, the average will never reach one hundred percent. But God requires one hundred percent in order to be able to stand having us around him; or put more professionally, to have us eternally connected to him. Thus there was the need for some way to make our failures irrelevant; which was this very justification through substitution via Messiah.

It is important to note here that the concept of "hell;" which is in actuality eternal separation from God; is not the result of any punitive intentions on the part of God. He does not condemn us because of our behavior as a punishment. It is simply because He cannot have our "messes" around Him and still remain perfect. Since we cannot undo our transgressions; and He really wants us to be connected; justification was His only option without breaking the rules. Justification loosely meaning; "just as though one never sinned."

MEEKRAKER *Beginnings…*

# Chapter 4

## You the Man!

A quick recap from the previous chapter:
Genesis 2: 6 told us:

> *"But a mist used to rise from the earth and water the whole surface of the ground."*

"This is a description of a condition; actually descriptions of two conditions. (Said) description of which was written in the past; but it was about a condition that existed in an even more distant past. At the time this passage was written; it was a time when the mist no longer rose, as it is described as "used to rise." The word "but" can reasonably be translated here as "because;" as it is offered as an explanation as to how the plants were watered without rain, as indicated in the previous (Gen 2:5) verse.
Genesis 2:5 told us:

> *"Now no shrub of the field was yet in the earth, and no plant of the field had yet sprouted, for the LORD God had not sent rain upon the earth, and there was no man to cultivate the ground."*

So when the mist was rising, there was no need for rain. But at the time of its writing, it seems there was no more rising mist; but nowhere is it actually stated as to what replaced the mist. You have to jump back and forth in time to get the meaning.

Back when the mist was rising, there was no need for rain. But the "no rain" was before the "used to" or rather when the mist "still was." So when the rain was not yet; then the mist necessarily still was. Once the status of the mist became "used to;" (no more mist) then either the rain or something else had to water the ground. Since there is no reference to any way of watering the ground other than mist and rain; and since the mist was no more; it is most likely that rain began; at some point, the "yet" being fulfilled. This is clearly an indication that time had passed and circumstances had changed.

Genesis does not tell us what happened. Since we have rain today, we have plants in fields today; we have to till and work the fields today; it is likely that this same change remains with us today."

Clearly there was an unspecified change in circumstances here. Probably the best way to try and gain insight with respect to what this change actually was; or rather what precipitated (no pun here) this change; would be to see what happened next.

Genesis 2: 7 tells us:

> *"Then the LORD God formed man of dust from the ground, and breathed into his nostrils the breath of life; and man became a living being."*[4.1]

At this juncture, it would be more than fair to ask two questions: Firstly: Is Yogi Berra in the house? And then naturally of course, the second question: Is this déjà vu all over again? This is now

Genesis 2:7, and didn't we just earlier learn the following in Genesis Chapter 2 verses 1-4:

> *"Thus the heavens and the earth were completed, and all their hosts. By the seventh day God completed His work which He had done, and He rested on the seventh day from all His work which He had done.*
> *Then God blessed the seventh day and sanctified it, because in it He rested from all His work which God had created and made.*
> *This is the account of the heavens and the earth when they were created, in the day that the* LORD *God made earth and heaven."*[4.2]

As previously stated, verses 1-4 clearly read like an epilogue or a recapitulation. The word "completed" appears; and clearly the closing of a series of events is stated. The actual word translated as "completed" is: "3615 kalah a prim. root; to *end*, whether intrans. (to *cease, be finished, perish*) or trans. (to *complete, prepare, consume*)..."[4.3]

Could it be that Chapter 2 verse 7 is merely a flashback? Thus far, Genesis has been written, albeit with gaps, in chronological order. Did that order change, or is something else happening?

There are two words worthy of note:

In the previous chapter, back in Genesis 2:5, (Now no shrub of the field was yet in the earth ...); this verse begins with the word "*Now.*" Here in Genesis 2:7; this verse begins with the word "*Then.*" So in these verses; remembering that the Bible was written in continuous form; we have the use of the terms "*now and then.*" Of course the question arises as to precisely when was "now" and when was "then." They are not used together in a common phrase or expression as they might be used today such as: "Now and then I go to church;" meaning occasionally. But even in this common usage, a lapse of time or duration is generally implied.

In Genesis 2:5, the use of "now" necessarily indicates the present. "Now no shrub;" or perhaps also stated as *at that time* no shrub.... The subsequent use of "then" in verse 7 implies duration; and signifies the occurrence of another event; said event being the one described after the word "then." But God created man all the way back in Genesis 1:26, with much happening since that time.

Here we see the use of the word "now" in Genesis 2:5; and the subsequent use of the word "then" in Genesis 2:7; this clearly indicating some duration of unknown quantity between verses 5 and 7. This is written from the standpoint of "now, describing present; with the subsequent "then," as some time after this "now." Thus, this cannot represent a flashback to Genesis 1:26; as evidenced by this duration and based upon the sequence of events. Furthermore, it is unlikely that God would have given the order to multiply; as well as given food to life forms, for which an account of their origin did not yet exist. Neither is the flashback view consistent with the following:

Here, in Genesis 2:7, the Lord God "formed" man; He did not create man. Back in Genesis 1:26 God created man, *bara,* created man out of nothing—he did not form man. Three times in verse 27 we are told that man was created or *bara*. Here in Chapter 2 verse 7, the word "formed" and not "created" is used.

This original word used here is not bara, but is actually the word: "3335 Yatsar prob. identical with 3334 (through the *squeezing* into shape); ([comp. 3331]); to *mould* into a form; espec. as a *potter;* ... 3334 yatsar a prim. root; to *press* (intrans.) ... 3331 yatsa a prim. root; to *strew* as a surface..."[4.4]

The use of the term *yatsar* or to form here is clearly not *bara*. This word *yatsar* by definition, requires something from which to make something else. In fact, in that sense *bara* and *yatsar* are mutually exclusive; in that *bara* precludes the use of any raw materials, and requires by definition that the product be made from nothing; and *yatsar,* means only to squeeze mould or form, thus requiring something to begin with to be used to make the product; as with *yatsar*, must be formed from something. It is the forming or pressing of something from something else; and not the creation of the something from nothing; that is the process involved with *yatsar*.

In addition, God did not speak here. He did not say "Let man be formed from the dust from the ground," or anything else for that matter, as he did with *bara*. The account is more of a third person narrative of what transpired.

We are also told precisely what man was formed from; which again precludes *bara*. Man was formed from *"dust from the ground."* Dust is the translation for: "6083 aphar from 6080; *dust* (as *powdered* or *gray*); hence *clay, earth, mud*: - ashes, dust, earth, ground, morter, powder, rubbish." "6080 aphar a prim. root; mean. either to *be gray* or perh. rather to *pulverize*; used only as denom. from 6083, to *be dust*: - cast [dust)]."[4,5]

The sense here of the word *aphar*, seems to be one of useless matter. No precise definition of the word "morter" is readily available; but it appears to be similar to the word "mortar" in English. The common belief is that it was the soil or ground from which this man was formed; but that is not really a fair interpretation of this word. Dust is really otherwise useless matter. It is believed that most people who are allergic to "dust" are not really allergic to the particulate matter, but rather the mite waste contained therein. The use of the terms "powder" and "rubbish" gives a good understanding of the meaning of this word, which is translated as "dust." So God formed what is considered to be the greatest of his creations, from what is generally considered to be otherwise useless and undesirable material.

It should be noted that there is a twofold process going on here. First God formed the man from useless dust, but that produced only the vessel. After He formed the vessel, He "breathed into his nostrils the breath of life; and man became a living being." The second half of the process was bringing the vessel into a "living being." Some translations use the words "living soul." This could also be termed into connected soul. When God breathed into man's nostrils this breath of life, the soul and the body became connected and physical life began.

Thus, it is reasonable to say that the respiratory system is the system by which physical life is begun and maintained. This life entity must then necessarily be contained in the blood. Clinical death is when the heart stops beating. Being the pumping mechanism for the blood which contains the breath of life; this also makes some sense spiritually. Death by asphyxiation would ultimately have the same result, but as long as the pumping mechanism is still working, even poorly, technically, clinically, life still exists.

Genesis 2:8 tells us:

> "The LORD God planted a garden toward the east, in Eden; and there He placed the man whom He had formed."[4.6]

Common belief is that Eden and the garden are synonymous; but verse 8 does not actually read that way. It reads that the garden was a section of Eden in the East, or at least toward the East. So then Eden; which is generally believed to mean delight; or de-light, or "of or from" the light; was necessarily larger than the garden; this garden then being a subsection of Eden.

The word garden is a bit misleading. The actual word for garden is "1588 gan from 1598; a *garden* (as *fenced*): - garden. 1598 ganan a prim. root; to *hedge* about, i.e. (gen.) *protect*: - defend"[4.7]

*Chambers* states that "garden" is "… related to *gart* enclosure, YARD; congnate with Old Saxon *gard*, Old English *geard*, Old Icelandic *gardhr*, Gothic *gard-s*, all with the meaning enclosure;…"[4.8]

The use of this term seems to have much more to do with security or protection, rather than simply a place to grow plants. A better definition would likely be a "guarded area;" the term "guarded," probably coming from the same (garden) root. But guarded in the sense of an enclosure, fence, hedged, protected etc, (not by a guard such as personnel) resulting in a protected area.

The word "planted" is "5193 nata a prim. root; prop. to *strike* in, i.e. *fix*; spec. to *plant* (lit. or fig.): - fastened, plant (-er)."[4.9]

Planted or plants in the sense we use it as relating to horticulture; is a specific use of the broader meaning of the term "plant," relating to that specific (horticultural) purpose. In actuality, one does not in fact "plant a garden" when placing plants in a garden. The acts of selection of an area, preparing the soil, fencing in the area, etc., is the creation of the guarded area, garden or gan; these actions are entirely different and separate from placing the plants in said area.

The use of "plant" in the general sense is to fix or fasten. As in "plant your feet firmly on the ground." The plantar surface of the foot being another related example. The word "supplant" or "supplanter," as in the meaning of Jacob's name, does in no way refer to a garden or gardening activities.

So a better translation would be that God fixed or fastened a fence or hedge in East Eden, which resulted in a protective enclosure. And into that protected area, "He placed the man whom he had formed." It does not merely state that He placed *a* man. Nor does it state that He placed the man he had *created*. Neither of these can be true, because of the qualification by use of the term to describe this man. What He actually did place there, was the man He had "*formed.*"

This does not really seem to make very much sense. Why would God create a protective area to place this formed man? What is it or was it that God could possibly need to protect this man from?

As previously stated, the Bible contains little or no direct revelation as to what actual events transpired between the Genesis 2:5; beginning with the word "Now," and Genesis 2:7; beginning with the word "Then." But by jumping ahead to when the formed man sinned in chapter 3, we can get an idea of at least some of the result of sin, as we do know some of the changes that took place at that (Chapter 3) time.

Genesis 3:17-19 tells us:

> "Then to Adam He said, "Because you have listened to the voice of your wife, and have eaten from the tree about which I commanded you, saying, 'You shall not

> *eat from it'; Cursed is the ground because of you; In toil you will eat of it All the days of your life. "Both thorns and thistles it shall grow for you; And you will eat the plants of the field; By the sweat of your face You will eat bread,..."*[4.10]

Here in Chapter 3, we see some of the results of the sin. Simply put, the serpent or hisser, (explanation of this term to follow) got to the woman; and then the woman got to the man. As it currently reads, the ground *then* became cursed. Because the ground became cursed, there no longer was harmony in the plant world. Because of the disharmony weeds would proliferate. Adam would now have to work not just the ground; but actually work the field for sustenance. Here we clearly have a man to work the "field" announced to Adam. There clearly is now a man to serve or work the field(s).

Many believe that these words represent God announcing Adam's punishment. It seems more likely that this was not punishment; nor any announcement of the same; but rather a warning as to what conditions would be like outside the guarded area. Since Adam was ultimately expelled and God remained, it was actually not the guarded area that became cursed at that time.

Quite possibly, this ground cursing was precisely what happened between the aforementioned "now" and "then." But it was not this man who caused it; as at that time he was yet to be formed. It was likely the earlier *created* man or men or hosts who sinned; and it was at *that* time when the ground became cursed. This possibility will be described in much greater detail shortly.

Many years later, when Satan is speaking to Jesus and refers to what was delivered or given unto him, most believe this was this formed man; later referred to as Adam; who was in this garden in East Eden at this time, who did this very delivering or giving to Satan. It likely was not; but rather was delivered to him (Satan) by the original "created" men or hosts. There is no evidence that the guarded area where Adam was originally placed, actually became cursed; rather the formed man was expelled to an area outside the "gan;" an area which was already cursed; hence God's warning. We know that at least the area around and the tree of life remained guarded, this time by cherubim. As to whether this included how much, if any, of the rest of the originally guarded area is unclear.

That is likely one reason why God had built a protective area. It was to protect the man from the cursed ground; meaning that cursed ground had necessarily existed before the formed man was formed, and before this protected area was "planted." The other reason likely being: in order to keep Satan, or this serpent or hisser away from Adam; or was it?

Here we have a bit of a conundrum. God made this protected area or *gan*, for the man who is now in Genesis 3:17 being called Adam; (rather than adam); as a place in which he was to exist. For a while, we know not how long, it was literally a paradise; this term from "paradeity," meaning next to God. It could have been for half an hour, or millions of years that he was there before he fell; unless it is certain that the 130 years of age attributed to Adam when he had Seth, refers to his formation and not his expulsion.

The problem; is that it appears that this protected area both did and did not work. If the purpose was to provide an area which would keep the formed man away from the cursed ground; then this was successful. But if the purpose included keeping the formed man inaccessible to the serpent; then this is another matter. The "hisser" ultimately found his way in and caused trouble. But, we all know that God is omnipotent and omniscient. In this case; being omnipotent meaning that he could have provided this protected area with any level of protection in any way he wished. There would have been nothing that could have gotten in, had God *"planted"* it so. Being omniscient, He also knew ahead of time whether or not it would fail. It is important to remember that this protected area was *not* about Adam's free will or bad choices; but rather about anything unwanted being able to get in to the protective area in the first place. As Dave Hebler once profoundly asked: "How do you protect a man from himself?" It is important to remember that before Adam could even be confronted with temptation, the "hisser" had to get to him, as Adam knew no evil. This protective area; which appears to have ultimately failed; by its very definition should have stopped this, but it did not work.

So then the question becomes: Why would God; who is omnipotent, knowingly build a protective area that failed; even when He had to know ahead of time that it would fail; instead of building it to be impregnable? Again, this does not in any way refer to Adam's failure when confronted by temptation, but rather the failure of the *"fence, hedge, or protection"* to shield him.

In order to determine success or failure in any endeavor, one must necessarily know what the desired outcome is to be. Since it is understood by most that God can do anything but fail, why does it appear that this enclosure did not work? Perhaps there is a misunderstanding in precisely what the actual intended purpose was for this protected area; this "garden," or *gan*.

In 1 Corinthians 15:45 Paul refers to Jesus as the "Last Adam."

> *"So also it is written, "The first* MAN*, Adam,* BECAME A LIVING SOUL*." The last Adam became a life-giving spirit."*[4.11]

This gets a bit tricky; as we are comparing words between Greek and Hebrew; as Paul wrote in Greek, and Genesis was written in Hebrew; but this is extremely important.

It is very difficult to ascertain whether or not the use of the name Adam, (Capital A) ever actually occurs in Genesis, until perhaps Chapter 5. It does not appear as such in *The Interlinear Bible*, which contains the original Hebrew script. Rather, it is presented as 120, adam (lower case) not 121 Adam, (upper case) a proper noun.[4.12]

The term adam is: "120 adam, from 119; *ruddy*, i.e. a *human being* (an individual or the species, *mankind*, etc.): - x another, + hypocrite, + common sort, x low, man (mean, of low degree), person."[4.13] This is generally translated as "the man," or is also used in the plural as the definition indicates.

The Greek word that Paul uses which is translated as Adam is "76 Adam, of Heb. or. [121]; *Adam*, the first man; typ. (of Jesus) man (as his representative): - Adam."[4.14]

Thus there appears to be a relationship between the use of Adam as a proper noun to Messiah; as opposed to the use of adam; this use of adam occurring throughout these portions of Genesis, and simply meaning human being, person, or man.

The Greek word that Paul uses for "first" is; "4413 protos, contr. superl. of 4253; *foremost* (in time, place, order or importance): - before, beginning, best, chief (-est), first (of all), former."[4.15] This word appears as a root in the word "prototype." Here the usage is suggestive of a precursor to something else.

As stated, Paul clearly indicates that there were some similarities between Adam and Messiah. When referring to the "second coming" it is not referred to in the Scriptures as the "last coming," even though it is believed to be such. So then the question arises as to why it is that Paul refers to Jesus as the last Adam, and not the second, third, etc. Adam? Although some highly questionable commentary could be found referring to Messiah as "Second Adam;" nowhere could this term be located Scripturally. This commentary is likely the result of the use of the term "second" by Paul in an entirely different context, when comparing spiritual and natural in verse 47.

This use of "last" is particularly interesting, since there were many beings who would fit the description of "adam" (the man or mankind) who existed after Adam, as well as many more who existed after Jesus. Thus, it cannot mean "last" in that sense.

The actual Greek word used here for "last" is "2078 eschatos, a superl. prob. from 2192 (in the sense of *contiguity*); *farthest, final,* (of place or time): - ends of, last, latter end, lowest, uttermost."[4.16]

In English we have the word "eschatology" which is concerned with final destinations, not physical destinations, but the ultimate or final destination of the soul. Here, by the choosing of this particular word *eschatos*, the definition indicates that there is also the sense of something continuous or in actual contact with.

The word which is not used here is the Greek word telos

which is and defined as "5056 telos from a prim. tello (to *set out for a definite point or goal*); prop. the point aimed at as a *limit*, i.e. (by impl.) the *conclusion* of an act or state..."[4.17]

As an example: the word telophase in biology refers to the last phase in mitosis or nuclear division, which is usually followed by cytokinesis, which is the actual cell division. Although mitosis technically is not cell division, but nuclear division; nevertheless, telophase is in fact its last or final phase of mitosis.

Thus, by use of the word *eschatos* and not *telos* when describing the last Adam, it seems likely that whatever the first/last sequence was, it had something to do with the ultimate destination of the soul; rather than merely the end of some physical process, state or act. There is also a sense that there is a continuousness or contiguousness in this transition; rather than two separate events. Of course it simply makes no sense that this sequential relationship consists of merely Adam sinning in order to give Messiah something to salvage and redeem.

So then it is fair to question or inquire as to precisely what it could have been that Adam and Messiah had in common; perhaps uniquely, perhaps not; which would then justify placing them as the first and last in a sequence; as well as to question precisely what that sequence might be.

We do know that neither was brought into existence with a biological or physical father in the "natural" sense. If it is believed that "original sin" is carried by the natural father, then neither was born with original sin. But the original "Hosts," who were brought into existence by creation, (*bara*) and not formation, via dust, or maternally, or any other method; they necessarily also had no natural father, and therefore also could not have entered into the world with original sin.

These three examples; the original created hosts, (male *and* female); adam and the woman; and Messiah; are the only three examples that could be found in the Scriptures with no natural, i.e. biological, father. The only known exception might be Melchisedec (Hebrew) or Melchizedek (Greek) who is referenced in Hebrews 7:3 "Without father, without mother, without genealogy, having neither beginning of days nor end of life, but made like the Son of God, he remains a priest perpetually"[4.18] Although there is much speculation about "Mel," very little is known about him. "Without genealogy" may mean that he had none, or could very well mean that his genealogy simply was not known at that time; or for that matter, not known even today.

There are at least two ways to interpret the concept of being born or conceived "without sin." If it is the case that sexual intercourse is to be considered as sinful; then this could mean born without any sexual intercourse; and it is often interpreted this way. Alternately; if sin is passed on to the child by the father; then this would mean being born without this sin being passed along.

The former makes no real degree of sense, as it is the method by which humans multiply; which is both God's will and desire: after all, He did devise the system. The latter is only possible if either a male without this original sin, or arguably any sin for that matter, is the natural father; or if this is somehow achieved supernaturally.

Note; although both Jesus and Adam were brought into existence without sin, there were interesting differences. One being that Adam lived in a "world" where no sin existed, and yet ultimately sinned. Jesus lived in a world rampant with sin, and yet sinned not.

But back to Genesis Chapter 2, and why God made this protected area or *gan*; and did it succeed or fail. And moreover, precisely what are or were the possibilities from which the man needed protection? There seems to be a limited number of these:

Could it have been protection from the plant life? This seems unlikely as the very next thing God did according to Genesis 2: 9 was:

> "Out of the ground the LORD God <u>caused </u>to grow every tree that is pleasing to the sight and good for food; the tree of life also in the midst of the garden, and the tree of the knowledge of good and evil."[4.19] *(emphasis added)*

Now it is true, this does not mention any vegetation other

than trees, but is seems a bit of a stretch to suggest that protection was required from vegetation; and particularly; only from vegetation other than trees.

Could it have been protection from the "beasts?" This also seems unlikely as according to Genesis 2: 19-20:

> *"Out of the ground the LORD God <u>formed</u> every beast of the field and every bird of the sky, and brought them to the man to see what he would call them; and whatever the man called a living creature, that was its name. (emphasis added)*
> *The man gave names to all the cattle, and to the birds of the sky, and to every beast of the field, but for Adam there was not found a helper suitable for him."* [4.20]

The sea beasts are not mentioned here, but it does not seem reasonable that sea creatures would be likely to come out of the oceans to this protected area or *gan*.

Could it have been protection from the original created (bara) "hosts?" Possibly, but the Scriptures provide no information about this. If this were so, there is no indication whatsoever that this *gan* failed, because nowhere is it written, suggested, or implied that any of the created "hosts" were ever present in this protected area.

What else is left? Can one have sin and not have the influence of enemy; AKA the hisser? Probably not, as that was the very situation or environment, that adam, or the man, was actually in prior to this sinning. Can one have the hisser and not have sin? Yes, but only one man ever succeeded in this.

It seems by Hobson's choice that it was from the enemy that this protection was afforded. This same enemy being the opponent, or adversary, or slanderer (devil); depending on ones perspective. The next question being of course, was it designed to ultimately succeed in this protection? Or, was it a trap?

There are many possibilities with respect to the purpose for which God formed adam. One possibility being that he was to begin the genetic line from which Messiah was to come. Another possibility being that it was adam himself who was originally and by divine plan supposed to be Messiah; via formation; to be the Messiah for the created hosts.

With respect to the latter, adam met perhaps two critical conditions for this. He was brought into existence without sin. He was tempted, but it does not seem in all ways—as he failed the first time; at least as far as we know.

It appears that he actually sinned more than once though, as when he was caught, according to Genesis 3:12, adam actually stated: "The woman whom You gave *to be* with me, she gave me from the tree, and I ate."[4.21]

Thus, according to adam, his sinning was God's fault and not his. In adam's view had God given adam a better woman, it would not have happened. As though the woman somehow held a weapon to his head. So now there is not only disobedience, but the pride as well. Which one is or was more serious is a matter of opinion.

Although by no means conclusive, it seems that adam having begun the genetic line for Messiah is the more reasonable explanation. The problem is that had adam not ever sinned, he probably would have lived forever in the *gan*. In fact, as previously mentioned, we have no idea how long he was there prior to sin. It is true that he was about 130 years old when he fathered Seth; but we do not know for certain when the counting actually began.

God was paving the way for the salvation of mankind. How could this have happened if adam had remained sinless in the gan for eternity? The only way would have been to allow the enemy access to him, for one of two possible outcomes:

1) If adam had sinned, as he did, then he would be expelled from the area, as he was.

or

2) Had it been the case that adam did not ever sin; which means he may arguably have been a suitable

candidate for the process of salvation of the created hosts and their offspring via substitution; how could temptation have happened without the influence of the enemy?

Either way, the enemy had to gain access. Thus the *gan* did not fail; or rather it "failed" by design; thus, succeeding by "succeeding" as a trap.

Genesis 2:10-14 tells us:

> *"Now a river flowed out of Eden to water the garden; and from there it divided and became four rivers. The name of the first is Pishon; it flows around the whole land of Havilah, where there is gold. The gold of that land is good; the bdellium and the onyx stone are there. The name of the second river is Gihon; it flows around the whole land of Cush. The name of the third river is Tigris; it flows east of Assyria. And the fourth river is the Euphrates."* [4.22]

Although this gan was made as a protected area, there also was flora and "shortly" there would be fauna present; although here, all of these would be made by formation and not creation. But it appears that there was no rain in this area, as we are told that a river watered the garden, and there is no mention of rain. As discussed earlier, here again, there appears to be that relationship between rain and sin. Or rather; this represents a correlation between the absence of rain and the absence of sin; and the presence of rain and the presence of sin.

Prior to this, there was no rain as a "mist used to rise," then after sin, there was rain. Here there appears to be no rain, but instead a river waters the area. As is well known, a bit later there would be a great amount of sin, and a great amount of rain.

It is also interesting to note that for some reason this river is unnamed. The four branches are named, but not until they leave the gan, and go out to the "unprotected" and previously cursed lands. The very subject of verse 10 is how the gan is watered, and yet we know not the name of the river which accomplishes this; but yet we are told the names of the four branches after the branching. This seems a bit odd, nevertheless, at this time it would be pure speculation as to why this is so. Upon researching the original terminology for the word "river," it seems to just mean river.

An important distinction should be made here. As previously stated, Genesis 2: verse 8 tells or told us that: "The LORD God planted a garden toward the east, in Eden; and there He placed the man whom He had formed."

But Genesis 2:15 now tells us:

> "Then the Lord God took the man and put him into the garden of Eden to cultivate it and keep it."[4.23]

It reads as though for some reason God did the same thing twice. This cannot be a recapitulation of the same event, because in the interim; plant life and the trees of life and the knowledge of good and evil had been introduced; and nowhere does it state or even imply that God had ever removed the man.

A note about the use of the terms "cultivate" and "keep." It was not the fields here that were to be "worked," but rather the existing garden, here garden and plants being used in the more conventional usage, as a protected area with plants. Some people cultivate very expensive roses, but that is not the same as working the earth.

This is also odd, because in the beginning, first God created the environment and the food, and then he created man. Here God first forms man, and *then*, He makes the protected environment with food as a place for the man to live.

Verse 8 ("The LORD God planted a garden toward the east, in Eden; and there He placed the man whom He had formed.") seems to indicate that it was the gan, in which God placed the man; meaning that the word "there" refers to the gan. But another reading could suggest that the word "there" actually refers to Eden and not the gan. The sequence of events then being: that God formed the man, placed him in Eden, staked out a protected area, caused the tree of life to grow, caused a river or had previously caused a river to flow into this protected area; and He *then* placed the man in this protected area with the trees.

The second placement (or put), but not the first placement referring to the man's placement in this protected floriferous area. The Bible is a book about redemption and not a historical text; so or but unfortunately, there seems to be no mention of what adam may have been doing until he arrived in the gan, or why. Thus it follows that whatever Scriptural evidence may have existed regarding this was either removed at some point; or is likely not directly or even indirectly related to redemption. Neither is there any indication as to how much time lapsed between when he was formed, and when he actually arrived in the gan.

Genesis 2:16-17 tells us:

*"The LORD God commanded the man, saying, "From any tree of the garden you may eat freely; but from the tree of the knowledge of good and evil you shall not eat, for in the day that you eat from it you will surely die."*[4.24]

These are pretty clear instructions. It must be pointed out however, that the prohibited tree was not the tree of good and evil, but the tree of the *knowledge* of good and evil. Whatever death(s) awaited, do not appear to be the result of evil, but rather merely the acquisition of the knowledge of good and evil. There is also no mention of fruit here. One might argue the irrelevancy of this, perhaps correctly, but there is a minor point about this later.

Also, much is attributed to Eve later eating; suggesting that this command was not given to her, and therefore it was only adam who sinned. In support of this, obviously she was not yet there, or even formed, when this command was issued.

The word here for day is again "yowm" (yom) which again does not necessarily mean that he would die on that very day, but rather an indication of some period of time. [4.25]

Genesis 2:18-20 tells us:

*"Then the LORD God said, "It is not good for the man to be alone; I will make him a helper suitable for him."*

> *Out of the ground the* LORD *God formed every beast of the field and every bird of the sky, and brought them to the man to see what he would call them; and whatever the man called a living creature, that was its name. The man gave names to all the cattle, and to the birds of the sky, and to every beast of the field, but for Adam there was not found a helper suitable for him."*[4.26]

There is one striking point here, beside the fact that these beasts were formed and not created. Verse 19 tells us that God formed theses life forms and brought them to adam. This implies that they were formed somewhere else; in some other part of the gan, or somewhere other than in the gan. We are not told where. The most likely place being in Eden, somewhere other than the protected area. Otherwise, it is likely that God would not have formed these creatures, but merely brought in the previously created ones or their offspring.

And contrary to common usage, not good does not necessarily mean bad. It refers to the absence of good, rather than the presence of bad. There can be neutrality. But generally, God is never about neutrality.

Verse 19 reads like a naming session. God brought the beasts to adam, and permitted adam to name them, and whatever he named them then became their names. The problem is that in verse 19 there is an implication that God did not know what names adam would call these life forms; and so God brought them to adam in order to find out. It does not state to see him call them, but to see *what* he would call them. But this really does not seem to make very much sense given an omniscient God.

Furthermore, the sandwiching of the formations of these life forms in verse 19, between verse 18 where God states that he would make a helper for adam, and in verse 20 the not finding of a suitable helper, implies that a suitable helper may have been anticipated to be found in these formations, but was not. Since this term "helper" is: "5828 ezer, from 5826; *aid*: - help." " 5826 azar, a prim. root; to *surround*, i.e. *protect* or *aid*: - help, succour.";[4.27] it does not seem reasonable that one could be

found; neither would one reasonably be expected to be found.
Genesis 2:21-25 tells us:

> *"So the LORD God caused a deep sleep to fall upon the man, and he slept; then He took one of his ribs and closed up the flesh at that place.*
> *The LORD God fashioned into a woman the rib which He had taken from the man, and brought her to the man.*
> *The man said,"This is now bone of my bones, And flesh of my flesh;She shall be called Woman, Because she was taken out of Man."*
> *For this reason a man shall leave his father and his mother, and be joined to his wife; and they shall become one flesh.*
> *And the man and his wife were both naked and were not ashamed."*[4.28]

The word "fashioned" is the word "1129 banah, a prim. root; to *build* (lit. and fig.): - (begin to) build (-er), obtain children, make, repair, set (up), x surely." [4.29]

Again, this is not *"bara,"* but rather *"banah,"* which may sound similar but is not; as the raw materials utilized are also disclosed here in Genesis.

Here again the fashioned or built life form is brought to adam, as were the other life forms to be named by him. Although adam named her too; called her woman; it is not clear if this was just out of habit; meaning that God did not necessarily bring her to adam for the purpose of being named. Given the statements made by God in verse 24, naming her does not seem to have been the main reason.

It is not stated where this banah took place prior to her being brought to adam. In addition, this was the only life form known to be made from a part of adam.

And Verse 25 clearly attests to their innocence at that time.

# Chapter 5

## Thoughts, Ideas, and Suggestions

In today's age, when examining the quality or appropriateness of behavior, many criteria necessarily must be considered. Supposedly; the system of law under which we live is derived from Scriptural law. Unfortunately, man's system of law has far deviated from this standard; often to the point where it is no longer recognizable; and may at times, in fact, actually contradict the word of God.

Man's laws generally fall into two separate and distinct categories: Actions or inactions which are considered wrongs because they are morally wrong; and actions or inactions which are considered wrongs merely because of man's prohibition of the same. As a result, we end up with a "two tiered" system of officially judging human behavior.

One tier is based upon what God said, or is genuinely believed to have said. The other being based upon some consensus of the opinions of some group or groups of men about what constitutes right and wrong. One serious problem with this arrangement; is that what God said is unchanging, but man's views are very often subject to change. Thus we have one system based upon unchanging objectivity, the other being largely based upon subjectivity, which can be quite fickle; the institution of "prohibition" being a prime example:

The NAS Bible version of Proverbs, 20:1 tells us:

*"Wine is a mocker, strong drink a brawler, And whoever is intoxicated by it is not wise."* [5.1]

In this version the word "intoxicated;" for whatever reason(s); was substituted for the original word which essentially means "errs."

The original word that was substituted with the word intoxicated is: "7686 shagah, a prim. root; to *stray* (caus. *mislead*), usually (fig.) to *mistake*, espec. (mor.) to *transgress*; by extens. (through the idea of intoxication) to *reel*, (fig.) *be enraptured:* - (cause to) go astray, deceive, err, be ravished, sin through ignorance, (let, make to) wander."[5.2]

So with the substitution of the word "intoxicated" for the word "errs," the focus is now shifted from one's behavior during or after consuming alcohol; to the quantity of actual alcohol consumed. Conclusion: "The Bible says it is unwise to become intoxicated." The problem is that this is not at all what it says. Although in a general sense, the wisdom of becoming intoxicated with alcohol would be a fair discussion; but what is actually stated in Proverbs has nothing to do with the level of intoxication; but rather one's behavior after consumption of any amount of alcohol. The word intoxication does not even appear, and is relevant only by extension and context.

If the consumption of "wine" or "strong drink" by an individual is contributory to transgression, mistake, error, etc.; then it is simply not wise to drink it. In this regard it is a binary; it matters little if one is intoxicated or not. If you are prone to err by it, best leave it alone; irrespective of the quantity of consumption. Although it is generally understood, that the level of consumption can usually be related to both the likelihood and severity of error. The entire concept of "drinking responsibly" is to try and ensure that the environment surrounding the consumption of alcohol is one that would minimize the opportunities to commit error; errors such as driving an automobile after consumption of alcohol.

To be perfectly clear; one should not ever drink any amount of alcohol and drive; period. That is not the issue under discussion at all. Staying alive and well in an automobile; even while perfectly sober is not easy; and thus only a fool would ever drive otherwise.

When Jesus turned the water into wine, this took place at a wedding, and was necessary because they had run out of wine. In fact, criticism was offered because the wine He made was superior to the wine that had already been served; their conclusion being that it should have been served first. But of course this miracle did not happen until the wine ran out. Nevertheless, it is difficult to understand how the supply of wine could have been exhausted, had the guests not already been drinking large quantities of it. It is doubtful that Jesus did this to facilitate the guests being unwise.

Thus, the constitutional amendment instituting prohibition did not become a reality because it was God's will that we do not drink alcohol. There are many similar laws today: Laws about fireworks, concealed weapons by upstanding citizens, confiscatory taxes on certain products, etc.

To be considered a miscreant, it used to require that one in some way disobeyed God. Now one can be considered such; simply by behaving in a manner which merely disagrees with the consensus of a group of individuals; without any requirement of causing any type of harm to anyone or disobeying God.

But at the time in question; the time of adam, this mess did not yet exist. It was the commands of God that determined right from wrong; which in actuality; is still the case today irrespective of any views to the contrary.

Genesis Chapter 3:1-3 tells us:

*"Now the serpent was more crafty than any beast of the field which the LORD God had made. And he said to the woman, "Indeed, has God said, 'You shall not eat from any tree of the garden'?"*
*The woman said to the serpent, "From the fruit of the trees of the garden we may eat;*
*but from the fruit of the tree which is in the middle of the garden, God has said, 'You shall not eat from it or touch it, or you will die.'"*[5.3]

The original word used for "serpent" is again: "5175 nachash, from 5172; a *snake* (from its *hiss*): - serpent." "5172 nachash, a prim. root; prop. to *hiss,* i.e. *whisper* a (magic) spell; gen. to *prognosticate*: - x certainly, divine, enchanter, (use) x enchantment, learn by experience, x indeed, diligently observe."[5.4]

Clearly this term "serpent" refers to the enemy, by whichever or whatever name one chooses to call him. It is important to again make the distinction that this word "nachash;" when it is used as a term to describe a snake; it is not by appearances, but rather by the sound it makes; and or its or his capabilities.

The first logical question is: How did the enemy have knowledge of this command issued by God to the man? Clearly he obtained it somehow. Perhaps he had been paying close attention when God issued this command to adam. And it is interesting to note the manner in which he twisted this command. If he heard the command, and he must have; then he knew quite well what the command was and what it was not. Although Satan may want his enemies to believe that he can read their minds, this is not commonly believed to be true. This of course is not the same as a non-verbal or mental communications to him, such as: "get lost" or "shut up;" any of which it appears that he can receive quite loudly and clearly, if that is our intention.

The serpent's or hisser's statement, which is presented here as a question; is proffered in order to begin a conversation with Eve. It should be noted that her name was not yet Eve at this time, so perhaps "the woman" would be more appropriate. Had "the woman" stuck to the military "name rank and serial number," this conversation likely would never have taken place.

The second question being: how did "the woman" know of this command? She had yet to be formed when God issued it to adam. There is no evidence that God told her; neither is there any evidence that adam ever told her; yet somehow she knew. Perhaps she learned it through the man's behavior, or perhaps at some point He or he issued a warning to her. But "the woman" did not recount this command accurately.

What God had actually said back in Genesis 2:16-17 was:

> *"The LORD God commanded the man, saying, "From any tree of the garden you may eat freely; but from the tree of the knowledge of good and evil you shall not eat, for in the day that you eat from it you will surely die."*

God made no mention of "touching" it; neither to adam nor to her. Neither did God mention any "fruit" in this command. It could be reasonably assumed that He meant fruit, but that is not what He said. It is also at least arguable that the tree of the knowledge of good and evil was actually in the middle of the garden; as the "also" ("...the tree of life also in the midst of the garden, and the tree of the knowledge of good and evil") can be read both ways. The "also" may refer to the food trees and the tree of life; but not necessarily the tree of the knowledge of good and evil; with respect to being in the midst of the garden.

Furthermore, she did not state that it was the tree of the knowledge of good and evil from which they were not to eat or touch, but rather only the tree in the middle of the garden.

As crazy as this may sound; it is quite possible that it did not matter from which particular tree they ate, as far as the nature of the tree is concerned. Both of them were truly innocent. They did not know evil, evil here meaning not only acting; but even the possibility of acting against God's will. This evil was introduced to them. Their first sin was disobeying God. That *possibility* was the knowledge of evil, and this knowledge did not come from a tree. They both knowingly chose to act against the commands of God.

The nature of the tree seems irrelevant. Meaning: precisely how would the outcome have been different if God had chosen another tree to prohibit, or if Eve picked a different tree? Had God picked a fortune cookie tree to prohibit; the disobedience would have been the same. Had the man and woman been mistaken about which tree was prohibited; the disobedience would likely have been the same, because of the nature of their intentions. In that case it would not have been because of the nature of the tree. This is a key point. Evil is acting against God's will; irrespective of whether or not the actual act in itself seems; or perhaps even is; good or bad.

Genesis 3: 4-5 states:

> *"The serpent said to the woman, "You surely will not die!" For God knows that in the day you eat from it your eyes will be opened, and you will be like God, knowing good and evil."*[5.5]

Here the enemy actually told two truths. Not *"the truth"* but rather a pair of *"truths;"* appropriately each singularly referred to as *"a truth"* but clearly not *"the truth."*

If by this death, or "die" he meant physical death; the separation or disconnection of the breath of life from the vessel formed to contain it; surely that did not happen at that time. But surely does not mean immediately; immediately being used as a description of the timing; but instead "surely" is used as a description of the degree of certainty.

If by this death or "die" he meant spiritual separation or disconnection from God; because barring justification; God can only have perfection connected to him, then the serpent, or the hisser clearly lied; in that is exactly what happened at that time.

The second statement made here is also very misleading. Firstly, the man and the woman already knew good. Whether they knew that they knew good is another matter; as this usually requires a point of reference; of which there is no suggestion was present. But until they disobeyed, all they knew or could have known was good; irrespective of whether or not they knew it was good. So the part of the statement about being like God by knowing good as an individual condition, is essentially superfluous.

Regarding knowing evil on the day they ate from the tree, this was also *"a truth."* But could the woman have had any idea what this really meant? It is likely that she considered being similar to God (which was actually already true) a desirable thing; but how could she even have known what knowing evil represented? So she heard the be like God part; but it seems doubtful that she even knew what was meant by good or evil; but whatever that meant, it meant to be like God, so it was desirable thing. After all, wanting to be like God, in and of itself, is not a bad thing.

It would have been interesting at this point if the woman had simply inquired or suggested to the serpent; that if this was so good, then why don't you eat it? The woman at this point knew only good, and the serpent only evil. Whoever ate would reach the condition of knowing both "good and evil." Had she made this suggestion, the serpent would likely have run away and waited for a more "opportune time." But had the serpent eaten, he would then have known good as well as the evil he already knew.

This gets even more interesting, because to this serpent, he is superior to God. Thus in his own warped way, his will represents good to him; and thus God's will represents evil to him. So he would have learned what would have been evil to him; which is actually good; while already knowing his good, which is actually evil. But no matter what he thought, the dynamics would have changed. But although this is interesting to ponder; it is an academic exercise, as she did not make this suggestion.

It does not seem that God could or would actually "know" evil. This knowledge of evil of course, is entirely different than knowing *"of"* evil. It seems that when evil takes place, often the first thing God does is disconnect Himself from it or destroy it; depending on the circumstances. Therefore, it seems fair to say that although God can and does know good, he either cannot or will not know evil; but only know "of evil." Anything that is good is of God. If it is evil, then by definition, it cannot be of God; as a thing cannot simultaneously be both consistent with and against His will.

It seems not long ago, that we were told that man was made in the image and according to the likeness of God. Thus by design, we are only capable of knowing good by this very same design. When we become evil, capable of knowing evil or even capable of knowing "of evil;" this is not by design, but contamination; this being precisely what the man and the woman were protected from by the *"gan;"* at least for a time. It must be remembered that it was not the tree of good and evil, but the tree of the *"knowledge"* of good and evil from which they ate.

Evil means against the will of God. Thus wicked and evil are not synonymous. The crucifixion was a very wicked thing, but it was God's will. Thus by this definition it was wicked, but not evil. It gets even more complicated because those involved in the crucifixion were being wicked for certain, and were acting out of evil subjectively; meaning they genuinely believed that they were thwarting the will of God. Why? Because they feared the social and economic upheaval Messiah might cause; and so by mistake; they actually acted consistent with the will of God; all while trying to do the opposite.

And during that time, the devil simply could not make up his mind what he was doing. First he was all behind it, and then when he realized what was actually happening, most likely in Gethsemane, he tries to talk Jesus out of it. It seems he had a tough time figuring out just what the evil course of action was supposed to be.

Genesis 3:6-7 tells us:

> *"When the woman saw that the tree was good for food, and that it was a delight to the eyes, and that the tree was desirable to make one wise, she took from its fruit and ate; and she gave also to her husband with her, and he ate.*

*Then the eyes of both of them were opened, and they knew that they were naked; and they sewed fig leaves together and made themselves loin coverings."*[5.6]

The first half of Verse 6 does not seem to make very much sense. Are we supposed to believe that she never before saw the tree, or that never before knew that it could have been used as food? She had already admitted that it had fruit that should not be eaten. Why would she have ever stated this if she did not think it could have been good for food at the time she stated it; which was before this time?

Neither was there any suggestion that this fruit was atypical looking, meaning that it's appearance was deceiving, because although it was fruit, it actually looked like balls of writhing maggots. Thus, neither of these statements seems to represent any revelation.

It is the third statement in this sentence which is the key, and provides the turning point for the remainder of the sentence; that statement which appears after the second "and;" "And that the tree was desirable to make *one* wise." The devil never mentioned what the fruit looked like or whether it was good for food. In fact the devil never even mentioned fruit at all. Her choosing to believe that the tree would make one wise, represented the completion of the seduction.

After filtering out all of his gibberish; that; (the belief it would make one wise); was what he was actually saying; and this (disobedience AKA sin) was the result he was after. Once that happened the rest just followed.

All of this represents very important and actionable intelligence as to how the enemy works.

And where was the man while all of this was going on? The way it reads he was right there. It does not say that she had to find him. It does not say that she decided to save some to give him for dinner when he came home from the office. The way it reads, he was right there and yet it seems that he did nothing except eat too.

Genesis 3:8-13 tells us:

> *"They heard the sound of the LORD God walking in the garden in the cool of the day, and the man and his wife hid themselves from the presence of the LORD God among the trees of the garden. Then the LORD God called to the man, and said to him, "Where are you?" He said, "I heard the sound of You in the garden, and I was afraid because I was naked; so I hid myself." And He said, "Who told you that you were naked? Have you eaten from the tree of which I commanded you not to eat?" The man said, "The woman whom You gave to be with me, she gave me from the tree, and I ate." Then the LORD God said to the woman, "What is this you have done?" And the woman said, "The serpent deceived me, and I ate."*[5.7]

Verses 8-13 read pretty straightforward except for a few points: Firstly, they were hiding from God.

There is no way that an omniscient God would have to ask any of these questions. Since we know God is omniscient; why then did He choose to make an inquiry regarding information He had already known since forever? The reason is unclear. Perhaps this was a merely means of justice; meaning giving them a chance to explain themselves. Even though He knew what the answers were to be, they had to be afforded the opportunity to answer. Would or could the outcome have been any different had they repented at that time when afforded the opportunity?

What is even more interesting is why they thought God needed this information; and actually answered Him; as though they believed that He did not know. It seems the answer is pride, which is revealed in verses 12 and 13.

In verse 11, God asks the man if he has eaten from the tree, and the man's answer (in verse 12) is not whether or not he did it; but rather that it is God's fault that he did it. It was because of that woman that You gave to be with me, she made me do it. Meaning that had God given him a better woman, then of course things would have turned out differently. Therefore it is all God's fault. There is no remorse, or even any appearance of remorse.

And when God asks her, she essentially says that the devil made her do it. Neither is there any appearance whatsoever of any remorse here, nor any need for repentance on her part. In fact, the way it is written, it could have ended with the woman asking "Yeah so?"

This is not dissimilar to a student receiving a low grade in a class. If it is an A it is, "I got an A." If it is a D, it somehow becomes "he/she gave me a D." The woman changed the subject from what she did, to what the serpent did. I wasn't deceived, but rather "he deceived me."

Genesis 3:14 tells us:

> "The LORD God said to the serpent, "Because you have done this, Cursed are you more than all cattle, And more than every beast of the field; On your belly you will go, And dust you will eat All the days of your life;"[5.8]

Because of what the serpent did, God cursed him. Or did He? What God stated was that the serpent was cursed. It does not say that God cursed the serpent. Perhaps it was God who cursed the serpent, but either way; either as an announcement of God's action; or the merely the announcement of a result; the serpent was cursed.

If, strictly for the purpose of better understanding, we were to add another "because;" this one between the words "field" and "On;" it would then read: "Because you have done this, Cursed are you more than all cattle, And more than every beast of the field; *Because* On your belly you will go, And dust you will eat All the days of your life." This would then establish a cause and effect relationship between the ground and the dust, and the degree of cursing.

This may not be quite as flippant a suggestion as it may appear to be. A bit later on, in Genesis 3:17, the word "because" appears twice in the NAS version. According to *Strong's*

*Exhaustive Concordance*, the word because only appears once in Genesis 3:17.[5.9]

The actual word translated as "because" is "3588 kiy, a prim. particle [the full form of the prepositional prefix] indicating causal relations of all kinds..."[5.10]

Of course establishing the fact that this word "*kiy*" which is translated as "because" indicates a causal relationship; does little to prove or disprove where or when it should occur. Nevertheless, its inclusion or exclusion in different translations does seem to indicate some degree of latitude with respect to this.

A few words must be said about this serpent. He is generally believed to have been a snake; but this is not exactly correct; and furthermore this belief may in fact be a bit dangerous. The only apparent reason that he is believed to physically have been a snake, is because of one of the definitions of "nachash" is "hisser."

When God told him that he would go on to his belly; obviously he was not yet on his belly at that time. Thus if he was actually a snake, he was not a snake who was already on his belly. How could it be that a snake could be other than on his belly? Levitation, or some sort of legs seem to be the only possibilities. Thus, whatever this manifestation originally was, it seems highly unlikely that it was a snake; at least as we know them to be today.

A fair argument can be made that this particular event actually was only about 6 thousand years ago; give or take a few centuries or more. Thus, there would likely be evidence of snakes with legs available to herpetologists. (Herpes means to creep.) This would render the old saying: "I need that like a snake needs shoes," invalid. But even if this were so; we are still left with the fact that the definition of nachash as a snake, is solely because of its "hissing."

Snakes do not generally whisper magic spells, or prognosticate. They are not divine, they do not enchant. They may, to a limited extent, learn by experience; but do they actually diligently observe? All of these represent additional definitions of nachash. The relationship of whatever manifestation in the gan that was the devil to a "snake's" physical appearance; would likely be similar to the relationship a human's physical appearance has when he or she is referred to as a "snake" by someone today. There is likely none.

The bulk of the definitions of nachash sound much more like the characteristics of the "seam" addressed in Chapter 2.

Relative to other "cursed" life forms, how much was the serpent cursed? Verse 14 tells us more than the cattle or the beasts of the field, and the way it reads, this seems to be presented as a superlative. There is a slight problem here however; because no other direct account of the cattle or the beasts of the field ever being cursed had ever appeared before this time. Yet it must have been so, because God used this as a reference regarding precisely how cursed the serpent was to be.

The following is a recapitulation of the two Scriptural sources as the origins of these beasts:

Genesis 1: 24-24 tells us:

> *"Then God said, "Let the earth bring forth living creatures after their kind: cattle and creeping things and beasts of the earth after their kind"; and it was so. God made the beasts of the earth after their kind, and the cattle after their kind, and everything that creeps on the ground after its kind; and God saw that it was good."*[5.11] *(The first time, the beasts outside the gan.)*

Genesis 2:19 tells us:

> *"Out of the ground the LORD God <u>formed</u> every beast of the field and every bird of the sky, and brought them to the man to see what he would call them; and whatever the man called a living creature, that was its name."*[5.12]
> *(The second time, the beasts who were formed and brought inside the gan.)*

There is no other recorded event in Genesis, thus far, that refers to these beasts ever being cursed. If we consider the circumstances; or rather the change in circumstances as evidenced in the beginning of Genesis Chapter 4; specifically by the tilling of the ground by Cain, and the keeping of livestock by Abel; as well as the following reference Luke Chapter 4; some light on this appears.

The following passage from Luke is concerned with the time when Jesus was being tempted by the devil:

Luke 4:5 tells us:

> "And he led Him up and showed Him all the kingdoms of the world in a moment of time. And the devil said to Him, "I will give You all this domain and its glory; for it has been handed over to me, and I give it to whomever I wish."[5.13]

Many, if not most believe that here the devil is talking about the earth as was handed over to him by adam. But it seems that before adam was even formed, the change or the act of the earth being "handed over" had already happened; arguably twice. The first time resulted in the earth becoming without form and void; as well as the establishment of the cover and the seam. The second time because of the created hosts, thus necessitating the need for Adam's formation.

If so, this means prior to adam's sin, the ground was already "cursed;" and depending on circumstances; so were all of those life forms on it. As stated, this being a minor or early version of what caused the original "without form and void" condition; but this time God would not and did not permit it to go that far. He had a different plan.

It seems that because the original hosts were engaging in sinful behavior. Even the mist could no longer be used for watering, as it became contaminated from the cursed earth or ground. This contamination or cursing also caused the need for the protected area or *gan*, in order to facilitate the formation of the man and the woman. This sin of the created hosts was likely the reason for the need for the first and ultimately the last adam; the initiation of the redemptive process being God's plan.

The issue again rises as to what effect this cursing may have had on the earth, land, ground, or soil. The reference to being cursed more than the cattle or the beasts, *is* probably related to the serpent being relegated to being on his belly and eating dust. The serpent's cursing would then be related to contact with the previously existing cursed ground. How much closer can one be to the cursed ground than by being on ones belly and eating the dust? The same rules apply to radioactive fallout. The closer any animal is to the ground, the greater the radiation absorbed dose.

You see this concept with the references to the type of hoof an animal has, with respect to the same being related to edibility. You see this with the prohibitions on eating shellfish, as they are close to the ground, albeit underwater; and they essentially eat, albeit wet, "dust." You see confirmation of this in Exodus when Moses is required by God to "take off his shoes;"

Exodus 3: 4-5 tells us:

> " *When the* LORD *saw that he turned aside to look, God called to him from the midst of the bush and said, "Moses, Moses!" And he said, "Here I am." Then He said, "Do not come near here; remove your sandals from your feet, for the place on which you are standing is holy ground."*5.14

If Moses had to remove his sandals because of the holy ground, then clearly the ground outside that particular area must have been unholy at that time. How could God or why would God have created unholy ground when He made the earth? The answer is that He did not.

If we try to say that it was still cursed from the "without form and void" period; then we are left with problems, because in early Genesis there is no evidence of any cursing with the plant or animal life; nor any evidence of any disharmony whatsoever. No need for a field etc. In fact, the actions originally undertaken by God very early in Genesis with respect to the darkness/cover/seam reads much more like a major "de-cursing," rather than cursing.

If we try the approach that it was the "adamic" sin that caused this change; then we have the problem with the need for a protected area; as from what was it to be protected? This is in addition to all the issues presented earlier. To address this question, it is necessary to jump ahead a bit:

The latter half of Genesis 3: 17 tells us: "Cursed is the ground because of you." (adam) Genesis 3:23 tells us "therefore the LORD God sent him out from the garden of Eden, to cultivate the ground from which he was taken."[5.15] But as will be seen shortly, the expulsion was not because of sin.

This tells us one or perhaps two things: Firstly, adam was made from the cursed "dust of the ground," likely from outside of the gan. Secondly, perhaps God was not only showing His power; but also simultaneously rubbing the devils nose in this fact.

As will be seen later at the time of the crucifixion; punctuation; all of which was added later by translators, can change meanings dramatically. The following is all of Genesis 3:17 in paragraph form, here again with the verse numbers removed for easier reading.

Genesis 3:17 tells us:

> "Then to Adam He said, "Because you have listened to the voice of your wife, and have eaten from the tree about which I commanded you, saying, 'You shall not eat from it'; Cursed is the ground because of you; In toil you will eat of it All the days of your life."[5.16]

In fact, there is no evidence that the ground in the gan ever became cursed during adam's lifetime; and precisely which ground is not specified here. It may be that the garden perished with the flood, but the flood is believed to have been God's will and not the enemy's.

This leaves a bit of a dilemma. Since the only reasonable explanation of the previous statements and actions by God; would clearly be that the ground outside the gan was cursed prior to adam's formation; and since there is no evidence that the ground inside the gan became cursed at any time during adam's lifetime; then precisely what is the correct interpretation of this passage?

If three minor changes are made, this would all seems to make a bit more sense. If a period is placed after "from it," as well as after "ground," and another "because" is added before the "cursed," The latter then could represent a declarative sentence offered as additional explanatory information; unrelated to any causal relationship previously believed to have been established.

Thus it would read: "Then to Adam He said, "Because you have listened to the voice of your wife, and have eaten from the tree about which I commanded you, saying, 'You shall not eat from it. *Because* cursed is the ground. Because of you In toil you will eat of it All the days of your life."

Incidentally, this verse also arguably represents God advising adam that as of now, there may be a finite number of days of his life.

A quick recapitulation:

If it were the case that adam had actually cursed the ground, it then also must necessarily be the case that although adam cursed the ground; or rather that the ground was cursed because of him; he did not actually curse the ground where he was placed, but rather only the ground where he was not placed. This being the area to where he was ultimately expelled; wherein likely resided the cursed beasts God had referenced.

Although there are no direct Scriptural statements regarding any cursing or contamination; at least from the point when God began establishing life forms until sometime before the formation of adam; there is no other reasonable explanation.; other than the ground had been cursed prior to adam. We have the issue of the absence of the mist outside of the gan; a likely gap in the recollection of events; as well as having no explanation for the purpose for the protected area or gan; as well as the formation of adam after the creation of the original hosts.

Again, there is also the problem surrounding the event when God advised the serpent as to how cursed he was to be in verse 14. There would have been no reason for this, unless He expected the serpent to know what he was talking about. How would the serpent have had any idea what God was even talking about, or what this cursing; and more specifically what this degree of cursing, could even have meant; if the ground cursing was happening for the first time? The serpent would have had to have known what being cursed meant, prior to being advised as to precisely how cursed he was to be now; or else it would have been a useless exercise on the part of God; and God does not engage in useless exercises.

God's advice to adam about the ground being cursed occurs in verse 17; and it was there that God then explained to adam precisely what this would mean to him. But God did not have to explain to the serpent what this meant.

Ergo, here again; the only thing that makes any degree of sense, is that the ground outside of the garden was already cursed. The only reasonable explanation being that it was the original created hosts who were responsible for this cursing.

Genesis 3:15 tells us:

> "And I will put enmity Between you and the woman,
> And between your seed and her seed;
> He shall bruise you on the head, And you shall bruise
> him on the heel."[5.17]

At this juncture, there is no evidence that the woman knew what enmity meant. Not just the definition of the word, but rather the emotion of extreme hatred. It is also noted that God put this hatred between the devil; to whom He is speaking here; and the woman. Thus, the hatred was placed between the devil and the woman; meaning he (the devil) would hate her, but the feeling was not necessarily mutual; at least not as a direct result of God's intervention.

The use of the term "her seed" is generally believed to refer to Messiah, and is considered by most to be the very first reference to Him; and what follows does support that viewpoint. Specifically, the otherwise lack of any other reference as to whom the "He" refers, with respect to the bruising, does make this quite likely. It is also fair to assume that a relationship exists between the two "bruises;" in that they may occur simultaneously; rather than sequentially over a period of undefined time. Meaning: that while the serpent's head will be bruised; (some translate as crushed) Messiah's *heel* will be bruised in the same action. It seems reasonable to believe that this is because the serpent's head remains on the ground, up and until the time it is bruised or crushed by Messiah. But it is important to remember that this condition of the serpent's head being on the ground was not the condition prior to his indirect attack upon adam.

While it is perfectly understandable as to why the devil would hate Messiah; it is fair to ask: why then would it be necessary for God to put enmity between them? But it does not state that the hatred was placed between the devil and Messiah; but rather the devil's *seed* and Messiah; once again assuming "her seed" means Messiah.

This may refer to those who choose the devil as their spiritual father. One must choose God as their spiritual father, or they get the devil by default. Some actually knowingly choose the devil as evidenced by their "walk" or lifestyle; *knowingly*—this despite the fact that they intuitively and/or tacitly know better. It may also have to do with whatever the devil may sow. Except for perhaps only arguably the nephilum; it is not likely that the devil can reproduce "according to his kind," or in any other manner, as there is no evidence that would even remotely support this. And those who follow the devil do in fact hate Messiah; although this feeling is never mutual.

The last two lines are subject to interpretation, again sometimes being found with the word "crush" substituted for the first "bruise." But it is in fact the same word: "7779 shuwph, a prim. root; prop. to *gape*, i.e. *snap* at; fig. to *overwhelm*: - break, bruise, cover."[5.18]

According to Strong's, the word "bruise" appears only seven 7 times in the Old Testament. Two of these seven appearances are in this passage; but this passage is the only time, where the original word that is translated as "bruise" is 7779 "shuwph."[5.19]

This reference to "He" is generally considered prophesy

regarding certain events surrounding the crucifixion.

Genesis 3:16 tells us:

> *"To the woman He said,"I will greatly multiply Your pain in childbirth, In pain you will bring forth children; Yet your desire will be for your husband, And he will rule over you."*[5.20]

The Interlinear Bible translates the word as "Sorrow" as relating to childbirth, and not as the word pain.[5.21]

The actual word translated as pain is: "6093 itstsabown, from 6087; *worrisomeness*, i.e. *labor* or *pain*: - sorrow, toil." "6087 is atsab, a prim. root; prop. to *carve*, i.e. *fabricate* or *fashion*; hence, (in a bad sense) to *worry*, *pain* or *anger*; - displease, grieve, hurt, make, be sorry, vex, worship, wrest."[5.22] This is also the same actual word used in Genesis 3, verse 17, where the word toil appears: ("In toil you will eat of it...")

The second "pain" is also translated as sorrow according to the Interlinear Bible,[5.23] but here the original word is: "6089 etseb, from 6087; an earthen *vessel*; usually (painful) *toil*; also a *pang* (whether of body or mind): - grievous, idol, labor, sorrow."[5.24]

What this statement by God means is not particularly clear. Although the use of the word pain is understandable given the context; with that translation, the meaning would reasonably refer to physical pain. With the use of the term sorrow, this can reasonably refer to mental state of sadness, rather than physical pain. Rephrased it could read "I will greatly multiply your pain and worry in having children, and in sorrow you will bring them into the world; nevertheless, you will still desire your husband. And you will be subject to him." A likely explanation; (for her worry or sorrow) being because of the conditions of their new world, as compared to their previous situation.

There are three interesting points here:

Firstly, it is not clear how "the woman" would or could know what this increased or multiplied sorrow or pain relating to pregnancy would actually be, because there is no evidence that she ever had borne any children at this point in time. Thus she had no reference as to what the level of sorrow or pain might have been before it was increased. It does not state that you will have pain or sorrow, but rather that the level would be multiplied.

Secondly: Strongs does not list the word childbirth as being present anywhere in the Bible. It seems the actual word translated as childbirth is: "2032 herown or herayown; from 2029; *pregnancy*: - conception." "2029 harah, a prim. root; to *be* (or *become*) *pregnant*, *conceive* (lit. or fig.); - been, be with child, conceive, progenitor."[5.25]

This represents more than just semantic latitude. The process of becoming a progenitor can really be considered a series of processes: conception, implantation and childbirth; for example. The implantation and subsequent development through the embryo and fetus stages ("being with child") ends with the childbirth process. The pain or sorrow does not appear to be in anyway related to childbirth as commonly believed; but rather to conception; or "being with child;" AKA pregnancy. There is no reference to childbirth in these definitions. Thus the common understanding that God is advising her that the pain of childbirth will be multiplied clearly seems to be erroneous.

With the addition of the "Yet," this seems to suggest that a relationship exists between the fact that she will be sorrowful while pregnant, yet she will still desire the very thing that will make her become pregnant. The word nevertheless may arguably be used in lieu of "Yet."

Unfortunately, other than revealing that God does not appear to have cursed women with painful childbirth—at least in this passage, there seems to be no reasonable explanation as to what this means.

Finally, the actual word used for children is "1121 ben, from 1129; a *son*..."[5.26] Common use of this word can be found in names such as "Benjamin;" meaning son of the right hand. Thus, this seems to limit these admonitions to male children rather than all children. Whether this refers to original sin, or is a foreshadowing of Mary's sorrow is unclear. It may also refer to the conditions outside the *gan* with regard to survival and/or raising a family, which would affect both sexes; but perhaps is expressed in a manner which is based more upon its effect on males.

As a note, there is no other mention of any conceptions, pregnancy or childbirth up to and including this point in Genesis. One might reasonably assume that the created hosts had children, after they were commanded to "be fruitful and multiply;" but these are not mentioned. This does not necessarily mean that it did not happen, as it likely did, but perhaps only that it is not related to redemption.

Just a few points about Genesis 3:18–19:

> ""Both thorns and thistles it shall grow for you;
> And you will eat the plants of the field;
> By the sweat of your face You will eat bread,
> Till you return to the ground,
> Because from it you were taken;
> For you are dust,
> And to dust you shall return."[5.27]

Back in Genesis 3, verse 17 was the first time the man is referred to as "Adam," and there the woman was for the first time referred to his wife. Here we have the man (now Adam) in serious trouble for two reasons. In a sense, this is because of both obedience and disobedience. The man did not merely hear the voice of his wife, but he "listened" to her. This is not technically obeying her, but the result was the same. There is a key message here with respect to how the enemy works. The term "listening" has a component of paying attention to what is being said, and not merely hearing. The enemy is the master of thoughts, ideas, and suggestions. If he cannot "catch your attention" with whatever it is he is trying to "con" you with, he will find someone else who he believes you will listen to. He will then try some type of "con" using them as an intermediary, in order to get to you. This is a classic example.

The disobedience part is of course with respect to God's command. In essence, Adam chose to obey the enemy, with the woman as the intermediary, and then necessarily disobeyed God.

The remainder of the passage is essentially antithetical to God's original gifts and intentions. Because the ground is cursed, (again, it does not state *this* (gan) ground) Adam would now have to work to eat, weeds would be a problem, fields would be necessary and would have to be worked, and physical death was introduced. This is a clarification of the "All the days of your life" statement.

Genesis 3:20-24 tells us:

> *"Now the man called his wife's name Eve, because she was the mother of all the living.*
> *The LORD God made garments of skin for Adam and his wife, and clothed them.*
> *Then the LORD God said, "Behold, the man has become like one of Us, knowing good and evil; and now, he might stretch out his hand, and take also from the tree of life, and eat, and live forever"—*
> *therefore the LORD God sent him out from the garden of Eden, to cultivate the ground from which he was taken. So He drove the man out; and at the east of the garden of Eden He stationed the cherubim and the flaming sword which turned every direction to guard the way to the tree of life."*[5.28]

It was the man who named the woman Eve. It is quite elusive as to the reason why. There is no record of any other humans (except adam, but he came first) being present. Neither is there any record of any offspring anywhere; at any time; at least as of this juncture. Clearly she was not the mother of any; much less all of the other life forms, either inside or outside the *gan*. It is not stated that they had any contact with any of the created hosts, and it seems likely that they did not at this point in time.

Perhaps this refers to Messiah and the eternal life that He would bring, but how Adam would have known that is also unclear. In a sense, and if viewed from a distance, this could represent a foreshadowing of Mary and Messiah. Clearly Mary must have had some misgivings about becoming pregnant and delivering child while unmarried— particularly in those times. And Joe must have been a bit beside himself when he received the news about the child that was not his; he clearly having sufficient enough misgivings for God to send an angel to assuage his concerns. Normally, any woman; including Mary, would have been killed by stoning for this type of "crime."

And since Mary was the mother of Jesus, and Jesus brought eternal connection or eternal spiritual life, technically Mary was the mother of all the spiritually living via her son. It is not known whether it was this; or perhaps that Adam just assumed and believed at the time he named her Eve; that all humans that would ever exist would necessarily have to be her offspring; just as so many still believe today.

Even after their sins, God still provided for them with coverings and clothed them. Whether this was because of their "nakedness" or for protection or both is not stated. This passage is often cited as evidence as the first animal sacrifice. This can be inferred, but does not appear to be a certainty. If God was capable of all that he had done thus far, creating fur coats from nothing seems to be a minor matter.

God stated in Genesis 3, verse 22: "Then the LORD God said, *"Behold, the man has become like one of Us, knowing good and evil;"* Back in verse 3, the devil had said: *"For God knows that in the day you eat from it your eyes will be opened, and you will be like God, knowing good and evil."* Since the devil is not omniscient, one might ask how the devil knew this would happen before God had said it? Perhaps he had seen it before. And it must be noted that the devil had not told them all of the rest.

The use of the plural *"us"* is generally explained by the Trinity. There cannot be found either a Strong's number, or a word corresponding to the word "us," for this passage.

The remainder of verse 22 states: *"and now, he might stretch out his hand, and take also from the tree of life, and eat, and live forever"—"* This "line" at the end seems to represent an unfinished sentence. Thus we do not know all of the facts supporting the "therefore" in verse 23, and preceding God's decision "send him out" of the gan. It is also arguable at this point that irrespective of the fact that this statement appears here, that this may have been the main reason for expulsion, rather than merely sin.

Based upon the part of the sentence included, many believe that this phrase has something to do with Adam attaining eternal life in sin. Of course this explanation really seems to make little sense. Had he or they physically lived forever, there still would have been a Messiah who brought salvation and redemption for all; they, (Adam &Eve) likely just being the oldest to be offered salvation and hit the rapture. This is so, unless of course, Adam's exodus was a prerequisite for the bloodline for Messiah.

So unless eating of this tree and living forever would somehow have interfered with the arrival of Messiah, it would seem to matter little with respect to their salvation and redemption. Had they received salvation and redemption while physically alive; regardless of their age; as many ultimately did; it seems to matter little how old they would have been when this happened.

Had either physically died prior to Messiah, *which they both did*, it also seems to matter little if they died and waited for salvation, as the great men of the Bible did, or lived physically until the time of Jesus.

Nevertheless, God did say what he said. The translation seems to be accurate until the appearance of the word "forever." This word translated as "forever" is "5769, owlam or olam, from 5956; prop. *concealed*, i.e. the *vanishing* point; gen. time *out of mind* (past or fut.), i.e. (practically) *eternity*; ...." "5956 alam, a prim. root; to *veil* from sight, i.e. *conceal* (lit. or fig.): - x any ways, blind, dissembler, hide (self), secret (thing)."[5.29]

Thus is appears that the primary meaning of this word is concerned with concealment, or to veil or cover from sight, rather than a measurement of infinite time. There is perhaps a secondary meaning of eternity; but it is the concealment and not the eternity that seems to be the main meaning. So had the man eaten from *this* tree, he would have lived concealed for a long time—perhaps forever; and not merely "lived" forever.

This concealment must mean concealed from someone or some thing. Could it mean concealed from God? This is admittedly is a difficult concept. This "time out of mind" definition could possibly refer to God not calling Adam to His remembrance. It is a fair question to ask what is or would be the difference between being disconnected from God because of sin; and being disconnected and concealed, if that were even possible, from God because of sin and the effect of the tree of life?

One explanation could be that if this disconnection were made permanent and thus not "salvageable;" because the man was veiled or hidden, then this indeed would have been a bit of a mess. Presumably this would also be a problem, because this formed "man" is presumed by many to have been the first, and thus believed to be the only source of or for mankind.

Alternatively, if concealment means concealed from the outside world; and Adam was part of God's plan for redemption; and had remained concealed from the outside world in the gan; this would then mean that God's plan for man's redemption could not continue through the bloodline to Messiah. (The Last Adam)

As previously referenced, Genesis 3:23-24 tell us:

> "therefore the LORD God sent him out from the garden of Eden, to cultivate the ground from which he was taken.
> So He drove the man out; and at the east of the garden of Eden He stationed the cherubim and the flaming sword which turned every direction to guard the way to the tree of life."

Therefore, or because of this, or all of this, God sent him out of the *gan,* to cultivate or here work the ground from which he was taken. Again, this indicates he was not formed from any "dust" that may have been contained in the *gan*. This also further supports the fact that this *gan* was an area which one could be sent or driven out of, hence an enclosed area.

Verse 24 tells us "So He drove the man out;..." This is not the same as telling the dog to get out of the flower garden. Here we have Adam being expelled from one area which was the protected area, to the very area where God had obtained the raw materials (*aphar*) to form (*yatsar not bara*) adam. (capitalizations chosen carefully)

There must have been a bit of disagreement here, because as it reads, first God sent him out; but then "so" He drove him out. It sounds very much like Adam did not want to leave.

But this tree of life was then to be protected from all sides.

Some "Genesis Gaps:"

1. Created Earth → Without Form and Void - unknown duration
2. Without Form and Void → Restored Earth - unknown duration
3. Restored Earth → Creation of Life – unknown duration
4. Creation of Life → Formation of Adam – unknown duration
5. Formation of Adam → Adam's Sin – unknown duration

MEEKRAKER *Beginnings…*

# Chapter 6

## CJHG

$$C = J + M \quad \therefore \quad J = C - M$$

"Fear Not!" According to the movie "*Facing the Giants*," this phrase appears 365 times in the Bible. At the risk of sounding sophomoric, it seems more than fair to say that it is God's will that we fear not; or perhaps phrased in a more contemporary manner; "do not fear." This is presented in the Scriptures as a general and all-inclusive advice regarding fear.

Why then are we in the same Book advised so many times about how one should "fear the Lord?" We hear, it seems as though incessantly, about how he is a "God fearing man," and "the fear of God;" or how some event "put the fear of God in him or you." We were never advised to; "fear not; except of course God." But rather, through the Scriptures God advises us to fear not.

Period. Of course that is much easier said than done; but nevertheless that is our instruction.

Fear can be defined as "anxiety caused by approaching danger."[6.1]

This is clearly not something one would wish to experience when approaching the throne or when in the presence of God. This particular "approach" of course, being relative to the petitioner; as it is he who is actually moving toward the throne and not the reverse.

Fear is the opposite of faith, and will even obey the rules of faith in terms of manifestation, which is precisely what happens in the Book of Job. To the extent that we have one, we cannot have the other.

Hebrews 11:6 tells us: "And without faith it is impossible to please *Him*,"[6.2] Thus, it simply makes no sense that we are to fear God at the same time we have faith in Him. Neither does this seem even possible.

Whenever this word "fear" appears with respect to God, this is an incorrect word. The correct word is *revere* or *reverence*. A word which perhaps is not in use very often today, except when discussing the American revolution, or purchasing cookware. The word "revere" is defined as "a feeling of deep respect, love, awe and esteem."[6.3] Whenever the word fear appears with respect to God or the Lord, the simple insertion of the word REAL makes it much easier to remember. That it is <u>R</u>espect <u>E</u>steem <u>A</u>we and <u>L</u>ove that is expected of us, and most certainly never fear.

In fact, 2 Timothy 1:7 tells us: "For God hath not given us the spirit of fear; but of power, and of love, and of a sound mind."[6.4]

Faith is what it takes to please God. The revelation of this fact is by Paul, who is believed to be the author of Hebrews. And although in the chronology of the Scriptures this may be somewhat new; nevertheless this fact was always so, even long before it was revealed in this manner.

The equations listed at the beginning of this chapter refer to the relationship between the Christian and Jewish faiths: wherein C = Christianity, J = Judaism, and M = Messiah. The title CJHG refers to Christians, Jews, Hebrews and Gentiles; each in actuality being a separate entity or classification.

Christianity is Judaism plus Messiah; it is nothing more and nothing less. Therefore, Judaism is Christianity minus Messiah; it is nothing more and nothing less. Thus an inextricable relationship exists between Christianity and Judaism. In a very real sense, one cannot be a Christian without also first being a Jew. Today, Judaism generally is considered to merely mean not recognizing Jesus as Messiah; but this view seriously sells short the important commonalities of Christianity and Judaism.

In fact, sometimes those of the Jewish faith represent Judaism as a system of faith that is apart and entirely different from the roots or beliefs of Christianity; but that is not so. Some even try to introduce doctrines into Judaism from other religions, and represent them as Judaism. Whether this is done because of lack of knowledge or otherwise; is unknown.

This is stated with the utmost degree of respect: Judaism is really incomplete Christianity. Granted that represents a major difference; but nevertheless, Christians believe in all that Judaism professes, and much more.

In a timeline sense, complete common ground exists between Judaism and Christianity from Genesis through Malachi, Machabees, or whatever one determines to be the last book of the Old Testament. Thus, those proponents of Judaism actually believe in only part of Christianity; but in a very real way, also hope and believe that someday they will be like Christians.

This is because the words "Christos" and "Messiah" are essentially the same word; the former from the Greek; the latter Hebrew; both meaning "anointed one." Those of the Jewish faith believe that Messiah will come but has not yet arrived; but that one day He will. And all of the prophesies that to Christians were in fact fulfilled by Jesus, would at that time be fulfilled by the Jewish Messiah. This must be so, because all of these Messianic prophesies actually come from the same texts.

Christ was not the last name of Jesus, but in fact means "the anointed one." This stands in contradistinction to "an anointed one." The correct contemporary terminology is not Jesus Christ, but rather Jesus the Christ. He was also known as Jesus the carpenter's son, Jesus of Nazareth etc. Thus any Jewish person who believes the Messiah has already come; and that Jesus was He; would in a literal sense become a Christian, if choosing to use the Greek term Christos; and some who believe Jesus was this Messiah in fact already have. This would not however likely be used on a mass scale because the term is already in use; but is merely used to illustrate the principle involved.

Today there are in fact "Messianic" Jews. These believe that Jesus was not just an average man or merely a prophet, but that He was in fact the Son of God. Although largely shunned by the "orthodox" Jewish community, these "Messianic Jews" generally are welcomed by the Christian community; but not necessarily by all of the Christian community.

It is understandable that the Jewish community would reject these Messianic Jews; as the belief that Jesus was not the Messiah, (as well as all that necessarily follows) is the prerequisite for being on the Jewish side of Judeo-Christian. Being Jewish is a self-limiting position in that once belief in Jesus as the Messiah is established; at least by today's definition; one can no longer be considered of the Jewish religion. This of course was entirely different in Old Testament times.

But it is fair to ask for what possible reason(s) would Christians ever reject Messianic Jews? Surely it cannot be based upon a belief system, as Jews and Christians both share belief in the Old Testament writings as the Words of God. And Messianic Jews embrace Jesus as Messiah, and likely all of His teachings as well.

It does not seem to be differences in belief, as in sectarian battles, that makes some Christians reject Messianic Jews. Rather, it is the fact that some of these Messianic Jews still believe in, as well as practice, some Old Testament mandates.

Salvation is based upon faith, and is never based upon works. This is an undisputed tenet of Christianity. No one (Jesus excepted) is ever good enough to be saved and redeemed by works; and no one can possibly ever be bad enough to be denied salvation and redemption by works. Yet parts of the Christian community reject Messianic Jews seemingly because they still observe certain holidays and rituals contained in the Old Testament writings; things that Christians believe are obsolete. So although God will never reject anyone who believes in His Son simply because of works; nevertheless it seems some parts of the Christian community will.

Furthermore, as will be seen in detail the in next "intermission," what one does can easily be dwarfed by the reasons for which one chose to do it. If Messianic Jews believe that God still wishes that they engage in observation of certain Holy Days and rituals; and then engage in the same for that very reason; this in no way abrogates their belief in Jesus. For example: Celebrating the Festival of Lights, which happens to fall near Christmas— because one believes it is God's will that it should be celebrated; does not in any way preclude the celebration of Christmas; neither does this necessarily affect one's belief in Jesus.

Many Christians are not really Christians, but perhaps more accurately described as "Jesusites;" as they believe in Jesus, but not necessarily recognize the Christ. To be perfectly clear, this does not mean failure to recognize *Him* as the Christ, but failure to recognize the Christ. The Christ here used as meaning the anoint-*ing*, as opposed to the anoint-*ed one*. Perhaps phrased a bit better by saying that they are familiar with Jesus, but they do not know the Christ. Many Scriptural translations use erroneous terminology by assuming that Christ and Jesus are always interchangeable; which they are not. This can lead the reader to believe that the passage is actually about the Son, when in fact the passage is actually concerned with the "Holy Ghost."

One prime example of this is the common belief that the church is the body of Christ, with Jesus as Its head. Here the use of the term "Christ" is generally believed to mean Jesus. So, this view must necessarily mean; that "the church is the body of Jesus, with Jesus as its head." In any other common usage, one would not need to advise anyone that: "This is the body of xyz, with xyz as its head;" since we generally identify persons this way. It would seem silly to say this; as precisely whose head would one expect to find on xyz, other than xyz's head; given the fact that the main way we identify someone is by their cranial features; and almost exclusively by their face? The reason we are told this is because here the body of "Christ" refers to the body of the Anointing, or the Holy Ghost, and Jesus as the head refers to the Son. Thus this statement includes two parts of the Trinity, and not two different names for the same one part of the Trinity.

Christianity is named such because of the Christ, the anointing, or the Holy Ghost.

It is interesting to investigate why those of the Jewish faith believe that they are God's "chosen people." Clearly there is ample evidence to suggest that this is or at least was in fact so. The question then arises as to from precisely what other alternatives were they chosen, and why? More specifically: What was the set or group from which this subset or subgroup of people was chosen? What were the characteristics God used to determine which people were the people he wished to choose; and also why did he not choose the people who were not chosen? The question also necessarily arises as to specifically what was the purpose for which these people were chosen?

It would be very easy to substitute a term indicating "superior" or "better" for the term "chosen;" but this would also be very dangerous, because this type of substitution is not necessarily always accurate. Choosing is often based upon intended purpose, and not necessarily overall quality; except as related to its suitability for a particular purpose. If one needed to change a flat tire in the desert, would one choose a lug wrench of 24 karat gold, or steel? Gold is very valuable and also very soft. As much as a lug wrench of 24 karat gold would be very valuable, and make an interesting item to own; it would not likely withstand loosening the first nut on the tire mount, much less the rest. If you wish to ever change this tire, 24 karat gold is not suitable; and as valuable as it might otherwise be, it has little or no value for this purpose; and thus would be a poor choice. Likewise steel lug wrenches are relatively inexpensive, but invaluable if getting that tire changed is the objective.

Thus, if a means of storing wealth by an inflation proof, time proven method, where the ability to store a large amount of value in small amount of matter is desired; choose the 24K gold lug wrench. If you wish to change the flat tire in the desert, choose the steel. Which one is superior? It all depends on the intended purpose.

The *"Illustrated Dictionary of the Bible"* defines "chosen people" as: "a name for the Hebrew people, whom God chose as His special instruments..."[6.5]

Who are the Hebrew people, any why does this definition not state "Jewish"? The very first time the word Hebrew appears is in Genesis 14:1**3**: *"Then a fugitive came and told Abram the Hebrew. Now he was living by the oaks of Mamre the Amorite, brother of Eshcol and brother of Aner, and these were allies with Abram."*[6.6]

This takes place before God had even changed Abram's name to Abraham. The term Jew or Jewish is believed to be derived from the tribe of Judah, who was the son of Jacob, who was the son of Isaac, who was the son of Abraham (formerly Abram). Thus to refer to the chosen people as the Hebrews and not Jewish or Jews appears to be correct; just as the above definition states.

In the context of Genesis 14:13, it seems that there may have been more than one Abram, as he is referred to as Abram the Hebrew. Why is Abram referred to as the Hebrew? Hebrew means from the other side, or one from the other side. This is generally explained as a river; whether this refers to the Tigris or Euphrates seems to be a matter of contention. In a certain sense, this particular interpretation is probably not dissimilar to one who is from "the other side" of town.

Remember what happened to Adam.
Genesis 3:24 told us:

> *"So He drove the man out; and at the east of the garden of Eden*
> *He stationed the cherubim and the flaming sword which turned every direction to guard the way to the tree of life."*

This garden, which is actually a protected area or *gan,* likely had a means to control access; else how could it have been a protected area. When God drove the man (Adam) out, either the entire gan or part of the gan, remained protected by the cherubim and the flaming sword. We are not told how much of the gan remained protected. Likewise, neither are we told that any part of this gan or protected area was in any way relinquished.

But clearly the man or Adam had to cross some type of threshold; as something was circumscribing this protected area or *gan* when he was driven out; and we know that some amount of this remained; at a minimum with respect to the tree of life. Thus Adam necessarily went from one side of the gan, across some type of threshold, to the other side of the gan, or non-protected area.

Many if not most people have no idea what happened to Adam after he was driven out of the *gan.* But Adam actually physically lived a minimum of 930 years,[6.7] with at least 800 years spent outside the gan. This is known because Genesis 5:3 tells us: *"When Adam had lived one hundred and thirty years, he became the father of a son in his own likeness, according to his image, and named him Seth."*[6.8]

This happened after he left the *gan.* No information can be found as to when the counting began. Meaning no information can be found about whether the 930 years was counted after he was formed, sinned, or was driven out. If either of the latter two, then no information is provided as to how long he was in the *gan* prior to the fall.

Genesis 4:17-22 tells us:

> "Cain had relations with his wife and she conceived, and gave birth to Enoch; and he built a city, and called the name of the city Enoch, after the name of his son.
> Now to Enoch was born Irad, and Irad became the father of Mehujael, and Mehujael became the father of Methushael, and Methushael became the father of Lamech.
> Lamech took to himself two wives: the name of the one was Adah, and the name of the other, Zillah. Adah gave

> birth to Jabal; he was the father of those who dwell in tents and have livestock.
> His brother's name was Jubal; he was the father of all those who play the lyre and pipe. As for Zillah, she also gave birth to Tubal-cain, the forger of all implements of bronze and iron; and the sister of Tubal-cain was Naamah."[6.9]

Counting the generations, there is a grand total of 8 generations, or generally about 160 years, perhaps slightly more, perhaps much less; from the beginning to the end of these passages. In 160 years these people went from knowing nothing but God and knowing when (but not necessarily what) to eat; to the father of those who live in tents and have livestock; father of musicians of lyres and pipes; and a forger of all bronze and iron forged implements. Not to mention where the furnaces or even the sources of heat for the forge came from; what type of implements were to be used how to forge them, or how Cain, the farmer, knew how to build a city; or how he even knew what a city was.

This represents a rather remarkable, if not miraculous series or group of achievements, in an amazingly short period of time.

This must be so, unless of course they were taught these things by the people who were on the *outside* of the *gan.* These very same people who named Adam et seq. "those from the other side;" or in their language, or what would ultimately be translated from their language: "*the Hebrews.*" These people on the outside of the gan being the descendants of the original created (bara) hosts, who had existed and multiplied on the earth for an unspecified length of time. It is kind of ironic, because if this is so; then the word Hebrew is one word that was likely not originally part of the Hebrew language. There have been dubious attempts to attribute the word "Hebrew" to "Hebrew" or other sources; but thus far, all such attempts remain unconvincing.

There is also the issue of Cain's wife. There is no information regarding who she was or from where she came. We do know that after he was cursed, Cain dwelt in the Land of Nod on the east of Eden.[6.10] There is no suggestion that God "formed" this woman; neither is there any suggestion that Cain married a sibling; nor is their any evidence that there even existed any sibling whom he could marry.

It is difficult to imagine what the scene must have been like when Adam et. al. crossed the threshold of the gan. Perhaps this was similar to a time warp, or *someone* being "beamed," in this case "out," rather than "up," just like in a science fiction movie. Suddenly, this couple comes out of somewhere; or perhaps what appeared as though out of nowhere; wearing what very well may have been animal skins. Was it like some type of "worm hole" that closed up after they passed through it? And then behind them remains this cherubim perhaps wielding (it does not actually state this) a flaming sword in all directions. Even if they came out at night, surely that flaming sword would be tough to miss. To be clear, this is in no way meant to be disrespectful, or in any way suggesting that this is other than true as written. Nevertheless, it must have been quite an event.

If these were the Hebrews; the very people from the other side "whom God chose as His special instruments," then it must have been by genetics and not belief. Adam, the formed man, and all those descendants of Adam; with their main purpose being to establish the bloodline for Messiah, all being these very Hebrews or chosen people.

It is also a requirement that in order to have an "other side," there must be at least two sides, or perhaps better phrased; a side from which ones perspective is that any person or persons not from that or their side, (the observer's); must then necessarily be from the other side.

Today, the word "gentile" is usually defined as non-Jewish. Thus, to be considered a gentile or a *goyam,* all one has to do is not be Jewish. So today, it is based totally upon belief and not genetics. It is true that some distinction might be made with respect to one who is Jewish by birth, as opposed to one who becomes Jewish by conversion. But, that distinction cuts both ways; as that person then became Jewish, or non-gentile, by choice, effort and belief; rather than involuntarily and solely as a result of birth. Nevertheless, it is one's system of belief or lack thereof, which from this standpoint, qualifies one as a gentile today.

But the roots of the word gentile are: "Late Latin *gentilis* foreign, heathen, pagan, from Latin *gentilis* person belonging to the same family, fellow countryman, from *gentilis*, adj., of the same family or clan, from *gens* (genitive *gentis*) race, clan; …"[6.11]

Based upon the above etymology contained in *Chambers*, the progression (or regression depending on one's point of view) can easily be seen. The *Late* Latin is more based upon belief; as precisely how does one become a heathen or pagan except by belief; including no belief?

But the original, or Non-Late Latin meaning of *gentile* is based upon belonging to a race, family or clan. Thus the meaning of *gentile* originally was based upon *genetic* considerations, and not one's system of belief. In civilized nations, religion is generally considered sacrosanct. When one chooses to attribute other personal characteristics to individuals based upon their religious beliefs, we call this prejudice; because we then prejudge these other personal attributes solely based upon religious belief.

It is inarguable that there were two different groups of humans existing at the time Adam had left the *gan*. One group was brought into existence by *bara*, necessarily made from nothing. These were the created *hosts*. Another group of at least two, (A&E, no more are mentioned) were brought into existence by formation, or *yatsar*, from something; that something being dust; or *aphar*; useless matter.

Thus the actual genesis of these two groups is or was entirely different and mutually exclusive; as one cannot engage in a process that requires making something out of nothing and yet simultaneously requires that it be made or formed out of something. Depending on who was doing the naming, when these groups first encountered each other, it seems logical that one or the other or both would be considered from the other side; as Adam had left the *gan* or a protected area; and the other being considered as the already existing countryman, race family or clan who were outside this *gan*.

It is entirely possible that Adam could have thought that these gentiles were actually the ones from the "other side," and from his perspective they may have in fact been so. Thus *he* could have named these gentiles, the *Hebrews*, or whatever word in his language may have meant from the "other side;" considering himself to be the gentile. This is because from his perspective, it was likely that the *gan* was all he had ever known at this time. He likely thought the inside of the *gan* was all there was. But that is not how it transpired.

The most logical order of events being that the "Hebrew" was formed because the created gentiles had already fallen. Then as we all know, whether by design or by error, the Hebrew(s) fell.

# 2nd Intermission

## Laws of Compensatory Blessing - Saying and Sowing

"As above so below." Perhaps a hackneyed expression; but nevertheless one which essentially contains as much revelation as one is willing to seek. It really could not be any other way. Perhaps another phrasing of this concept would be: Thy will be done, on earth, as it is in heaven." This is approached from a bit of a different angle though, because it is phrased in a manner suggesting that it is hoped or desired that God's will be done here on earth, in the same way and manner as it is done in heaven.

All that was originally brought into physical existence; was brought into existence because of, and completely consistent with, the will of God. Thus from the other viewpoint, when examining the known physical realm as the accomplished *result* of God's will, this physical realm necessarily was already done on earth as it is or was in heaven, according to His will.

Therefore, the physical laws we know to exist on earth, necessarily have their origins in the will of God. For each physical law, then there must be a corresponding law in the non-physical or immaterial; some might choose to use the term supernatural, realm.

Although the following is a subject about which many do not enjoy hearing; it is raised not with the intention of in any way attempting to solicit contributions; but rather to analyze the processes involved.

In Malachi 3:10 God tells us:

> *"Bring the whole tithe into the storehouse, so that there may be food in My house, and test Me now in this,"* says the LORD of hosts, *"if I will not open for you the windows of heaven and pour out for you a blessing until it overflows."*[12.1]

The most striking words or phrase in this passage is the phrase "test Me." God does not state that we are to examine or quiz Him, but rather to "test" (*bachan*)[12.2] Him. This is not an invitation to inquire as to the nature of God. Neither is it an invitation to quiz Him to see how much he knows; but rather is an invitation to actually test Him. This "test" is in the sense of finding out; not if He actually is what *we* say He is; but rather if He is actually what *He* says He is. This is similar to the acid tests for testing precious metals such as gold. In those tests one is generally trying to determine if the metal is actually what the metal is being proffered to be.

The nature of this "test" involves the very same physical principles or laws we encounter in our everyday existence:

The following may at first appear very complicated, but is not. For some reason, many people seem to become intimidated when confronted with symbols. Nevertheless, the following is really quite simple:

<u>Newton's Second Law of Motion:</u> "The acceleration of an object as produced by a net force is directly proportional to the

magnitude of the net force, in the same direction as the net force, and inversely proportional to the mass of the object."[12,3]

All this really means is that if you push on something with enough force, it will move in the direction in which you pushed it. It is expressed as **F=MA**, where **F**=force, **M**= mass and **A**= acceleration. It really is that simple:

When something is moving, it has either velocity or speed. This is a change in the distance it travels in a certain amount of time. A car traveling 60 MPH will travel sixty miles in one hour. *($v=\Delta d/\Delta t$ velocity or speed equals change in distance or displacement divided by the change in time; for speed and velocity respectively.)*

In order to make an object such as a car (or a blessing) change it speed or velocity, this requires some type of acceleration. This acceleration, or **A**, is considered to be the change in the object's speed or velocity. This happens when one pushes down on either the gas pedal (accelerator) in a car, or the brakes. The gas pedal provides positive acceleration and the car increases its speed or velocity. The brakes provide negative acceleration (deceleration) and will slow the car down. *($a=\Delta v/\Delta t$ acceleration equals change in speed or velocity divided by the change in time)*

Force equals mass multiplied by acceleration. All this really means is that if the object is a large mass; then it takes more force to accelerate it (change its velocity or speed), a given amount, as compared to a smaller mass. If the mass is small, given the same force, its acceleration will be greater, and so on. When the car is carrying a heavy load, the gas pedal has to be pushed farther down in order to get more force from the engine to cause the car to increase its speed (accelerate), as compared to an empty vehicle. Although not technically exactly correct, if we consider the weight of the car to be **M**, this is all that **F=MA** means. (Technically mass and weight are different, but skip this for now.)

The "test" in the passage from Malachi previously cited, refers to 4 things:

1) the window
2) the tithe
3) the blessing

4) the pouring

The window is a binary, in that it must be either open or closed. It is essentially allegorical, as it is far from certain that literal windows, at least as we know them to be, actually exist in heaven. This "window" really means merely a route for something to travel from the immaterial to the material.

Assuming this route exists, meaning the window is open, this leaves the tithe, the blessing and the pouring. These can be expressed in the terms of Newton's second law, $F = MA$ or more specifically here, $F_T = MA$ where:

$F_T$ = total value of faith
$M$ = the quantity of the blessing (how much stuff)
$A$ = the pouring or movement. (the increase in velocity of the blessing from zero, to some speed or velocity) This determines how fast the blessing will get to you.

The "test" referred to in this example from Malachi refers to the results of tithing. $F_T$ or total faith value in this context is essentially "putting your money where your mouth is." It is equal to the amount you tithe, multiplied by the reasons for which you tithe; or, more simply put; how much did you tithe, and why did you tithe it.

We generally can easily calculate the amount we tithe, but this multiplier; meaning the value of actual reasons for tithing, and thus also necessary for determining the total amount which $F_T$ represents; can only be calculated by God.

Perhaps a better way to describe this, would be that the value of the faith total is calculated in this manner: $F_T = F_A \times F_R$ The faith subscript $A$ representing the amount of a tithe or other "good works," and subscript $R$ representing the reasons. The value of this $F_R$ is the factor by which the thirty fold, sixty fold and one hundred+ fold realms are calculated. Reading Matthew 13:8 provides insight into these realms of increase.

This reason, or "why factor" is extremely important. This is not only because this factor largely determines the quantity of the blessing; but also because of our material limitations for the actual amount (how much) of the giving. One cannot give more than 100% of what one has. In the tithing example, even if one tithed all of their increase instead of the required 10%, this in itself would result in only a tenfold increase in the blessing. But the "reason" or why factor could easily result in a return in the "hundred fold realm."

This concept is further illustrated by Proverbs 16:2 where it tells us "All the ways of a man are clean in his own sight, But the LORD weighs the motives."[12.4]

Weight is actually a force. (It itself is technically a function of mass and acceleration.) Proverbs is telling us here, that God determines the value of the motives or reasons. This *is* the **F**$_R$. Weighing something is merely determining the resultant force of its mass multiplied by the acceleration of gravity.

In the **F=MA** equation, **M** is being used here to represent the blessing, or precisely what it is that travels through this "window," from the immaterial to the material.

The use of the term "Blessing" here meaning "increase *consistent* with natural law" This is to be distinguished from "increase *inconsistent* with natural law," which is better termed a "miracle."

**A** is representing the actual acceleration resulting in the movement or pouring out of this blessing. This is actually acceleration which is the direct result of God' intervention.

Newton's First Law of Motion states: "An object at rest stays at rest and an object in motion stays in motion with the same speed and in the same direction unless acted upon by an unbalanced force."[12.5]

This essentially means that an object that is moving will stay moving unless acted upon by another force. Or an object that is not moving will continue to not move unless a sufficient force is applied to make it move.

This is the initial status of **M**, or the blessings which are in heaven. They are already there, but will not move or change their direction of movement unless a force is applied. For those who might argue that these blessings might already be moving, it would seem that if this were so; then said movement is definitely not towards this window, or God would merely open the window, and would not have to pour them out. Thus, let's assume they are stationary. In order to move, they must have a change in velocity from zero to something. For any mass, any change in velocity with respect to time represents an acceleration, and requires a force.

Here is where Newton's <u>Third Law of Motion</u> comes into play. "For every action, there is an equal and opposite reaction."[12.6] This law probably represents the most fundamental law of compensation, or "karma."

When the value of $F_T$ is established, this represents the force of faith, which we cause by tithing or giving; this being something which is always done for some type of reason. The amount or value of the gift ($F_A$) is one factor; the other being the reason ($F_R$) we are doing it. It must be clearly stated here that the value of this reason is not the reason we may tell others, it is not necessarily the reason we tell ourselves; but rather the true reasons, which God always knows no matter what we may say or do; and it is God alone who "weighs" this.

Thus our action or $F_T$, represents the first action as referenced in Newton's third law. When this action is consummated; when we tithe; an equal but opposite reaction is undertaken by God. This results in another $F = MA$. It is important to remember that it is not just how much we give alone, but the value of that gift (or $F_A$) *and* the reason(s) as the multiplier ($F_R$), which determines the total value of this force.

This $A$, (change in velocity) of $M$, (the blessing), is the result of the equal and opposite action undertaken by God as a direct result of our actions. It is equal to His calculation of $F_T$, but opposite in direction, as now; instead of going *from* us, it travels *to* us.

The rest of this equation also holds. The acceleration is inversely proportional to the mass of the object. In the physical world this means that given whatever the total force applied may be; the greater the mass, the less the acceleration, and the slower the resultant movement to you. Likewise: the lesser the mass; the greater the acceleration, and the faster the resultant movement toward you.

This same relationship holds in the immaterial realm. The mathematical product of the God induced **MA** must remain constant, and equal to but is opposite in direction to the original $F_T$ (original tithe and reasons) for this particular event. Thus, the greater the blessing you are to receive, the longer it may take to get to you. If the blessing is received quickly, the amount or mass of the blessing is sacrificed in exchange for the rapidity with which it is received. This is necessary to keep the equation in balance.

How does God decide whether to provide a smaller blessing quickly, or a larger blessing more slowly? Only He knows this for sure, but in the initial stages of faith, rapidity can be very important; as it is evidence to the "neophyte" that the system actually works. Once the system is known to work; even with a relatively small amount of increase, but an extremely rapid increase, the system becomes confirmed as functional by the believer; and he or she is much more likely to permit this to ascend to higher levels.

With subsequent tithing or giving, as the amount of ones faith (God in fact passed the test) increases, then God may choose to increase the magnitude of **M** at the expense of **A,** but again this must equal the new $F_T$. This is a different result (more quantity of blessing) than the above process, but God's priorities may be different. With this increased *quantity* of blessing, the acceleration will be less in order to balance the F=MA equation. This means the velocity or speed of the blessing will be less, and this greater amount of blessing will take longer to arrive.

Whenever this results in a much greater, but slower to arrive, blessing being returned; of course the enemy knows this. He (the enemy) also has a way to sense when "due season" is near. During those dry periods, when it looks like God forgot all about you, and it appears that He isn't doing a thing; this is the dangerous period. That is when your faith is attacked, and it is not examined but actually "tested."

The enemy will remark with something like: "See, God aint gonna do nuthin. If God was gonna do sumthin he (sic) would have done it by now." Is this because the devil does not know of this **F=MA** function? No, it is because he knows precisely of this function. All the while this huge mass of blessing is heading toward you with a relatively slow acceleration having been applied; but with the magnitude of this mass or blessing being beyond your ability to think or imagine. The devil likely can also sense this, and he is trying desperately to get you to do something; to get you to do anything that will cancel out your receipt of this blessing.

To be clear, this is not about storing up blessings in heaven; but rather in the here and now; in this material plane; most particularly, if $F_A$ is in any way material in nature.

This **F=MA** law is not unique to tithing. Rather, it applies to any action or inaction undertaken; and is sometimes referred to as karma. Anything we choose to do or not do has quantities that are calculable and the same rules apply. We should do unto others as we should do unto ourselves if for no other reason; because that is precisely what *will* be done unto us; and done according to the aforementioned rules. If something is undertaken for this reason alone however, the value of $F_t$, and the subsequent value of the returning **MA**, is likely to be smaller; as the reason or motive value is diminished if it is largely a selfish act.

2 Corinthians 9:7 tells us:

> *"Each one must do just as he has purposed in his heart, not grudgingly or under compulsion, for God loves a cheerful giver."*[2.7]

Why does God love a cheerful giver? Because it is His will that we prosper, and this gives Him license, arguably requires Him, to bless us not only based upon what we do; but more importantly why we do it.

This law cannot be changed; neither can it be avoided. It makes little difference what we say the weight of our motives are, as we are not in charge of weighing or calculating them; and thus our opinion of their value is essentially irrelevant.

One very reliable way to short circuit this process is to name your own blessing. If boasting about the amount of the tithe, (or whatever it may be), is undertaken, that is precisely what can easily happen.

How does any of this in any way relate to speech, and precisely what is speech?

# *Part II*

Despite the fact that in today's world, when perhaps 99% of the time this does not appear to be so; whenever an otherwise lucid person speaks, there is a reason for which they are doing this. More often than not; although not necessarily always for particularly sensible reasons; nevertheless, the fact remains that there is or are a reason or reasons for the speech.

S→ R→ S→ R → S→ R → S→ R → S→ R ...

This represents what used to be called conversation: stimulus and response. A thought or idea leads to a decision (free will) being made to speak; the thought leading to the decision being the stimulus; the response being the spoken word. This speech then provides a stimulus for the listener or listeners who then generates a response or no response; either of which still being a response, which will then provide a stimulus to the original speaker and so on.

There is a very old joke about a couple who are out on a date.

One says to the other: "I've been talking about myself all night. Let's talk about you for a while— what do you think of me?" Instead of laughing, most people *today* would likely say in response to this joke. "I don't get it."

What is a thought or idea? Probably an age-old question, but in this sense, different aspects of this question arise. How much does this thought weigh? What are its measurements? How big a container is necessary to carry it? Of course these are seemingly idiotic questions, but they do illustrate a point. A thought or idea is immaterial by its very nature.

It is interesting to note a few of the terms used to describe certain thoughts or ideas: Inspiration: breathing in. Invention has a similar meaning. Discovery: dis-cover, removing a cover; a cover which was over something that already existed; but this "something" was not previously visible or detectable because of the cover. Revelation is similar to discovery; but is less specific in terms of the nature of the method of the concealment.

When a thought or idea is the basis for speech, said speech represents the transition of this thought or idea from the immaterial realm to the material realm. The impetus for the speech is expressed in the material by vibration. This vibration can be measured; and is measured with respect to time; and thus necessarily requires time in order to exist.

Therefore, it is not so much the actual words that are used; but rather the intention(s) behind these words which is the major basis for the material manifestation. This sounds quite familiar. This is similar to the **F=MA** law with respect to actions, and is very similar to what God did in the beginning of Genesis.

Proverbs 18:20-21 tells us:

> *"With the fruit of a man's mouth his stomach will be satisfied; He will be satisfied with the product of his lips. Death and life are in the power of the tongue, And those who love it will eat its fruit."*[2.8]

And in Matthew 15:11 Jesus tells us:

> *"It is not what enters into the mouth that defiles the man, but what proceeds out of the mouth, this defiles the man."*[12.9]

"But words will never harm me?" That is clearly not what Proverbs tell us. Death and life being in the power of the tongue, sounds a bit more serious than any sticks or stones. And Proverbs makes it clear, by being unclear about precisely what "it" is. "It" can refer to either life or death, and we get to choose. The fruit is the **M**; and when it arrives is determined by the **A**.

Neither is that what Jesus tells us. A man's mouth produces this fruit, by bringing forth into the material realm, that which exists in the immaterial realm. When speech is instituted, the sound vibrations bring into the material, the immaterial purpose or intention for the speech. This "intention" is based upon our free will, and our free will is respected.

There is also another aspect to speech; this being when additional "fruit" is produced; not by the direct manifestation of force of the speech itself; but rather the result of the interaction of this force on something else. In this case, a change in the status of something in the material is produced as a result of its interaction with this force.

"A force is a push or pull upon an object resulting from the object's *interaction* with another object. Whenever there is an *interaction* between two objects, there is a force upon each of the objects."[12.10]

This is a very useful definition, The problems with this definition, is that it concerns itself with only two objects, one event, and takes into account only the physical or material, realm.

As a material illustration: When a cue ball receives the force imparted by the "shooter," it generally does not simply strike another ball and stop; the second ball thus receiving 100% of the kinetic energy of the cue ball. Neither does the second ball generally move and interact with nothing else, even if it were to receive all of the kinetic energy of the first ball. This initial action begins a process, affecting anything that is in the paths of the various objects. If the original force is great enough, (say if the shooter is angry) a ball may actually become airborne and interact with something unintended, such as a body part or an expensive furnishing.

With respect to the impact of words, person A genuinely and sincerely says to person B: "You look so pretty when you smile," causing B to smile. Known or unknown to A, B was suffering a bout of depression at that time. Because of what A said and meant; B is now in a much better state of mind. All of the people who encounter B from that point onward, will encounter a much different B than they would have encountered had A not expressed that sincere opinion. Each of the individuals B encounters "down the line" will ultimately be affected by B; and thus is actually affected indirectly by A's speech via B in a different and more positive way because of what A said to B.

As with actions or inactions, *all* speech results in the beginning of a process, or processes. Whomever receives these spoken words, will receive the force of these words; and a long process will begin, as the "impact" of these words likely will not end with their initial reception or recipient.

In addition; corresponding to what was said, and more importantly precisely why what was said was actually said; similar "reverse" processes are instituted in the immaterial realm for all of those who receive this original force; even "down the line." Here again, Newton's F=MA law comes into play. The quantity of this force is again being determined by the product of what was said, and the reasons why. And again, as in the tithing example, an equal but opposite force is generated in response to the initial force, returning to the speaker. It is likely that this ultimately represents some degree of "karma" for all of those affected by the speech; including the original speaker.

Conclusion: Exercise extreme care with everything one says or does. Most people exert little self-control over what they say or do. Particularly with speech, most people will quickly say things because they "feel good." When this happens, this is usually because there is a desire to "show someone something;" which is usually quite successful.

Unfortunately, what is often shown resembles not at all what the "show" was supposed to be; but rather something or things that were supposed to remain concealed. And in the process, they are setting up a "karmic" debt that definitely will not prosper them. They are creating a cesspool all around them and do not understand how or why.

There is a saying in common use today, perhaps best expressed euphemistically as "Stuff Happens." This of course, if taken literally, represents no revelation whatsoever. The alternative being that "stuff" does not happen. "Stuff" represents a rather large number of possibilities. Even if the actual word is used, this still represents no revelation—albeit in a rather crass manner.

Thus, a better meaning of this phrase as it is normally used, would be "stuff just happens;" implying that there is no rhyme or reason for this "stuff" to occur, it just does. Generally used as though this were merely some type of random event. "Oh well, stuff happens!" This statement includes a bit of resignation to this "fact," as well as a large degree of personal impotence being implied therein. Likely this would be accompanied by some body language such as shrugging of the shoulders and turning one's palms upward.

"I just called to see how you were doing." This can often represent concealed pride: "(I didn't call to ask you what I really called to ask you about) but just called for your benefit." Nevertheless, if it is actually true, a better terminology would be: "I *only* called to see….."

These uses of "just" are dissimilar and not interchangeable. To state that stuff only happens, simply makes no sense. Neither do: "only stuff happens;" nor "stuff happens only;" make any degree of sense; again remembering that the use of "stuff" represents a euphemism.

"Stuff" does not just happen. Simply because one is unaware of the relationship between the "death" that one is sowing into the immaterial with their mouth; and this cesspool surrounding their lives because of it's return to them from the immaterial; does not in any way mean said relationship does not exist. What is being reaped in one's life is a result of what was sowed; in this particular case, simply by the actions of their mouth.

Generally; the faster the response and the more "emotionally stimulating;" the more likely one is merely repeating what the enemy has very recently told them to say. Yes, the enemy fully understands these rules, and enjoys very much watching us exist in a garbage heap of our own creation. After all; he is totally incapable of manifesting anything even close to it without our help.

It is simply foolhardy to believe that the total resultant forces in the material can be calculated by the human mind. Accurately calculating the material forces; initial and subsequent, and thus accurately predicting the results is humanly impossible.

With respect to the immaterial response, no objective data is even available with which to calculate the immaterial quantities and/or the equal but opposite reactions. The only exception to this may be to be able to calculate the overall polarity. This can only be done by accurately determining how consistent any given speech or action; and particularly the reasons for the same; actually is with respect to the word of God.

# Chapter 7

## You're a Dead Man!

Abraham is generally considered to be the "father of faith." He is considered as such primarily; but certainly not exclusively; because he was willing to sacrifice his son Isaac, when he was asked or instructed by God to do so. (The name Isaac actually means laughter, or to laugh, or he laughs.) In the end, Abraham was never actually required to do this, but it was very close. Many believe that God just wanted Abraham to prove his faith, (it is unclear as to precisely whom); and that Abraham believed that God himself would have resurrected Isaac.

Woody Allen is attributed with having stated that: "90% of success is just showing up."

This is actually a scriptural principle; as Proverbs 21:31 tells us:

> "The horse is prepared for the day of battle, But victory belongs to the LORD."[7.1]

Faith is not just believing; as Hebrews 11:1 tell us:

*"Now faith is the substance of things hoped for, the evidence of things not seen."*[7.2]

The meaning of this passage can vary greatly depending upon where one may introduce a comma. Most would interpret this passage in this way: "Now, faith is the substance ... Or perhaps phrased in a more contemporary type of dialect "Now lookey here, I'm telling you that faith is ..."

But if the comma is placed after the word "faith," instead of after the word "now;" then "now," becomes an adjective that is describing; or even limiting the type of faith to which the rest of the statement necessarily pertains. If this were presented as the following question: Precisely what is "the substance of things hoped for, the evidence of things not seen?" The answer would be "now faith," or present faith. Not future faith or past faith, or even just plain old faith; but present faith exclusively. Whatever future faith or past faith may represent; neither is "the substance of things hoped for, the evidence of things not seen."

Now or present faith, is then described as two things: Substance and evidence.

Substance means something material or tangible. It is interesting that this word consists of two parts. The prefix sub, usually meaning below; and stance, as in how something stands; the prerequisite for stance of course being standing. Substance then meaning something that stands below. But stands below what? Most likely, whatever something is standing below something else; there necessarily is something that is above it. As above, so below.

But precisely what type of substance or what is it that is standing below? The answer we are given is: that which is hoped for. Hope is not merely wishing. In the use of the word hope, it is not merely desire; but hope includes an expectation that this desire will be fulfilled. But from where does this expectation of fulfillment of desire arise; and is it a reasonable expectation? The only way to know this is to actually know; and not just read; the word of God and His will.

If one is ever actually thinking, "I hope that God kills that fool," it would be best to stop wasting his or her time. This time would be better spent analyzing one's self; in order to find out precisely what fault or faults there is or are in yourself that this person is triggering. If it were the case that merely being a fool justified death; we would all be dead.

In order for this "thing" that is hoped for to have substance, or to be "standing below," it must exist; or in a sense, be "standing" above first. As above so below, does not necessarily translate into "as below so above." Everything that exists below; or in the natural or material world; had to first exist "above;" or in the supernatural or immaterial realm. If it does not exist "above" first, it cannot exist or stand below; at least if it is of God. God killing a person because someone else wants it; simply because they remind another person of themselves; or because this person has done foolish things, does not generally qualify. And even if it did, it would not be merely because someone had hoped for it. The basis for this request is not of God, and thus does not exist in the above. Ergo, it cannot stand below. And as an aside, it is fair to ask if it is not of God; then who would want it?

What then is the link between this hope and manifestation? In a word: faith. Do you believe that God is what He says He is, and will do what He said He would do? To the extent that one has this genuine belief; that is the basis of the expectation. If whatever you desire exists in the above; meaning it is of God and consistent with His will, and you trust that God is what He says He is, and will do what He said He would do; this is the basis for the manifestation of substance. It is not based on what you think your faith is, but what it actually is; and God cannot be fooled.

"Now faith," is also: "The evidence of things not seen." In the natural or material world, usually "seeing is believing," which sometimes can be very dangerous. In a court of law, evidence must be competent, relevant and material; but this is not a court of law. If we substitute "detectable by the five physical senses" for the word "seen," we have "Now faith is the evidence of things not detectable by the five physical senses." If the result of "now faith" ultimately is substance, then perhaps a better way of phrasing this might be: "Now faith, is the evidence of things not detectable by the five physical senses....y*et.*"

Most people will be willing to work at a new job for upwards of a month, trusting their employer to pay them as much as 30 days later. This could be after working 160 hours; when the fact is that it is quite possible that the employer may go bankrupt before ever issuing a paycheck to them. One will trust the gas station attendant to accurately measure how much gas was pumped into your tank, and pay him whatever is asked, without ever actually knowing. One will trust a surgeon; about whom they know very little; to save their life and not kill them in the process. But most people will not trust or test God; even though He asks that we trust Him, and actually tells us to test Him.

But back to Abraham. Genesis 20: 1-2 tells us:

> *"Now Abraham journeyed from there toward the land of the Negev, and settled between Kadesh and Shur; then he sojourned in Gerar.*
> *Abraham said of Sarah his wife, "She is my sister." So Abimelech king of Gerar sent and took Sarah."*[7.3]

Why did Abraham lie to Abimelech? He later states that it was because he did not believe that Abimelech was a man of faith, stated as "no fear of God in this place." The translation of the actual word for fear is: "3374 yirah, fem. of 3373; *fear* (also used as infin.); mor. *reverence*..."[7.4] This includes reverence as well as fear in its definition; and is likely one source for the "Fear God" error previously addressed.

Abraham believed that Abimelech would have had him killed in order to "take" Sarah, had Abimelech known that Sarah was his wife. This may seem reasonable, but in Genesis 15:1, God, in a vision, had already personally promised Abram to shield him; and to grant to him more descendants than there were stars.

Genesis 15:1 tells us:

> "After these things the word of the LORD came to Abram in a vision, saying, Do not fear, Abram, I am a shield to you; Your reward shall be very great."[7.5]

Genesis 15:4-5 tells us:

> "Then behold, the word of the LORD came to him, saying, "This man will not be your heir; but one who will come forth from your own body, he shall be your heir." And He took him (Abram) outside and said, "Now look toward the heavens, and count the stars, if you are able to count them." And He said to him, "So shall your descendants be."[7.6]

Now precisely how Abraham thought it would be possible that he could be the father of all of these descendants after Abimelech had him murdered, is unknown; probably because he didn't. Abraham, just like all of us sometimes have, had a faith failure. God had promised to be his shield and promised him many descendants; but Abraham became frightened, and then lied to get out of it. This was not the first time Abraham did this, as he had previously told Pharaoh the very same lie for the very same reason.

Why was Abraham so certain that neither Pharoh nor Abimelech were men of faith? Because if they had been; Abraham, the father of faith, would have been the one from whom they learned it; at least in his view. Thus Abe did not just *think* they were not men of faith; but rather in his mind, he *knew* they could not have been.

It must be noted here that at this time Sarah was ninety years old. She surely must have been one good looking "ninety year old."

For clarity, when Abimelech "took" Sarah, this does not in any way mean sexual intercourse. It is likely that "took" in this usage means physically took her and placed her in the area occupied by his other concubines at that time. There is no other reasonable explanation; as it seems that it was afterward; when he did try to have sexual relations with her, that he in fact did not succeed.

Genesis 20 3-7 tells us:

*"But God came to Abimelech in a dream of the night, and said to him, "Behold, you are a dead man because of the woman whom you have taken, for she is married."*

*Now Abimelech had not come near her; and he said, "Lord, will You slay a nation, even though blameless? "Did he not himself say to me, 'She is my sister'? And she herself said, 'He is my brother.' In the integrity of my heart and the innocence of my hands I have done this."*

*Then God said to him in the dream, "Yes, I know that in the integrity of your heart you have done this, and I also kept you from sinning against Me; therefore I did not let you touch her.*

*"Now therefore, restore the man's wife, for he is a prophet, and he will pray for you and you will live. But if you do not restore her, know that you shall surely die, you and all who are yours."*[7.7]

The use of the term "a dream of the night" is likely used to distinguish this from a vision, as when God came to Abraham. Usually a vision happens while one is awake, and dream occurs while one is asleep. The use of the terms "Come near her" and "touch her" are euphemisms. It does not seem likely that God meant that Abimelech would be killed for either merely being in her proximity, or for merely touching her. And it was not just Abimelech who would be killed, but also "all who are yours."

The conversation between God and Abimelech; as are many conversations; is revealing not only because of what is or was discussed, but also for what was not discussed. Abimelech had concubines; seemingly quite a few of them. Yet God did not comment on his concubines in general; or at all for that matter. God seemed to agree that Abimelech had acted with "integrity of my heart and the innocence of my hands," in not knowing Sarah was married. It appears that God was concerned solely with Abimelech's relationship with Sarah. Was this strictly because Sarah was married? Perhaps this is so; as there is no evidence concerning the marital status of the other women. It seems more likely however, that God's main concern was because God had promised Sarah and Abraham offspring.

Previously, in Genesis 15:4 where God had promised Abraham an heir; Abraham and Sarah had eventually taken it upon themselves to obtain offspring by Abraham having relations with their Egyptian maid Hagar. The result of their actions and the fruit of this union was a child, (Ishmael) who had Abraham as his father; but Hagar, and not Sarah as his mother.[7.8] This time, a child could have been born with Sarah as his mother; but Abimelech, and not Abraham as his father. It seems that God would in no way permit this. It must be noted that many believe that Ishmael is the father of either the present day Arabs, and/or the Muslims; depending on whom it is that is quoted.

Perhaps some other euphemisms are in use here. How was it that God "Kept you (Abimelech) from sinning," and did not let him "touch her?" The Bible does not say precisely how this was accomplished, but it later states at this time the wombs had been "closed fast" because of this. It also states that Abimelech was also healed. There is one sure way to accomplish this; that is making it impossible for Abimilech to engage in sexual intercourse, by affecting Abimelech in a reversible manner. The authors' use of the phrase: "affecting Abimilech in a reversible manner," represents another euphemism.

So here we have Abraham, who is the father of faith; whose faith has failed yet again: failing again about the very same matter and for the very same reason. First this happened with Pharoh, and now with Abimelech. And Abraham is *so* certain that Abimelech is not a man of faith; or a "God fearing or revering" man, as Abraham likely considers himself to be.

In fact, Abraham; as evidenced by *his* behavior; seems to more closely resemble the faithless man that Abraham considered

Abimelech to have been. And Abimelech; as evidenced by his behavior; more closely resembles the man of faith that Abraham considers himself to be; but whose behavior was clearly inconsistent with this alleged faith.

It is also interesting to note that there seems to be no element of surprise on the part of Abimelech when God came to him in the dream. The way it reads; it seems as though this may have been just one in a series of times that God had spoken with Abimelech. There is no indication that having a conversation with God; as opposed to the *subject* of this particular conversation; was in any way unusual to Abimelech.

Genesis 20:8-11 tells us:

> "So Abimelech arose early in the morning and called all his servants and told all these things in their hearing; and the men were greatly frightened.
> Then Abimelech called Abraham and said to him, "What have you done to us? And how have I sinned against you, that you have brought on me and on my kingdom a great sin? You have done to me things that ought not to be done."
> And Abimelech said to Abraham, "What have you encountered, that you have done this thing?"
> Abraham said, "Because I thought, surely there is no fear of God in this place, and they will kill me because of my wife."[7.9]

Abimelech asks Abraham three questions and makes one comment to him. Abimelech asks what have you done; how did I harm you to justify your behavior; and if not, what experiences have you had that could possibly justify your behavior? Abimelech also tells Abraham that he did things that ought not be done. And what is Abrahams answer? His answer essentially being: that it was because he thought they were all a bunch of uncivilized animals, who knew God not. Abimelech's men were greatly frightened, and it is fair to say that in all likelihood, so was he. Being told directly by God that you are a "dead man" would tend to be quite an attention getter. Abimelech also referred to what Abraham did as a "great sin."

What was Abimelech's response to Abraham's actions and defenses?

Genesis 20:12-13 tells us:

> *"Besides, she actually is my sister, the daughter of my father, but not the daughter of my mother, and she became my wife; and it came about, when God caused me to wander from my father's house, that I said to her, 'This is the kindness which you will show to me: everywhere we go, say of me, "He is my brother."'"* ,"7.10

First Abraham lies, and then we see the pride come out. "She actually is my sister." Abraham did not tell Abimelech that Sarah was his sister because he wanted Abimelech to believe that Sarah was his sister. Abraham lied only so that Abimelech would not think that Sarah was his wife. Abraham didn't care one whit about what Abimelech otherwise may have thought or believed, as long as Abimelech did not think or believe that Sarah was his wife.

Abraham did not originally tell Abimelech that Sarah was his half sister, which would have been the truth. Instead, he said "sister;" which of course is only *a* truth, arguably half of the truth, but certainly not *the* truth. Had Abimelech known *the* truth, he likely would not have assumed that they could not have been married; which of course they were. So in Abraham's mind, *the* truth would not have worked. If Abimelech would have believed that they were not married because Abraham convinced him that Sarah was an alien from Jupiter, he might have tried that one; had he had genuinely thought that it would have worked for him

Then when he gets caught, he doesn't have enough integrity to admit to what he did; instead he makes it worse. Like so many people that all of us know, he had to be "right," even when he knew he was wrong, and was caught in the act.

Here we also see another trait that is common today. The second defense was that the lie was okay because they both agreed to lie. Although it does not actually state this, the implication is that

Sarah agreed to the lie. She did in fact participate in the lie, and it was not she who ultimately told Abimelech the truth. The conclusion being: that if we both agree to lie, that somehow makes it acceptable. This is truth, or right and wrong by consensus. God had not committed the false witness prohibition to stone as of yet; but lying was sinful at that time nonetheless. But apparently Abraham believed that this prohibition does not apply to him, because they both had agreed to lie. This is the logical, but erroneous, conclusion of this second defense.

What was Abimelech's response to Abraham's actions and defenses? Genesis 20:14-18 tells us.

> *"Abimelech then took sheep and oxen and male and female servants, and gave them to Abraham, and restored his wife Sarah to him.*
> *Abimelech said, "Behold, my land is before you; settle wherever you please."*
> *To Sarah he said, "Behold, I have given your brother a thousand pieces of silver; behold, it is your vindication before all who are with you, and before all men you are cleared."*
> *Abraham prayed to God, and God healed Abimelech and his wife and his maids, so that they bore children. For the* LORD *had closed fast all the wombs of the household of Abimelech because of Sarah, Abraham's wife."* [7.11]

Today this might be translated as follow: "Abe, take your lying self and your lying wife and get as far away from me as possible. I damn near became a dead man because of you two. (or "youse two" depending on geographical area) Here are some servants, animals and some cash. Now—you *have* your trouble making wife back, land, servants, animals and cash, so go wherever you please. I don't care. I have given you everything you might ever need, so there is no excuse for you to do anything other than to get out of my sight and don't ever come back."

This passage also tells us that Abimelech not only had concubines, but he also had a wife.

Just as a note, if you later read through Genesis 26, it seems like there must be some strange mistake. But it is no mistake. It is ironic that sometime later, as recorded in Genesis 26:6-11, Isaac, Abraham's promised son, goes to Gerar; and here is what he does:

Genesis 26: 6-11 tells us:

> "So <u>Isaac</u> lived in Gerar. When the men of the place asked about his wife, he said, "She is my sister," for he was afraid to say, "my wife," thinking, "the men of the place might kill me on account of <u>Rebekah</u>, for she is beautiful."
> It came about, when he had been there a long time, that Abimelech king of the Philistines looked out through a window, and saw, and behold, Isaac was caressing his wife Rebekah.
> Then Abimelech called Isaac and said, "Behold, certainly she is your wife! How then did you say, 'She is my sister'?" And Isaac said to him, "Because I said, 'I might die on account of her.' "
> Abimelech said, "What is this you have done to us? One of the people might easily have lain with your wife, and you would have brought guilt upon us."
> So Abimelech charged all the people, saying, "He who touches this man or his wife shall surely be put to death."[7.12]

But returning to the story. Abimelech had given Abraham "a thousand pieces of silver."

The first time the word silver, meaning the precious metal silver appears in the Bible is in Genesis 13:2. "Now Abram was very rich in livestock, in silver and in gold."[7.13]

The actual word translated as silver is: "3701 keceph, from 3700; *silver* (from its *pale* color); by impl. *money*; - money, price, silver (-ling).[7.14]

The word silver does not appear again in the Bible until Abimelech gives these one thousand pieces of silver to

Abraham.[7.15] The first time the word gold, meaning the precious metal gold (*zahab*) appears, after being briefly mentioned in Genesis 2:11-12, is also in the above referenced passage in Genesis 13:2.[7.16]

The actual word translated as gold is: "2091 zahab, from an unused root mean. to *shimmer*; *gold*; fig. something *gold – colored* (i.e. *yellow*)..."[7.17]

The next appearance of the word silver is in Genesis 23:15-16:

> *"My lord, listen to me; a piece of land worth four hundred shekels of silver, what is that between me and you? So bury your dead." Abraham listened to Ephron; and Abraham weighed out for Ephron the silver which he had named in the hearing of the sons of Heth, four hundred shekels of silver, commercial standard."*[7.18]

This passage describes the circumstances surrounding Abraham paying for a place to bury Sarah. Whether or not this is this some of the same silver that was given to him by Abimelech; or if this was some of the same silver referenced in Genesis 13:2; or both; is unknown. There is no evidence that Abraham received any additional silver in any other manner; neither is there any evidence that up to this point in time, he had ever spent any of the silver he had obtained.

The use of the term "commercial standard" clearly indicates that silver was in use for commerce. This term is defined as silver "which passes with the merchant and (is or was) certified"[7.19]

Except for the aforementioned references, it does not seem likely that precious metals were any significant part of Abraham's culture. There is no evidence other than his possessing it, that Abraham had any real idea of the use of silver in commerce. We only have three references to silver as of Genesis 23, where: Abraham *had* silver in Genesis 13:2; Abraham was *given* more silver in Genesis 20:16; and Abraham, for the very first time recorded, *spent* it in Genesis 23:16.[7.20]

The problem is that nowhere are we told the source of the silver and gold described in Genesis 13:2. After Abraham had told the "sister lie" for the very first time to Pharoh; Genesis 12:16 tells us: "Therefore he treated Abram well for her sake; and gave him sheep and oxen and donkeys and male and female servants and female donkeys and camels."[7.21] There is no mention of silver here.

If the argument is used that this is because the Bible is a book of redemption and not a history book; then it necessarily follows that sheep, oxen, donkeys, servants, and camels are related to redemption; but somehow silver is not. Further exploration into this line of thinking then may result in statements such as "sheep are important because Jesus was the lamb;" but would then likely be countered with: "but He was betrayed for silver," and so on.

It seems likely that the use of silver as a medium of exchange, simply was not a normal part of Abraham's culture. Yet at the same time, the use of silver was so ubiquitous that even at that time, commerce had a means of certifying it. Ergo; the Hebrews, likely did not trade in silver, but the gentiles did. Although Abraham may have had been given silver by Abimelech, and perhaps by Pharoh; there is no evidence that he even knew what it was. (Gifts can sometimes be like that.) Or, Abraham might have known what it was, but he or they did not generally use it as a medium of exchange; and did not use it until the burial cave was purchased.

With respect to faith, what can be determined about the level of faith of Abraham, as compared to the level of faith of Abimelech? It is important to understand the time frame surrounding this story of Abimelech. It was in Genesis 12, when Abraham listened to God and left. We are now only in Genesis 20. Isaac had not even been born yet, much less been taken up the mountain to be sacrificed. Faith is a process; not an event; but rather a series of events. Faith grows over time, and from level to level. Abraham, the "father of faith;" was a relative neophyte at this time.

Abimelech's faith seemed to be much stronger and more mature than Abraham's was at that time. This can be seen by both Abimelech's actions and his words. Clearly Abimelech was a blessed man. His name essentially means father of kings. It seems that communications from or with God were not out of the ordinary for him. He took the death pronouncement from God very seriously. He referred to Abraham's actions as a "great sin." He asked Abraham how he (Abimilech) had sinned against him (Abraham) that he brought on him and on his kingdom this "great sin?" He referred to Abraham's actions as things "done to me things that ought not to be done." Abimelech did not say things that should not be done *to him*, but rather things that should not be done. He even remembered the death penalty, when he discovered the same lie from Abraham's son Isaac some time later.

Thus, this very important question then necessarily arises: If Abimelech did not learn about faith from Abraham; who is considered the father of faith; who clearly at this time did not possess a high level of faith; then from where did Abimelech obtain such a high level of knowledge and such a mature level of faith?

The only answer being; that since he could not have obtained it from the "father of faith" who was one of those from the other side, (the Hebrews); then it must have come from those who were from the other side of the other side; ie: the same side. Thus, the only possible source of Abimelech's faith then necessarily must have been the gentiles.

# Chapter 8

## The Case for Adultery

Granted this is probably not considered news, but Exodus 20:14 tells us: "You shall not commit adultery"[8.1]

This is a seemingly very simple commandment, with a seemingly relative ease of compliance. Just be sure to avoid certain types of physical relationships with certain types of persons, and you are good to go with this one.

But, in Matthew 5:27-28 Jesus tell us:

> *"You have heard that it was said, 'YOU SHALL NOT COMMIT ADULTERY'; but I say to you that everyone who looks at a woman with lust for her has already committed adultery with her in his heart."*[8.2]

Things suddenly seem to have gotten a lot more complicated. Clearly it does not sound like anything physical yet took place; nevertheless, under certain conditions, adultery could have already been committed; but in one's heart. Perhaps a better way to interpret this might be to substitute the word "in" with the word "to," now reading; "has already committed adultery with her *to* his heart."

Precisely what is adultery? The word *adultery is* derived from the Latin *adulterare*, meaning to corrupt. The word *adulterate* is from the "Latin *adulteratus*, past participle of *adulterare* to corrupt, give an altered form to."[8.3] What is noticeably missing in both of these etymological sources of the words adultery or adulterate is any reference to any type of sexual behavior.

The word "ultimate," is "borrowed from Medieval Latin *ultimatum* last possible, final, from Latin *ultimatum*, past participle of *ultimare* be final, come to an end, from *ultimus* last, final, superlative of *ulter, ulterus* beyond."[8.4]

The word "perfect" is "from Latin *perfectus* completed, past participle of *perficere* accomplish, finish, complete (*per-* completely, to the end + *facere* perform, DO). It is also probable that *perfect* was influenced in its formation by earlier *perfection*. -v Remove all faults from."[8.5]

If the word adult is split into ad-ult: it then translates into "to or toward" followed by the meaning of the word "ult." If "ult" is reasonably considered to be the same root as ultimate, then adult means to or toward last possible, final or most beyond. "Last possible" really meaning none better; or no chance of improvement resulting in "another" is possible at that time.

Thus, there seems to be a relationship between the meanings of the terms ultimate and perfect. Perfect essentially meaning to complete or to finish. It is not possible to literally complete something if there is anything missing; or if it contains any faults; as the faults would have to be remedied, or else there is not completion; but rather partial or semi-completion, which may actually be an oxymoronic term. Unless of course these faults were by design, but then of course they would not be considered faults. Pants sold new with wear or holes from the factory by design, (and likely more expensive) being an example of the latter.

If it is possible that there can be an improved model at a given current time; then whatever currently exists at that time cannot simultaneously be the ultimate at that same time.

As previously alluded, adulterant is another term that contains the same root. This describing something that participates in, and results in contamination or impurity—sometimes purposely, sometimes not. Hard to believe that something would be deliberately contaminated, isn't it?

Conclusion: there are two mutually exclusive meanings for the seemingly related terms of adult and adultery. One meaning to or towards the ultimate, or best possible; and the other meaning corrupted or altered form; both terms containing the word "adult."

One term meaning what God wants; (adult) the other being what he actually gets; (adulteration). One meaning being based upon the way humans should be by design; the other being based upon what we actually are because of our choices. The key word here is "choices," as by design we are the image and likeness of God. It may also be fair to ask if something that is already adulterated can still be adulterated; as opposed to further adulteration; which is not the same thing.

In Matthew 5:48, Jesus is quoted as saying "Therefore you are to be perfect, as your heavenly Father is perfect."[8.6] Note that this statement includes the phrase "to be," and not just the word "are." And of course, by design; or perhaps better stated by purpose; we are in a constant state of war, and unfortunately we do not prevail in each and every battle.

This really can appear a bit unfair though, because the word is *ad*-ult, really means *to or toward* this ultimate condition. The recognition that this is a process is inherent in this word. We should be moving to or towards the ultimate or perfection. It is the *process* which is important, and provides the real distinction between saints and sinners. Saints not meaning a departed soul who by consensus is determined to have done exemplary works; but rather one who has chosen to "bear the cross;" or follow the word of God. Thus; when a "saint" sins; and all do, this constitutes a mistake or a failure.

Saints are not sinners, and sinners are not saints. These definitions are based upon intentions and not actions. When a saint sins; a mistake has been made, as his or her intention is to obey the word of God. When a sinner sins; this is not a mistake, as he or she intends to live by their own set of rules and not God's.

This is really the basis for salvation; which of course is entirely different than redemption. Although it could be reasonably argued that salvation is a part of, or a type of, redemption; then if so, salvation would necessarily be a subset of the larger set of redemption. Thus there are many other areas of redemption in addition to salvation; even as critically important as salvation may be.

The case for the need for salvation has been made many times by many people, but it is really quite simple. If the requirement to successfully complete a given class requires maintaining 100% average; then once one question is answered incorrectly on any examination; or one falls short in any other manner; then no longer can the class possibly ever be passed. No matter how may times 100% may be achieved on subsequent endeavors, the average can never be 100%, unless you round up; which God does not do. Since He is perfect, He can only have perfection around Him or connected to Him. Thus He had to institute a method by which scoring less that 100% became irrelevant. Ergo: He instituted salvation and/or justification through substitution.

Back to the commandment contained in Exodus 20:14 that told us "You shall not commit adultery." Rephrased it might read: "You shall not commit any action or inaction which will cause any corruption, contamination, impurity or alteration in form."

Proverbs 6:32 tells us:

> *"The one who commits adultery with a woman is lacking sense; He who would destroy himself does it."*[8.7]

There is some serious wisdom in this passage that reinforces this concept of the true meaning of adultery. Based upon the common understanding of adultery, the phrase "with a woman." seems superfluous; but is not. This Proverb refers to a more specific type of adultery than does the "commandment" in Exodus 20:14. The same necessarily more than implying of course, that there are other (non woman) types of adultery. Actually, this passage does not necessarily have to refer to any type of sexual behavior; but rather the source of, or perhaps better stated; the accomplice associated with this specific type of contamination, corruption, or pollution.

Jeremiah 3: 9 tells us: "Because of the lightness of her harlotry, she polluted the land and committed adultery with stones and trees."[8.8] In this passage, it is God that is speaking. The context here is such that "her" refers to the "faithless Israel," and not a physical woman. Is this to be interpreted as allegorical, or is it literal; with a much broader definition of adultery than is commonly believed? It does not state *"as"* one who committed adultery. It must be noted that there is also the reference to pollution.

Adultery is not necessarily any specific act; but rather any act that results in said corruption, pollution, etc.

And what about Abimelech back in chapter 8? Remember; he was doing fine with his concubines and his wife; until Abraham and Sarah came along with their "she is my sister" scheme. He was married, and yet was obviously having physical relationships with women other than his wife. By the common understanding of the term today, he was sinning with these women on a regular basis by committing adultery; irrespective of whether or not *they* were married, as *he* unquestionably was married.

It was solely because he took Sarah into his group or family of concubines, and tried to have relations with her, that God "restrained" him. Remember that God threatened to kill him and all those around him unless he restored her to Abraham. But once he returned Sarah to Abraham; Abimelech was then able to return to his "normal" relationships with his concubines.

The conclusion being that: "God healed Abimelech and his wife and his maids, so that they bore *children,"* deliberately and specifically; so that Abimelech could return to his "sinful" lifestyle. Of course this makes no sense whatsoever. And Abimelech is not the only person in the Bible who had concubines; as there were others, also apparently with God's permission. King David and King Solomon being other examples; with perhaps the exception of not having God's permission at the time when King David essentially murdered Bathsheba's husband in order to obtain her. (As a note, King Solomon had 700 wives, princesses, and 300 concubines.)[8.9]

When Jesus tells us: "but I say to you that everyone who looks at a woman with lust for her has already committed adultery with her in his heart;" the actual Greek word used here by the writer for "lust" is: "1937 epithumeo." This word means: "to set the heart *upon*, i.e. *long* for (rightfully or otherwise): - covet, desire, would fain, lust (after)."[8.10]

There is also another related word which is derived from epithumeo: "1939 epithumia, from 1937; a *longing* (espec. for what is forbidden)…"[8.11]

It seems unlikely that Jesus was referring to "set the heart upon rightfully," when He chose the word that is now translated as lust. The "otherwise" contained in the definition must then necessarily mean to set the heart on either neutrally or wrongfully. Unless one were to adhere to the "sliding scale" or "gray area" school of morality; neutrality is not really an option, and in this context would make little sense. Thus He was likely referring to the "setting one's heart on wrongfully" definition of this word.

Thus Jesus' admonition about adultery easily translates into "everyone who looks at a woman and wrongfully sets his heart upon her has already committed adultery with her in (or to) his heart." Read in this manner, the meaning becomes quite obvious. A wrong heart is a contaminated, polluted or adulterated heart, even in the absence of any additional action. Before anything physical even happened, the heart was already adulterated; which is why this longing for was entertained. To put this in quasi-legal terms, it means contamination "before, and even in the absence of the fact." It is important to distinguish this "lust" from merely a fleeting desire, which is quickly dismissed.

The key of course is how to determine precisely what constitutes "wrongfully." Wrongfully meaning: inconsistent with or against God's will. Sometimes lust is defined as evil (but not necessarily wicked) desire. Here again: evil meaning against the will of God.

How can it be determined what the will of God was for Abimelech? The will of God for Abraham and Sarah, obviously was to deliver on His promise of offspring to them. And obviously it was not His will to deliver on His promise via child with Sarah as the mother and Abimelech as the father; nor to allow said union for any other reason. Abimelech likely was a gentile and not a Hebrew. For the bloodline that must culminate with Jesus, this simply would not do.

It would be speculation to try and state precisely why another child like Ishmael, in the sense of not being the offspring of Abraham *and* Sarah would be so dangerous to God's plan. The "seed" God referred to was to be of Abraham's; but without any doubt, so was Ishmael; albeit by their maid Hagar, and not Sarah. Clearly Isaac was who God had in mind to be Abraham's son, but why would another "illegitimate" offspring have interfered with this? Perhaps the age of Sarah was a factor; but no clear information is provided regarding this.

But why was Abimelech not in any way rebuked for his extramarital activities? Perhaps God had another plan for Abimelech and his offspring that required many; perhaps many more than his wife would have been able to provide.

With regard to adultery, a fair conclusion can be made that anytime anyone one becomes contaminated by acting against the will of God *for him*; this is by definition some form of adultery.

In Matthew 19:6 and 19:9 Jesus tells us:

> ""So they are no longer two, but one flesh. What therefore God has joined together, let no man separate."...
> ""And I say to you, whoever divorces his wife, except for immorality, and marries another woman commits adultery"[8, 12]

This is a passage (verse 6) that is notoriously used at weddings. But often this is an example of the kind of hubris that is very difficult to surpass. It could be rephrased as: If God joined something together; then let no man separate it. The hubris of course, stemming from the assumption that because these individuals chose; for whatever reasons; to get married; then God necessarily joined these people together. The "if " or "what therefore" requirement is thus assumed to have been met; and this determination is solely being made because of the couple's decision to wed.

Nevertheless, it is not the assignment of any "*host*" outside of a couple's marriage, to take it upon themselves to determine that this condition of being "joined together" by God; is not in fact so; and/or to act upon any such determination made.

And in verse 9 above, it may not be clear whether it is the subsequent marriage; or the consummation of the said marriage; or both; that actually constitutes the adultery. But it does in fact state "marries;" with no reference to any consummation of the same or any other subsequent actions.

What is prostitution? The word pro-stitute is: "From the past participle of Latin prostituere "to expose publicly, offer for sale," from statuere "to set, place"[8.13] Or "pro" before and statuere set or place; to set or place before.

Thus, literally prostitution has nothing to do directly with any sexual act. And it is not exclusively used that way even today. Neither has prostitution anything to do with any acceptance of any such offering. "Soliciting prostitution" then means soliciting someone to "expose publicly offer for sale," or to stand before; rather than acceptance, or an attempt to accept, whatever the "offer for sale" may be.

In ancient Rome, the site for this public exposure or offering for sale by women, was under the city arches. These were similar to what we would refer to as "red light" districts today. An arch was and still is referred to as a fornix; or the plural is fornices. This is also believed to be the root of the word furnace. Hence *fornicate* is derived from the location where the prostitutes would offer their "wares."

Thus we have two related words: prostitution and fornication. Words referring to the "offerer" and the "accepter" of a trade of sexual activities for money or something else of value; acceptance here including willfully engaging in the activity.

If no type of payment is solicited or required, then whatever it may be considered, it cannot be considered prostitution. If there is no acceptance or agreement to pay, then whatever it may be considered, it cannot be considered fornication.

But today, everyone knows that fornication represents any type of sexual relations between people who are not married to each other. However, this "knowledge" is most certainly not consistent with the origins of the word.

So then what would be a suitable term with which to exclusively describe merely sexual relations between unmarried persons? Of all of the words commonly used to describe this type of activity; and although a myriad of expressions relating to other aspects such as: frequency, lack of selectivity, addiction etc. do exist; none can seem to be found that would fit this sole definition. Perhaps this is because sexual relations between unmarried persons; with nothing else attached; is in actuality such a rare phenomenon.

Generally; it seems that one does not always recognize prostitution and fornication when it or they occur(s). If there is *any* type of payment sought with respect to sexual activities, it is prostitution in that sense. The payment can be: self-centered physical pleasure, a young person getting out of the house, acceptance, getting someone to like you, or hurting another's spouse or mate. Whatever the payment desired may be; whether recognized as such or not; when this type of arrangement is offered, this constitutes prostitution. When payment is made; irrespective of the form; this constitutes fornication.

Marriage is both a contract and a covenant. The contract part; which is in reality a license granted by some agency of authority; is essentially worthless without the covenant. It is interesting that governing authorities believe that special permission (license) need be granted for persons to be allowed to marry. This likely arose from unreasonable dissolutions of the same. Nevertheless; except for allocation of assets and perhaps some degree of concern for offspring; the provisions of this contact are unenforceable without a covenant. And with a kept covenant, outside enforcement is unnecessary. Covenants are agreements. And based upon the scriptures, it appears that such covenants or agreements can have great degrees of variation.

Whether or not any given covenant is adulterous or contaminated; or is consistent with God's will; can often be difficult. This is made even more difficult; when the meanings of words are misunderstood; particularly when a much narrower view is believed. But, as in the case of Abimilech; if God's view of any given covenant can be known; then consistency or inconsistency with His will can be determined; at least retrospectively.

Clearly there can be prostitution within a marriage. There can be times in a marriage when sexual relations are prohibited by one party; unless and until the other party agrees to do or not do something. This is a kind of backwards version of prostitution, but prostitution nonetheless. A marriage based upon financial issues may result in sexual behaviors based upon maintaining this financial relationship, and nothing more. Whether or not these represent immorality; perhaps even the kind of immorality of which Jesus spoke, seems likely; although this could be argued depending on one's perspective.

Many forget that Joseph and Mary were not married at the time Jesus was born. And although there is evidence of siblings of Jesus, no evidence could be found which would reasonably indicate that they ever did in fact actually marry; at least with respect to the 66 books contained in the commonly accepted "version" of the Bible.

Right and wrong are not to be determined by man's standards, but rather by God's standards. When man's standards and God's standards conflict; it is God's standards that provide the ultimate moral standard and thus must prevail; and never the reverse.

# Chapter 9

## Job's Predicament

Job is probably the most often misquoted and misunderstood book of the entire 66 books that comprise the standard Bible; arguably more so than even the Book of Revelation—which is in no way any small accomplishment.

It is not so much the story of Job; but rather both the circumstances surrounding the Book of Job; (as opposed to Job himself), as well as the implications of the Book of Job, that are of greatest interest.

The name Job is the following: "347 Iyowb, from 340; *hated* (i.e. *persecuted*); *Ijob*, the patriarch famous for his patience: - Job."[9.1]

It is interesting to note that the name "Satan" appears only 19 times in the entire Old Testament; and 14 of 19 times this name appears are contained in the first two chapters of Job.

It is important to distinguish that there are often three separate "times" concerning many books of the Bible; which in the case of Job is especially interesting and illuminating. Firstly, there is time that Job lived; this being the actual years or time when this story took place. The second; being the time which this book was actually written. The third "time;" being the sequential appearance of this book in the Bible. They are all quite different.

Whenever traits and tendencies which otherwise might seem "ungodly" are attributed to God, Job is often the Scriptural basis for this claim. "Watch out; God is "gonna" do this or that to you; after all look at what He did to Job." "God will turn you right over to the devil, just like He did to Job," and so on.

The very first and most important requirement for understanding the Book of Job; is the realization, that one must first to try and filter out what is nonsense from what is truth. The following is what God ultimately told Job's friends; these very same friends whose words are often cited as "His" wisdom.

Job 42: 7-8 tells us:

> "It came about after the LORD had spoken these words to Job, that the LORD said to Eliphaz the Temanite, "My wrath is kindled against you and against your two friends, because you have not spoken of Me what is right as My servant Job has.
> "Now therefore, take for yourselves seven bulls and seven rams, and go to My servant Job, and offer up a burnt offering for yourselves, and My servant Job will pray for you.
> For I will accept him so that I may not do with you according to your folly, because you have not spoken of Me what is right, as My servant Job has."[9.2]

This sounds rather suspiciously like "You are a dead man," or perhaps in this particular instance dead *men*. Essentially God is saying: "You fellows had better do something and do it fast; *and* get Job to pray for you as well; or I will take you out because of the trash you have been talking about Me."

Thus, it seems that whenever some seemingly wicked or evil act is attributed to God; which does not sound anything like the God that you know; and then Job is cited as the source of the "proof;" it would be prudent to be certain that this "proof" is not in actuality contained in any part of the "folly" to which God was referring in Chapter 42 verse 8.

It is the mechanism involved with respect to the events contained in Job which is of greatest interest. Specifically and precisely: what was it that was happening that precipitated these events; and what can be learned from the same.

Job 1:5 tells us:

> *"When the days of feasting had completed their cycle, Job would send and consecrate them, rising up early in the morning and offering burnt offerings according to the number of them all; for Job said, "Perhaps my sons have sinned and cursed God in their hearts." Thus Job did continually."*[9.3]

Job had seven sons. A fair reading is that Job and his sons would have a feast everyday; each of the days of the week dedicated to each son for that or his particular feast. When the seven son/seven day/seven feast cycle was completed, Job it seems would then offer burnt offerings for all of his sons.

As previously indicated in Job 42: 7-8; burnt offerings are a serious matter. Some types of burnt offerings involve animal sacrifice and subsequent burning. There are strict rules about these types of offerings, with respect to the handling of the blood, fat, skin etc. They require a bit of effort, and are not the equivalent of merely lighting a candle, or today pushing a button in lieu of an actual candle. They often are used as an offering to God because of sinful behavior.

According to Job 1:5, Job *continually* offered burnt offerings; the subsequent "perhaps" meaning; just in case his sons may have sinned and cursed God in their hearts. So whether or not Job's sons had sinned or cursed God in their hearts, Job offered burnt offerings just as though, and/or in case they already had. One might reasonably ask why Job saw fit to do this?

Later, after the calamities Job suffered, Job 3:25 tells us:

> *"For the dreadful thing I dreaded has come on me; and that which I feared has come to me."*[9.4]

Here the *Interlinear Bible* translation is better, because it maintains the correct tense usage. In this passage, Job reveals what his motivation likely was for these continual offerings. It seems that it was in fact *fear* that drove Job to continually offer these burnt offerings. Not only were these offerings for sins for which he had already admitted uncertainty with respect to whether or not any of the same was ever actually committed; but in addition, these were in fact intercessory offerings. This meaning that it was Job; and not the suspected "sinners," who made the offerings on their behalf.

Job *feared* for his sons' welfare. Fear so great that he took it upon himself to continually offer burnt offerings irrespective of any knowledge of any level of sin or lack thereof.

Often, it is said that fear is the opposite of faith. If this is in fact true, then it is reasonable to assume that the rules for fear should be similar to the rules for faith. Job did not just have intermittent episodes of fear or doubt; neither does it appear that he merely experienced what may have been constant fear. But rather; that he undertook actions with respect to those fears; and he did so on a consistent basis.

The laws in different states vary with respect to what constitutes conspiracy. But the general rule is that merely discussing or cursorily planning a crime does not constitute conspiracy. Usually some action must be undertaken in furtherance of said plan, in order to qualify as conspiracy. A group of people merely discussing how, or making "vague" plans to, rob a bank; does not generally rise to the crime of conspiracy. But once one or more of them undertakes "an act in furtherance" of this planning; such as "casing the joint;" this can trigger the conspiracy statutes.

This is precisely what Job did with respect to his fears. If the rules for fear are similar to those of faith, then again we have $f_t =$ **ma**, using lower case letters here to distinguish fear from faith. Here $f_t = f_a \times f_r$, meaning the quantity of the total "force" of fear being equal to the product of the amount of action undertaken because of the fear (continual burnt offerings) and the reason for the fear (doubt). Again, the same rules apply with respect to the **ma**. But from this point on, the mechanism is a bit different. It seems that is not God who is actually in charge of the delivery of this **ma**, but rather the enemy, as the story continues.

So what happened? Job 1: 6-7, the very next verses begin to tell us:

> "Now there was a day when the sons of God came to present themselves before the LORD, and Satan also came among them.
> The LORD said to Satan, "From where do you come?"
> Then Satan answered the LORD and said, "From roaming about on the earth and walking around on it."[9.5]

Without digressing into who the sons of God were, or why God appears to be asking Satan a question; there are two important points here. Firstly, Satan shows up to discuss something with God. Secondly, wherever this conference took place, it was not on the earth.

The following is likely the first great misconception which is purported to be in the Book of Job; as appearing in Job 1:8:

> "The LORD said to Satan, "Have you considered My servant Job? For there is no one like him on the earth, a blameless and upright man, fearing God and turning away from evil."[9.6]

In this passage, God appears to be offering up Job to the devil, and inquiring as to whether or not the devil would be interested in Job; this being precisely what many believe to in fact to be the case. But this really does not make any particular amount of sense. Firstly, God is not going to help the devil by suggesting or offering up Job. And secondly, an omniscient God would have known from the beginning of time what Satan's answer to this question was to be; as well as the very reason for which the devil was approaching Him at this time.

In all fairness, it must be noted that some of the versions do contain a footnote to 1:8; which indicates that the original words that were correctly translated as "set thy heart on" were for some reason later supplanted by the word "considered."

The *Interlinear Bible* confirms this "Have you set your heart on" translation, as the correct translation of the original verse.[9.7]

Now it is also fair to say, that the same argument as to why God asked Satan something that God already knew, can be raised with respect to the proper translation and understanding of this question. (And as though somehow Satan would actually tell God the truth.) In fact, the very same question is repeated, and again asked of the devil again in Job 2:3.[9.8] Of course God knew the answer to this question. It was not asked twice or even once because God was in need of this or any other type of information from Satan; neither is Satan known to be a reliable source for truth.

The most reasonable explanation being that this was actually offered as a warning to the devil, in a question form. "Have you set your heart on my servant Job?" A more contemporary translation or translations being: "Are you really sure you want to do this?" or " Can I change your mind about doing this?" etc. Most people being given this type of warning by God would immediately reconsider. But not the devil, instead he starts complaining about how God is protecting Job etc.

Job 1:9-12 tells us:

> "Then Satan answered the LORD, "Does Job fear God for nothing? "Have You not made a hedge about him and his house and all that he has, on every side? You

> have blessed the work of his hands, and his possessions have increased in the land. "But put forth Your hand now and touch all that he has; he will surely curse You to Your face."
> Then the LORD said to Satan, "Behold, all that he has is in your power, only do not put forth your hand on him."
> So Satan departed from the presence of the LORD."[9.9]

This represents classic Satan behavior. First he pollutes Job's mind with all of this doubt and subsequent fear. Then, after falling for Satan's meanderings, Job becomes terrified about the welfare of his sons, makes these continual burnt offerings; which establishes the **f$_t$**, and then Satan comes to God for permission to deliver the **ma**. And deliver this **ma** he did.

But back to Job 1:8. The second part of 1: 8 is also interesting where God states: "For there is no one like him on the earth, a blameless and upright man, fearing God and turning away from evil." God did not state that there has or had never been anyone on earth who had those aforementioned attributes, but rather that there *is* no one like him. God did not state that there was never anyone like Job; neither did he state that there would never be anyone like Job; but rather at that time there was no one like Job.

Thus, given the chronological placement of the Book of Job in the Bible, (the 18$^{th}$ book), clearly God was not necessarily ignoring other persons in the Bible who had or would have these very same attributes; persons such as those whose existence constitute the "Patriarchal Period."

Abraham, Isaac and Jacob had the types of positive characteristics quite similar to those attributed by God to Job. After all, there is this entire Patriarchal Period of the Bible attributed to; arguably named after them. It seems that God was merely stating that *at that time*, there was no man on earth like Job. This likely being *a* reason, if not *the* very reason, why Satan hated Job so.

In fact, it would seem fair to say that Job *must* have had a much easier time with respect to the faith department. Based upon the Scriptural placement of Job, he would have had the benefit of

Abraham, Isaac and Jacob; as well as the benefit of at least the existence of the writings of Moses. Moses died in Deuteronomy 34:5, the fifth book of the Bible. Assuming Mosaic authorship; surely Moses must have written the books he wrote prior to his death, which is in the fifth book. And even if those books had been unavailable to Job, there must have existed "word of mouth" knowledge of some of their contents. Thus, it would be easy to understand how Job could, at that time, have had what could be considered a rather extensive knowledge of God; as well as God's covenant with His "hosts."

It seems the consensus is; that providing the specific time that Job actually lived is impossible, because no known historical events coincide with the known events of his life. Chronological placement is reputed to be between Genesis Chapters 11 and 12, or shortly after Abraham lived. Some conclude the life of Job was in the "Patriarchal" period; the time of Abraham, Isaac and Jacob. It is believed that Job's wealth being described in terms of tangible assets other than gold and silver is significant in terms of chronologically placing the events. Also of believed significance, is the position of Job as priest of his family, Job's offering of sacrifices, the structure of Job's family; as well as and the fact that historical events such as the Exodus, the life of Moses, or the tabernacle, etc. are not mentioned. The facts that the Chaldeans were not yet living in cities, and that "Shaddai," was used for the name of God, are also considered significant. Finally, it is believed that Job actually did exist, rather than the story merely being a parable.[9,10]

If there are no references to any known historical occurrences at the time of Job, this is very problematic. One might ask how this could possibly be so? It seems highly unlikely that there could not be *any* correlations made between any historical events contained in Job, and any other known historical events.

There are really only two possibilities for this: Firstly, that the Book of Job contains no such identifiable references; either because of mere coincidence; or because of the removal of these references; whether accidental or deliberate. The conclusion then necessarily being that it is the book itself that is missing any such reference; either by coincidence or deliberate omission.

The second possibility being: that the book itself *is* in fact replete with what would otherwise be contemporary historical references; but it is the historical knowledge of his time that is incomplete. Here we would be faced with having to make the decision as to whether these secular historical facts; the very facts which could have been used to determine the time of Job; were somehow lost, or were in fact *never* any part of known history.

If Job lived somewhere between Genesis 11 and 12, this would then represent the period after the marriage of Abraham, (at that time called Abram,) to Sarah, (at that time called Sarai); and well before God even instituted the Abrahamic covenant, which appears at the beginning of Genesis 12.

According to *The New Open Bible KJV*, "The covenant with Abraham is the first of the theocratic covenants (pertaining to the rule of God)."[9.11]

Consequently, if Job lived during this time period, (between Genesis 11 and 12), this was before the existence of the first theocratic covenant, and thus Abraham; the father of faith; could not possibly have imparted any of this information to Job; as Abraham was not yet in this role at that time. Thus, the question arises as to precisely what was the source of Job's faith and associated knowledge?

If Job lived shortly after the time of Abraham, there is no evidence that Job knew of Abraham; who at the time of his (Abraham's) death, it appears was quite well known. There is also no evidence that Job ever knew Isaac or Jacob. Again, the same question about the source of Job's faith arises.

We are also faced with another time discrepancy concerning the time that God made the statement: "For there is no one like him on the earth, a blameless and upright man, fearing God and turning away from evil." Obviously then, this description did not apply to Abraham, Abraham's son Isaac, Abraham's grandson Jacob, Abraham's great grandson Joseph; nor to anyone else at the time God had said this. This seems not just very unlikely, but impossible; had any of them been alive at the time God made this statement to Satan about Job. This is something that would necessarily had to have been the case had Job lived shortly after the time of Abraham.

The period of time when Abraham, Isaac and Jacob are believed to have lived is listed as circa 2090 to 1897 BC.[9.12] *The Illustrated Dictionary of the Bible* states that Isaac was 75 years old when Abraham died.[9.13]

Thus we can infer that Abraham did in fact live 175 years, as we know Isaac was born when Abraham was 100 years old. This same reference also tells us that "Isaac and Rebekah had twin sons, Jacob and Esau, who were born when Isaac was 60 years old," and that "Isaac lived to be 180 years old."[9.14]

At this juncture, this "Patriarchal" period is 280 years; based upon the lives of Abraham and Isaac alone. Jacob, the son of Isaac, lived to a very old age. Genesis 48:28 tells us: "And Jacob lived in the land of Egypt seventeen years. So the length of Jacob's life was one hundred and forty seven years."[9.15]

We already know that Jacob was 60 years old at the death of Isaac. Thus we can add another 87 years to this period, bringing the total to 367 years. This calculation does not even include Joseph, the son of Jacob, who lived to be 110 years old.[9.16]

Thus we have a period of time well in excess of 367 years when men lived who would have fit the description of Job as God stated to Satan: "For there is no one like him on the earth, a blameless and upright man, fearing God and turning away from evil."

To be fair, Abram (Abraham) was 75 years old when he listened to God and departed Haran.[9.17] Thus, if we use 2090 BC as the year for the birth of Abram (Abraham), this would mean that from 2015 BC (2090 minus 75) through 1723 BC was the time period when these (Abraham, Isaac and Jacob) good men walked the earth. Thus we can reduce the time period where God's words to Satan about Job could not have been true, and thus not uttered; at least not uttered by God, to a "mere" 292 years. Based upon this chronology, if it were in fact the case that Job lived shortly after

Abraham; then "shortly" would then have to be defined as a period of time greater than 292 years.

Given that Job could not have lived between Genesis 11-12; neither could he have lived shortly after Abraham; Job being like a priest of his family, offering sacrifices, and family structure is also problematic. This being so because there is no evidence as to how he otherwise knew or could have known any of this. Nevertheless, it seems that he somehow engaged in precisely the same family organization and practices.

The fact that there are no references to the Exodus, or the life of Moses, or the tabernacle is not surprising; as likely none of this had yet occurred. The real issue of course being how long it was to be before these things would come to pass

Job's family structure is really not that surprising; but really provides no evidence for dating the time of Job. It must again be noted that the word gentile is derived from the Latin *gentilis*, literally "of the same clan"[9.18]

Job's wealth being described in terms of tangible assets other than gold and silver, is not particularly revealing. Remember gold was mentioned back in Genesis 2:11. This belief about Job and gold and silver, could make it seem as though Job lived without any contact with cultures that used precious metals as a form of wealth.

In fact, the word "gold" appears in the translation of Job fifteen times, the word "silver" appearing six times. There are five different original words that are translated as "gold."[9.19] But as often is the case with the Book of Job, it is not quite that simple.

A few examples are:

*Job 3:15 "Or with princes who had gold, Who were filling their houses with silver."*[19][20]

Here again the actual word for gold is: 2091 *zahab*. This is the same word that appeared with respect to Abraham.

*Job 22: 24-25 "And place your gold in the dust, And the gold of Ophir among the stones of the brooks, Then the Almighty will be your gold And choice silver to you."*[9.21]

Here the word for gold is: "1220 betser, from 1219, "strictly a *clipping*, i.e. *gold* (as *dug* out): - gold defence."[9.22]

*Job 28:15 "Pure gold cannot be given in exchange for it, Nor can silver be weighed as its price."*[9.23]

Here the word for gold is: "5458 cegowr, from 5462; prop. *shut up*, i.e. the *breast* (as inclosing the heart); also *gold* (as generally *shut* up safely): - caul, gold."[9.24]

It is implied that because Job's wealth is not measured in gold and silver, that any use of these precious metals for valuation of wealth did not exist. Barring any subsequent adulterations of the book of Job, this clearly is untrue. But that does not necessarily mean that Job did not exist much farther in the past than suspected. For all of the foregoing reasons, any claims that Job lived between Genesis 11 and 12, or shortly after the time of Abraham, seem to have little or no merit.By Hobson's choice, if Job did not live at the time of Genesis 11 and 12; and neither did he live shortly after the time of Abraham, then he must have lived prior to Genesis 11 and 12. Unless of course, one were to argue that Job lived at a time that which was long after Abraham; this being an argument that no one seems to be making.

The first time period to consider would be from the time of Adam, until Genesis 11 and 12. This is very problematic because Job's genealogy is unknown. Surely, if someone were to be important enough to have an entire book of the Bible written about them, they would have been listed among the "begats" (KJV) or in the "became the father of" (NAS) sections. There are many people listed in these sections whose names never appear again in the Bible. Yet Job's genealogy is not referenced.

On page 586 of *The New Open Bible* the following appears: "The non-Hebraic cultural background of this book (Job) may point to gentile authorship."[9.25] It is also believed that Job did actually exist and the story is not a parable. This would likely be true merely on its face; as it is generally the case that parables do not name the individuals involved in the story. When actual names are used, this usually signifies that the events and the characters actually existed.

No evidence can be found that supports the contention that Job lived during the time between Genesis 11 and 12; shortly after the time of Abraham, or at any time after the formation of Adam. Thus, the most reasonable explanation being that he had lived *prior* to the formation of Adam.

# 9-B

# These Aren't the Chaldeans You are Looking For.

**Warning:** The following contains many names that are difficult to pronounce, much less spell or remember. There are also many words that seem quite foreign; and dates that can be even more difficult to follow—any of which can become very annoying and downright aggravating. Reader discretion is advised.

The fact that the Chaldeans who murdered Job's servants in the fields were not yet living in cities; seems to indicate the time Job could not have lived, but provides little or no evidence as to when he actually did exist. When they became city dwellers is supposedly known, but how long they lived as nomads seems to not be known. Similarly, it is likely quite true that neither Beethoven nor Bartholomew had ever heard of Elvis Presley; but although this would provide an era in which they did not live either during or after; this does little to ascertain when either of them actually did walk on the earth.

There are some minor problems with these Chaldeans. The first time the term Chaldeans appears in the Bible is in Genesis 11:28 wherein it states "Haran died in the presence of his father Terah in the land of his birth, in Ur of the Chaldeans."[9.26]

Terah was the father of Abram. Thus Haran and Abram were brothers; both being sons of Terah. As previously stated, it is believed that Abraham was born in approximately 2090 BC. Therefore, based upon this reference in Genesis 11:28, the Chaldeans must have existed at least as far back as about 2090 BC. This becomes a bit more complex, if one considers Ur of the Chaldeans to be a city; then it would otherwise seem reasonable that the Chaldeans were already living in the city by this time; this time being circa 2090 BC; this arguably necessarily placing Job prior to that time; at least by the Chaldeans/city theory.

According to *The Illustrated Dictionary of the Bible*, the first non-Scriptural historical reference to the Chaldeans occurs about 900-800 BC.[9.27]

Thus, a decision must be made as to whether or not these Chaldeans somehow could have existed for over a thousand years with no mention of their existence in secular history; at least according to this same reference. Other sources seem to reasonably confirm this recognized time period of the Chaldeans existence historically.

One possible alternative being that in Genesis; when Moses is describing the city of Ur as *"of the Chaldeans;"* that this is an erroneous attribution.  According to this theory, the Chaldean attribution or characterization was somehow added after 1000BC;[9.28] this appearing to be a position for which no evidence, other than circumstantial, can be found.  With respect to the Chaldeans; there then is a missing millennium— *how very embarrassing!*  The conclusion then being that Genesis must somehow be wrong.  Therefore, there appears to be sufficient motive for this position; that of suggesting that this characterization of Ur as relating to the Chaldeans, is erroneous, and thus should not be considered. However; there can be found no reasonable explanation as to why this designation would have ever been added incorrectly in the first place.

Although perhaps convenient at times; it can be very dangerous to suggest that the word of God is in error; simply because it does not agree with what one "knows;" what one believes is known; or what one simply believes at any given instant.

In this particular instance it is especially dangerous, because Nehemiah 9:7 tells us:

> *"You are the* LORD *God, Who chose Abram And brought him out from Ur of the Chaldees, And gave him the name Abraham."*[9.29]

Thus Nehemiah must have also been altered; again not by deletion, but by addition in order for this theory to hold.

The way this reads; "brought him out;" it seems like it was more of a rescue mission, rather than merely God desiring a change in location.  In addition, it was not just Abram (Abraham) that God brought out of Ur, but also Terah, Lot and Sarai; and they went to Haran.  In fact, it seems that it was really Terah who left Ur of the Chaldeans, and he brought Abram and the others "out" with him.[9.30]

There is of course one additional minor problem with placing the Chaldeans circa 900 BC.  That problem being: if so, then precisely from what source were the Chaldeans who attacked Job's livestock and servants? It would seem that there now must be three times the word of God is wrong; at least in order for this theory to hold.

It is important to remember that the time of Moses and the Exodus was approximately 1445 BC.[9.31] (We have to count backwards when using BC dates.) Nevertheless, this means, at least according to the actual Scriptures, that Moses *referred* to Ur as "of the Chaldeans," some 445 years before the Chaldeans are believed by secular history to have actually existed. This 445 years corresponding only to the date when Moses wrote this; and not to the time he was writing about, which was actually 600+ years *earlier*.

*The Illustrated Dictionary of the Bible* further indicates that Ur was already a highly developed "city" at the time Abraham had lived there. Furthermore, as a result of "Excavations of the royal cemetery, from about 2900 to 2500 B.C." many interesting items were found. These discoveries included; "beautiful jewelry and art treasures, including headwear, personal jewelry, and exquisite china and crystal."[9.32] It is assumed that this date refers to when they were actually made, and not when they were buried.

According to the online *Ancient History Encyclopedia*: "The earliest settlement of Ur dates back to the "Ubaid Period, or about 5300–4000 BCE." Shortly after the birth of Abram, Ur had 65,000 residents, making Ur the largest city in the world.[9.33] Even if the earlier date is off by 20%, this would place the formation of Ur at 4240 BC.

Irrespective of the possibility of Ur existing in the years stated above, the Scriptural date of "creation" is generally considered to be circa 4000 BC.[9.34] Yet Ur; with or without Chaldeans; somehow had "beautiful jewelry and art treasures, including headwear, personal jewelry, and exquisite china and crystal" buried in cemeteries somewhere between "2900 and 2500 B.C." This means that somewhere between 1100 and 1500 years after Adam and Eve were expelled from the *gan* possessing only animal skins; these items had existed.

To put this in proper chronological reference, if we add up the years from the emergence of Adam through the birth of Noah to the beginning of the flood, the total is about 1760 years. Subtract this from 4000, and this places the beginning of the flood at 2240 BC and the end of the flood at about 2239 BC. So by the time of the completion of the ark and the onset of the flood, these items had already been made, and perhaps also buried in these cemeteries of Ur; for a period of time ranging between 260 and 660 years. To restate this for the purpose of clarity; these objects had already been in existence at least 260 years *before* the occurrence of the flood.

Although not realized by most, Adam lived to be 930 years of age.[9.35] When the actual year count began is unknown; meaning whether this is based upon his formation or expulsion. It is assumed here that his 130 years of age when Seth was born, refers to 130 years from Adam's formation. Adam then lived for at least 800 years on the outside the *gan*. We know Seth was born outside the *gan*, because Cain and Abel were born first and were born on the outside. Seth was his third recorded child and was born when Adam was 130. Thus 930 minus 130 leaves at least 800 years that Adam had lived on the outside.

Basing this upon his formation, Adam's death likely translates into circa 3070 BC. Consequently, approximately 170 or perhaps even fewer years after the very first formed man died, these people in Ur were manufacturing and/or burying somewhat sophisticated treasures in their cemeteries. (This date could be much later if the date of expulsion is used as the starting point for the 130 years of age when Seth was born.)

But back to these Chaldeans. Both Moses and Nehemiah attribute them to the city of Ur, as of approximately 2090 BC; (with Job, possibly much earlier), yet, secular history states that they were not in Ur for at least another thousand years.

Thus, rather than suggesting that the word of God is in error, it seems possible that it may in fact be the case that: *"These aren't the Chaldeans you are looking for."*

There seem to be Chaldeans everywhere. The one certainty

about the Chaldeans is uncertainty. It seems that sooner or later the Chaldeans show up in the Scriptures; they are seemingly everywhere. It is like today when virtually everyone one knows; is somehow related to someone who is famous; or is directly related to those who were on the Mayflower. Much of the available information about the "later" Chaldeans is contradictory. Thus, there seems to be little value in trying to distinguish which Chaldeans are which: with the exception of distinguishing the Chaldeans who are referenced in the time of Job and Abraham, from those Chaldeans who "showed up" circa 1000 BC.

There appears to be several possible sources for the term "Chaldeans:"

Firstly is "3778 Kasdiy, (occasionally with enclitic) Kasdiymah *towards* the *Kasdites*: - into Chaldea), patron. from 3777 (only in the plur.); a *Kasdite*, or desc. of Kesed; by impl. A *Chaldean* (as if so descended); also an *astrologer* (as if proverbial of that people: - Chaldeans, Chaldees, inhabitants of Chaldea."[9.36]

This is not particularly revealing. Irrespective of one's view of astrology, it is a system that is learnable by anyone.

Secondly is: "3779 Kasday (Chald.), corresp. to 3778; a *Chaldean* or inhab. of Chaldea; by impl. a *Magian* or professional astrologer: - Chaldean."[9.37]

It must be noted here that the word *magian* is not a typographical error for magician, but rather that *magian* is an adjectival form of the noun magus; magus meaning "a Zoroastrian priest: a priest in the ancient Persian religion of Zoroastrianism or man with magical powers: a man with supernatural or magical powers, especially in ancient times"[9.38]

This adjective of *magian* is used here to indicate the type of astrologer. There is a distinction being made between a "professional astrologer," and a "magian astrologer;" the latter also having "magic" powers. This is a very important distinction. These were not just astrologers in the sense of "*Kasdiy*," but astrologers who also had supernatural or magical powers. This association is likely the source of revulsion by many "religious" people about astrology or astrologers.

When Aaron cast down the rod which transformed into a serpent in Pharaoh's kingdom, the "sorcerers;" who were present and who subsequently mimicked Aaron's actions; are or were: "3784 kashaph, a prim. root; prop. To *whisper* a spell, i.e. to *inchant* or practise magic: - sorcerer, (use) witch (-craft)."[9.39] To be perfectly fair, the sorcerers relating to Aaron are not called Chaldeans in the text, but the root of the word, (kas) is the same.

Thus the term Chaldeans, which Ur is qualified as being "of," appears to be related to the terms kasdiy, Kasdites, Kasday, and kashaph, in a progressive type manner—from astrologer; to astrologer with supernatural powers; to whisperers, sorcerers, and inchanters, with no mention of astrology.  To classify these apparent powers as supernatural may not be accurate, if this term relates to that above the natural, rather than beneath the natural; this of course referring to the source of the power; perhaps subnatural being a better term for the power and its source.


In chapter 4, verses 12-16 of the Book of Job, Eliphaz is speaking about a personal experience.
Therein he states:

> ""Now a word was brought to me stealthily, And my ear received a whisper of it.
> "Amid disquieting thoughts from the visions of the night, When deep sleep falls on men,
> Dread came upon me, and trembling, And made all my bones shake.
> "Then a spirit passed by my face; The hair of my flesh bristled up.
> "It stood still, but I could not discern its appearance; A form was before my eyes;
> There was silence, then I heard a voice:"[9.40]

What follows, is probably best described as typical Satanic propaganda. Simple astrologers do not do this. It also appears that his experience began with a whisper; and then progressed to a voice.

To again be fair; the reason that the Chaldeans, who engaged in what was actually the third attack on Job, are the subject of discussion; rather than the Sabeans, who engaged in the first attack; is because very little uncontroverted information can be found about these Sabeans. It must also be noted that the second attack was fire; the fourth attack was wind; and the fifth attack being boils;[9.41] again remembering that it was Satan who asked God's permission for him to engage in these attacks.

The meaning or meanings of the term "Ur" is or are:

1. "218 Uwr, the same as 217; Ur, a place in Chaldea; also an Isr.: - Ur."
2. "217 uwr, from 215; *flame*, hence (in the plur.) the *East* (as being the region of light): - fire, light. See also 224."
3. "215 owr, a prim. root; to *be* (caus. *make*) *luminous* (lit. and metaph.): - x break of day, glorious, kindle, (be, en-, give, show) light (-en, -ened), set on fire, shine."
4. "224 Uwriym, plur. of 217; *lights*; *Urim*, the oracular brilliancy of the figures in the high-priest's breastplate: - Urim."[9.42]

This may seem irrelevant; and in a certain sense may in fact be irrelevant; because at the time of Job, the Chaldeans were not yet city dwellers, and so not yet in Ur. But of course this then also definitely places the time of Job before the birth of Abram; but even roughly how long before cannot be determined by this alone. Qualifying Ur as "of the Chaldeans," strongly suggests that before the time when Ur was "of the Chaldeans;" that there was a time when Ur "was not of the Chaldeans;" and this qualification may have been used to distinguish the two. When Ur was of these

Chaldeans, it seems like a place from which it would be wise to be "brought out" of. But Job was attacked before even these Chaldeans were living in Ur.

Satan attacked Job with five forces: Sabeans, fire, Chaldeans, wind and boils. It is likely that these particular Chaldeans were those with magical powers, sorcerers, etc.; and not those who later took on the name Chaldeans. Whether these original Chaldeans were actually humans who were acting as agents of Satan, or actual demonic manifestations; remains unclear.

Thus, it is more than just speculation to suggest that Ur; when it was "of the Chaldeans;" was in fact a stronghold of the enemy, (Lucifer) with the Chaldeans being one group of those who did his bidding. It is important to remember that the enemy lost much of his power at Calvary, so it is difficult to comprehend the level of his power prior to this, although this will be addressed in the very next chapter. Once Satan or Lucifer, (adversary, or morning light before the sun) got the green light from God with respect to the lowering of the hedge around Job; he (Satan) then sent his representatives (including these Chaldeans) on the attack.

MEEKRAKER *Beginnings...*

# 3rd Intermission

## Antennas Work

The title of this intermission may read like something that truly need not be stated. Of course everyone knows that antennas work. Or do they? This question can be interpreted two different ways: Do all antennas work? Or alternatively; does everyone know that antennas work? If an antenna is an antenna, then it necessarily must function as such or it is not an antenna. Perhaps it is a broken antenna, but that is not the same. Despite the fact that there exists a plethora of antenna designs; if it is an antenna; it is such based upon function and not merely structure. It doesn't make much difference what it looks like, if it functions like an antenna, then it is an antenna; even if it in no way resembles such; or more importantly, even if it was designed or appears to be designed as something else.

Whenever there is current flowing through a conductor,

there is a magnetic field produced around that conductor. This behaves according to the so called "right hand rule;" which correlates the direction of the current with the direction of the field. As long as current flows in that conductor, the field will remain, its characteristics relating to the characteristics of the current. If the current increases, or diminishes, or changes direction; then this field will change accordingly.

If a second conductor then enters this field, a voltage will be produced in this second conductor. It makes little difference if the conductor physically moves into the field, or if the field expands to the second conductor; the result is essentially the same. The current flow in the second conductor however, will be in opposition to the flow of the current in the first conductor; a phenomenon explained by "Lenz's law."[13.1]

This forms the basis for antenna function. On radio transmission, the current flowing through the transmission antenna creates a field that expands and will "cut" into another conductor (receiving antenna) at a distant location. Here it is the field that is moving, and it is the conductor that is relatively stationary. Radio frequencies are alternating current, which means that they periodically change direction. The voltages induced in the receiving antenna will vary accordingly. Thus a faithful reproduction of the original current will result at the receiving end; albeit perhaps out of phase; as Lenz's law indicates.

An alternator or generator works similarly, but here it is the second conductor and not the field that is moving. In this case, the field is constant and produced by a magnet or a coil, and the second conductor is the moving part; whose energy for movement is supplied by something such as an engine.

Thus two rules can be established. Whenever electrical phenomena travel through a conductor, a field is created around that conductor. Whenever a second conductor enters such a field; or the field encounters a second conductor; an electrical phenomenon is induced into that second conductor. And of course it goes on as the secondary conductor produces a field; a field which would induce an electrical phenomenon in another conductor, as well as the original conductor and so on. Lenz's law merely explains that you cannot get something for nothing; else the world would explode.

It is also then fair to say that any field capable of producing a voltage in *any* conductor, would be capable of producing some degree of voltage in *all* types of conductors. It is true that some conductors specifically designed to convert the field produced by a specific frequency are more efficient at this task, but that is not the issue. An antenna that is trimmed to a specific frequency will do a much better job at this conversion at that frequency; but *any* conductor can and will have voltages produced in it when it enters or cuts this field, or the field reaches the conductor.

It would be quite understandable at this point to say: "That is very nice, but why do I need to know all of this? If I wanted a lesson in conductors, inductors, and induced currents I would consult an electrical or physics textbook."

The answer to this question is that human beings are conductors. If that were not so then no one would be able to receive an electrical shock. Neither would it be possible for anyone to be electrocuted.

Thus any time a human being is placed in this type of field; (or expanding and contracting fields are placed around a human); voltages are produced in that human being. Whether or not said voltages are of any significance would be a matter of opinion. Clearly if a human were placed in a strong enough field, undeniable changes would take place. So then it is not in any way an issue of *if* voltages are induced when a human is placed in this type of field, because that is a fact and thus a certainty. But the issue of whether or not said voltage or voltages is or are *significant* is another matter; and thus this remains the only real question.

The following from *Guyton's Textbook of Medical Physiology* may sound a bit complex and a bit verbose, but is provided to illustrate a point:

"Electrical potentials exist across the membranes of essentially all cells of the body, and some cells, such as nerve and muscle cells, are "excitable" - that is capable of self-generation of electrochemical impulses at their membranes and, in some instances, utilization of these impulses to transmit signals along the membranes."[13.2]

Guyton further indicates that the lipid portion of the cell membrane causes the cell to be similar to a capacitor in an electrical circuit. This lipid portion represents the dielectric or insulator portion of said capacitor, with electrical charges on both sides of this lipid or dielectric.[13.3] It is important to remember that whenever two electrical conductors are separated by an insulator, there is capacitance. Whether this capacitance is desired or not, it nevertheless remains. This is not to say that this necessarily represents a charged capacitor at any given time; but rather that capacitance exists.

Thus according to Guyton, cells have electrical potentials across their cell membranes, and some types of cells are excitable. These cells can also act exactly as electrical capacitors.

There seems to be little doubt that any voltages in these body cells; particularly nerve cells, will result in the production of magnetic or electromagnetic fields. Some may refer to this as an "aura."

There also seems little doubt that any voltages induced in these body cells, particularly nerve cells, which are the result of magnetic or electromagnetic fields, irrespective of the source, will have some type of an effect on the physiology of these cells.

Neurons have resting potentials measured in negative millivolts. When this voltage is changed, the neuron may become more excitable if this resting potential becomes less negative; or inhibited if this potential becomes more negative.[13.4]

So we have two possibilities: These induced voltages can cause a nerve cell to become less negative; more easily excitable; and aberrantly reach action potential or "depolarize" or "fire." This results in the nerve firing when it should not. Should these induced voltages cause the neuron's resting potential to become too negative; the nerve will become inhibited and not fire when it should.

In today's world, virtually everything that can possibly become wireless, is becoming wireless. The amount of radio frequency emissions on earth has never been higher. Frequencies that were never before usable because of technological limitations, today are in use incessantly. The "airwaves" are becoming saturated with these emissions; and every year, as technology improves, there are more and more frequencies being used. Thus, the level of the field intensities increases incessantly, as does the frequency spectrum in use.

To make matters worse, there is a phenomenon known as "heterodyning." When two frequencies are combined, the result is four frequencies. There are the original two; and one frequency equal to their sum; and one frequency equal to their difference. This not only produces unwanted frequencies, but may also produce frequencies beyond technological limits to detect. If two frequencies at the current technological high frequency limits heterodyne; this "sum" would be approximately double the frequency of the highest currently usable frequencies, and would likely be difficult if not impossible to even detect. Thus, any physiological effects would be impossible to determine.

The authors of this "Intermission" have discussed this "theory" for many years. This theory being that these types of induced voltages in the human body can have significant physiological effects. Recently, an excellent description of this phenomenon was "discovered."

> *"Doc Grimes alone had guessed that the present, general, marked preference for a sedentary life was the effect and not the cause of the prevailing lack of vigor. The change had been slow, at least as slow as the increase in radiation in the air...."*[13.5]

With all of the increasing electromagnetic radiations in our environment today, it was certain that eventually someone would have taken notice and written about this matter. Clearly this passage could easily refer to sedentary children today; and the resultant health problems; such as childhood obesity. The lack of any mention of playing video games, could be read as an effort to not single out any particular industry.

This is not exactly the truth; in fact it is not even close. This description was contained as an ancillary matter in a science fiction story; said being contained in the short story "*Waldo*;" written by Robert A. Heinlein, which was first published in 1942. How could it be that Heinlein had sufficiently noticed this phenomenon way back in 1942 to write about it, and yet no one today seems to pay much attention to it?

A reasonable answer would be that his base line was different. His perception of "normal" was based upon essentially no influence of electromagnetic radiation on human physiology and behavior; compared to those, especially the young, who became influenced by exposure to increasing levels. If a culture knew nothing about the existence of alcoholic beverages, it is likely that any member of this culture who was even slightly under the influence of alcohol would be easily noticed. Today it is *not* that the ubiquitous electromagnetic radiation and its physiological and psychological effects are accepted and merely considered as "normal;" but rather that they remain largely unnoticed. Unnoticed not meaning that the behavioral and physiological changes are not noticed, because they are. What is not noticed is any relationship between this electromagnetic radiation and the observed effects.

It must also be pointed out that the types of "radiation in the air" that Heinlein had written about, would by no means be considered in any way similar to the radiations of today. In 1942, "high frequencies" were generally considered to be those up to 30 Mhz. (Mhz. is one million cycles per second) Today, cordless telephones alone operate in the Ghz (billion cycles per second) range. Those frequencies previously considered as "high frequencies," would be considered on the low frequency end of the radio spectrum by today's technological standards. Generally the higher the frequency, the greater the penetrability; which is why an FM station being listened to in the car; unlike AM; will not be lost when driving under a small bridge or through a small tunnel.

All of this has been addressed for two reasons: Firstly, to draw attention to the fact that these ubiquitous physiological and behavioral changes which are seen today are not idiopathic; but merely have a source whose recognition continues to be evaded and avoided. Secondly, to provide a reasonable foundation for; as well as provide a segue to; some similar matters. Up to this point the concern here has been electromagnetic radiations from electrical devices such as radio transmitters, cellular phones, etc.

"When I walked into the room, it was so thick you could cut it with a knife." If the speaker were asked specifically what it was that was so thick it could be cut with a knife, the answer would probably be expressed with the inclusion of the word "like" or "as;" because no word commonly exists with which to describe "it."

Why is it that every time the bass player hits that note when music is being played perhaps a bit too loud, that the same window rattles in the same place? How does a microwave heat water; and why do material things that do not contain water heat very little in a microwave? The answer is the same for both; that answer being resonant frequencies.

When that person walked into the room, something had been going on in the room prior to their entrance. The individuals in the room were likely engaged in high amount of mental and emotional activity; here most likely "negative;" negative in the sense of the nature of the emotions or activities, as opposed to any relative electrical polarity. This neuronal activity; being electrical in nature, was producing a field or fields consistent with the nature of the activity; similar to a radio transmitter. When the person entered the room, their nervous system; being a conductor of electricity; "cut" into this field, with resultant neural impulses created; impulses which were then interpreted in a manner consistent with their (the negative impulses) original formation.

Why was it that the person entering the room (in this case) did not experience anything until they entered the room? There are two reasons for this. One reason is the "inverse square law." The intensity of the field is such that when the distance is doubled, the intensity is diminished as a square function; here resulting in $1/4^{th}$ intensity. Triple the distance $1/9^{th}$ etc. On approach, the same relationship holds. The intensity becomes stronger as a square function. At ½ the distance the intensity is 4 times as great, at 1/3 the distance 9 times as intense etc. One other reason for not experiencing this until the room was entered likely because of whatever level of shielding the wall may have provided.

In this case, the frequencies did not resonate with the nature of the individual at that time. Thus, "dis-ease" was the result, which made the person "uneasy." Had it been positive activities that were transpiring; the likely result would have been a positive experience in the person entering the room; as these would have been in phase or resonating with them. But in the first example that was not the case; as these "were out of phase."

Why do loudspeakers sound so much better when they are in an enclosure? It is because the sound waves coming out of the back of the speaker are 180 degrees out of phase with the sound waves emanating out of the front, and they will largely cancel out each other. An enclosure will either dampen those emanating out of the rear of the speaker; or find some method of making them in phase with those emanating out of the front.

Loosely speaking, Proverbs tells us that the upright find the wicked abominable, and the wicked find the upright abominable; abominable generally meaning completely repulsive. This is usually interpreted to exclusively mean that it is their respective "behaviors, or "ways" or "walks," or "speech" that result in this repulsion. But in situations similar to the above, (where no one had even said anything), the cause for this phenomenon can be much more subtle than behavior or speech.

"When I first met him, there was just something about him that I didn't like, but I couldn't put my finger on it. And sure enough he turned out to be no good." or, "I don't know why, I just liked him from the start." This is the resonant frequency or phase principle. There is nothing mysterious about any of this; it is merely a matter of physics.

It is a Scriptural fact that human beings are all made in the image and likeness of God. How could it then be that one could find another so repulsive in the absence of any objective evidence for this repulsion? How is it that one's "spiritual nature" could be so out of phase with another's? The only reasonable answer is interference; interference with the vibratory patterns of either one or both. And we all know that there is only one possible source from which this interference could emanate. Whether or not we know we know is another matter.

This "interference" should be clearly distinguished from matters such as those of say: taste or diurnal cycle. Simply because one may like blue, that does not make another who may like purple wicked. Neither is it righteous to awaken early, nor wicked to awaken late; else those who pave major highways are necessarily doing the devil's work; as would then be policemen, airline pilots and so on. Should one actually believe any of these things; said belief in and of itself represents clear evidence of interference in or with *their* manner of thinking. Uprightness and wickedness are not determined by what humans think is such; but only by what God *said* is such.

Furthermore, judging actions or ways is entirely different from judging a person. As "hosts," we are required to ascertain when there is evil, and either correct it or avoid it. But this is not the same as judging the person. We have all been fools at one time or another with some matter or matters; and we are all still fools with certain matters at certain times. A wise person will admit this, and a liar will not. If God treated us the way we feel like treating people who do foolish things, not only would there never have been any salvation; but the earth would be uninhabited; at least by H. Sapiens.

There is one additional interesting and even more controversial matter. This being the question of whether the fields emitted by humans and animals can impart changes to non-living matter. This concept or theory generally is referred to as *vibroturgy*. Does a funeral home absorb negative fields, and do said fields change the nature of emissions normally emitted by the matter contained therein? If so, can these stored energies produce any types of changes when a life form enters these environments. And of course, precisely what is the nature of the types of changes that are recorded with Kirlian photography?

# Chapter 10

## The Slanderer

If one could somehow place themselves as a true devils advocate; and then encountered a book whose main purposes were not only redemption, but also to provide a plethora of substantial and credible information with respect to your nature; and in addition, this same book included an elaborate instruction manual written with great precision as to how to defeat you; what would be the best course of action? Of course, attack the book. Change things, remove things, add things, and do anything else possible to stop the accurate transference of this knowledge. If you could not get to the book, then make sure that you get to those who have notoriety as being the "experts;" but preferably do both.

When attempting to find the first Scriptural references to "the enemy;" defining precisely what constitutes *first*, will of course have an effect on the result. First can mean the earliest book, whether when written or as it appears; or it also can mean a passage that refers to the earliest event, irrespective of when it appears. The first implied or tacit reference to the enemy; if first means earliest book; appears between Genesis 1:1 and Genesis 1:2. This is the time between when the heavens and the earth were created, and (then) the earth was without form and void.

Although this may represent the result of the actions of the enemy, this cannot be the first chronological event; because Satan had to have already been on the earth in order "facilitate" these actions. The next reference to Satan appears in Genesis 3:1 wherein it states: "Now the serpent was more crafty than any beast of the field which the LORD God had made."[10.1] The context in which this is stated, the way it appears, and the way it reads; it is as though this serpent somehow just kind of fell out of the sky.

Revelation 12: 7-9 tells us:

> *"And there was war in heaven, Michael and his angels waging war with the dragon.*
> *The dragon and his angels waged war, and they were not strong enough, and there was no longer a place found for them in heaven.*
> *And the great dragon was thrown down, the serpent of old who is called the devil and Satan, who deceives the whole world; he was thrown down to the earth, and his angels were thrown down with him."*[10.2]

A fair read of Revelation Chapter 12 *in-toto*, is that it is chronologically all over the place. This is not surprising. As previously discussed, John was permitted to enter the immaterial realm where there is no time. He then wrote what he recollected without any type of time reference for all or most of what he had witnessed.

But clearly Revelation 12:7-9 refers to a time when Satan was still in heaven. Although a bit scant on details, it does show us what happened and what was the result. Likely it was his expulsion; and his subsequent appearance while he was being thrown down to the earth, being the source from which the name Lucifer was derived.

It must be noted here that the original word translated as "serpent" in this passage from Revelation, is not the same word for the serpent (nachash) who orchestrated the "confidence game" against Eve back in Genesis. One might say: "of course not; as Genesis was written in Hebrew and Revelation was written in Greek." That is quite true, but the meaning of this word used for serpent is not particularly close. In Genesis nachash was translated as serpent solely because of hissing. Here the word is: "3789 ophis, prob. From 3700 (through the idea of sharpness of vision); a snake, fig, (as a type of sly cunning) an artful malicious person, espec. Satan: - serpent."[10.3]

There are some mixed tenses contained in this passage from Revelation. Most of it is in the past tense; but the "is called the devil" and "deceives the whole world" are stated in the present tense. Thus it seems fair to assume that the events recounted in the past tense are historical; and those stated in the present tense are current events.

We are told that Satan was thrown down to the earth along with his angels, because there was "no longer a place found for them" in heaven. But precisely when did this event occur? Unfortunately, it does not state the timeframe, but what we do know is that the earth must have existed prior to his shall we say, departure; as we are told that earth was his ultimate destination; whether by anyone's intention or not.

To be fair; depending on punctuation, this passage arguably *could* be read as though it was actually four entities which were thrown down. These four being: the dragon, the serpent, Satan; as well as his angels. However, the use of the phrase "he was" makes this unlikely, although not impossible. Likely the "he" refers to Satan; and it was he that was accompanied by his angels.

A cursory reading of this statement concerning being "thrown down" makes it seem necessary that someone or something actually and intentionally engaged in this "throwing;" most likely the same being Michael and company. However, the determination must be made as to whether in actuality this "thrown down" describes an action or a result. If it is an action, then this was done purposely: whether correctly or erroneously. But a cause effect relationship is implied with respect to "no longer a place found for them" and being "thrown down." A strong argument could be made that it was solely *because* there was no place for him; that this resulted in him being thrown down; as opposed to someone throwing him down.

This may be a similar relationship to the eternal life or connection with God, and eternal separation. It may be that simply because there was no place for Satan and his angels once he rebelled, the expulsion out of heaven was automatic; rather than a cognitive decision being made by Michael, God or anyone else.

One could describe a meteorite as having been thrown down, but this merely describes a result; and not necessarily an action. A meteorite appearing to be thrown down, particularly from the perspective of someone on earth; is or was simply the result of a wandering mass entering the gravitational field of earth; and this resulted in the meteorite being "thrown down." It was not necessarily the result of some entity actually making a decision, as well as undertaking an action to "throw" this mass down to the earth.

It does not seem likely that God would have purposely; whether directly or indirectly; thrown Satan and his angels down to the earth; the earth being created and designed as the place for the very greatest creations of His that we know of. The question then also arises as to why it was to earth that Satan and his angels were thrown down; instead of to a nice cozy place like Pluto; into the middle of a black hole; or into Mercury; this being an environment closer to what he will end up with anyway? Based upon early Genesis, it seems that there may have been nowhere else that he or they could have gone. It does not seem that the stars or any other planets existed at that time. Thus, when he rebelled, he could not stay in heaven; the immaterial realm; and it is possible that there simply was nowhere else he could go.

Was Satan ejected from the immaterial and merely caught in the gravitational field of earth? If so, then his being "thrown down" necessarily would represent a result, and not an action. First he was merely ejected, and then he was subsequently affected by gravitational pull. If this were true; could this then logically imply that Satan and his angels had become subject to some of the laws and limitations of the material world at this juncture? Did they become subject to mass, time, duration and distance?

This may sound nuts, but the alternative being that Satan would not be affected by gravity; thus likely floating around the universe forever. Granted, this may not sound like a bad idea, but that is not what happened.

When the spaceships in the science fiction movies blow up, they usually fall after breaking apart. Of course this falling downward is nonsense, in that there is no up and down; (except to the viewer), and there is no significant amount of gravity present that could cause them to move in any particular direction; at least not enough to be noticed. The movement of the parts of the spaceship would be the result of only the forces imparted to them; forces of which gravity is not of a significant quantity in outer space. The answer to the question of whether or not Satan and his angels acquired any of the properties of mass is unknown, but is something on which it is interesting to speculate.

There is also the issue of Satan's name as Lucifer, because of how he appeared when he fell; which we know is true because Jesus saw it.[10.4] He was not instantaneously "beamed down" to earth; but rather he fell. Thus this process took time, which only exists on the material realm; or rather to be more precise, does not exist in the realm whence he came.

It is likely more accurate to say that Satan was ejected from the immaterial realm, and thus thrust, at least partially, into the material realm; with earth as either the only possible destination; or perhaps merely the closest destination at that time. If so, then this presents a significant problem for him, because the life forms on earth were designed to exist in the material realm; but Satan was not.

This could mean that although Satan once resided in a realm where he had immense powers as an angel; at some point he became subject to at least *some* of the rules or limitations of the material realm. Perhaps this is why Peter tells us that: "Your adversary, the devil, prowls around like a roaring lion, seeking someone to devour." [10.5] There is clearly a consideration of space (prowling around) as well as time (seeking). It is true that part of Peter's statement may be read as a simile, but that would relate to the similarities to a roaring lion, and not necessarily the devil's actions. Or, and more likely; Peter is attempting to describe a phenomenon for which no correct word exists; thus a description using the word "like" to indicate the closest similarity is intended, rather than an actual comparison.

If it is assumed that devour means consumption of whatever is the object of the "seeking," then one might fairly ask why any animal would warn it's prey with roaring; prior to killing it for food? This would seem to substantially decrease the likelihood of success; or at a minimum, cause more effort to be required. If devour just means to destroy; to kill when it is not to be used for food; then likewise why would it make any sense to warn the prey?

But what if Peter really meant that the prowling and roaring constitutes the first effort in his seeking; is in a sense similar to radar? In the use of radar, a signal is first sent or transmitted; and then the returned signal is examined in order to gain information; "stealth" aircraft being specifically designed to minimize this returned signal. In a likewise manner, the enemy "roars;" here actually meaning those "thoughts ideas and suggestions" humans get into their heads; often knowing not from whence they came. He then watches one's reaction in order to determine their specific potential level of "devourability." His goal being to "get our attention" as he did with "the woman," so that he can get a foothold with which to continue the process. Thus, he does not like it when it is the case where little or no signal is returned; meaning that he has been largely or completely ignored.

But one might fairly ask: Is it not true that God and the angels also act in the material realm? This is true in the sense that they engage in actions that have *results on* the material realm, but generally they are not in any way acting *from* the material realm; and even if they were, that would be by choice.

This requires a bit of an explanation. God and the angels clearly undertake actions that have an effect on the material realm; the very realm where time and space exist. But when these actions are initiated, they are usually if not always initiated from the *immaterial* realm; the realm which has no such limitations. God and the angels have the ability to transverse time and space from the immaterial realm; and although while perhaps he once did, at this time Satan likely does not.

Another fair question would be concerning Jesus; Jesus being God on the material realm. This is an entirely different situation because in this case, as God chose to take on a human form; an "earth suit" if you will; a form just like the form he gives us to exist on this realm.

When Gabriel had visited Mary to inform her of what God wanted her to do, he was also asking for her permission.[10.6] Whether or not Gabriel already knew what her answer was going to be at this point was irrelevant; as this still had to be done because God respects free will; a willing vessel being needed. Some amount of time had then lapsed, before he went to Joseph. This visit being later was not because Gabriel (who was most likely the "an angel"[10.7] referenced), could not visit Joseph immediately after Mary, or even simultaneously; but rather, because a process first had to take place with respect to Joseph, and processes take time. Thus, this delay was purposeful; so that Gabriel would be advising Joseph at the most opportune time. Gabriel either knew or had access to information about all of what was to transpire; including Mary's answer; as well as Joseph's understandable jealousy; jealousy here meaning distrust of a spouse or other person, and not meaning envy. Neither Gabriel's delay, nor the necessity of a second visit had anything to do with any lack of knowledge, or any other type of failure on Gabriel's part.

Back in chapter 9, when Satan went to God about Job, he was essentially requesting permission to attack Job. This request was presented in the manner of wanting the protective hedge around Job lowered; but it amounts to the same thing. Satan had believed at that time that his scheme was sufficient to succeed; but nevertheless, it did not. Thus, Satan was forced to go back to God the second time, because his first scheme had failed. Satan had believed that he knew what Job's reaction was to be, but he was wrong; thus, the need for the second visit.

With respect to Mary and Joseph, Gabriel had access to knowledge from the immaterial realm. With respect to Job, Satan did not. Gabriel knew all he needed to know, and Satan had guessed. There are some key points about this:

Satan did not guess as one would choose "heads or tails;" but rather based this guess upon years of careful observation. Perhaps prediction would be a better term, but the key is that he did not know; and what he believed Job's reaction would be was in fact incorrect. Had Satan been able to read Job's mind, he likely would have chosen a different scheme; because it is not likely that Satan enjoyed going back to God pleading for another opportunity; because he had failed in his first attempt. Whatever else one can say about Satan, this proves that he is not *omniscient*; despite any attempts on his part to convince anyone otherwise.

There is also the issue of his two visits with God, with some amount of duration and some events in between. In both discussions with God, Satan indicated that he had been "going to and fro on the earth, and from walking back and forth on it."[10.8] Both of these require time and space, and thus he was subject to these material limitations. It appears that while he is on the material realm; i.e. earth; whether seeking, going, or walking; he has these limitations. And it appears that he is no longer permitted on the immaterial realm; except perhaps by dispensation. Whatever else one can say about Satan, this proves that he is not *omnipresent*; despite any attempts on his part to convince anyone otherwise.

Angels were created to serve man. Thus, angels must always respect the free will of men. This does not mean that they must always do what we want; but rather they cannot do what we do not want. The amount of angelic assistance received, depends upon our will; and whether or not said wants or desires are consistent with the will of God. Angels are incapable of forcing their will upon us; and God *will* not.

Satan used to be an angel; assuming that a fallen angel is not exactly the same as an angel; thus he was designed the very same way. Therefore no matter what else it may appear to be, it is likely that Satan must always respect our will; but it is never required of us to respect his. Whether or not he likes it, this is the way that it is; and there is nothing he can do about this arrangement. This is why he is incessantly seeking our consent.

Thus, in order to achieve his will; Satan must get us to agree with him. In a sense, to confess his will. Again confess meaning to agree with what was already said; in this case said by him. For example: It is one's actual will to obtain wealth. There is nothing wrong with this desire, as even Jesus had a treasurer. Of what use would be a treasurer if one has no money? But the enemy wants you to disobey God by taking someone else's wealth, rather than earning it. So he will tell you that the person doesn't need it; doesn't deserve it; won't miss it, etc. If he is successful, then his prey (potential sinner) and Satan are now in agreement. He could not and cannot get one to act against their will; so he merely *changes* their will. Now the person will be acting according to *their* will; but obviously, without receiving any assistance from God or the real angels.

"I am going to live to be over 100 years old"
*"No you're not, you will be lucky to see 50."*

"I do not accept that, I will live to a ripe old age."
*"It doesn't make any difference what you accept, facts are facts."*

"Then what are you doing here?"

or

"I am going to ask her out."
*"She will never go out with you."*

"I think she might, it is worth a try."
*"You will look and feel like a fool."*

"She's *already* not going out with me; and I already look and feel like a fool talking to you."

All of a sudden, the enemy of the hosts, that old serpent, is suddenly looking out for his enemy's welfare; at least that is what he wants you to believe. If this were so, then it would seem like there is very little left for God and the real angels to do. No—he is attempting manipulation by altering expectations.

Why didn't Satan just knock down that hedge around Job, instead of whining about it to God? The short answer is that he couldn't.

"Although you incited Me against him, to destroy him without cause." [10.9] This is God speaking to Satan in Job 2:3. This is commentary by God about Satan's desire to kill Job. God had forbidden Satan to kill Job. The reason this was "unjust" is because the quantity of fear Job practiced (*f=ma*) was insufficient to justify a death sentence for Job. Satan tried to purchase the death of Job; here demanding an *ma* quantity that was in excess of the value of the $f_T$ ; thereby attempting a purchase with what essentially amounted to "insufficient funds." So why didn't Satan just kill Job anyway, or kill him before he even met with God? The same answer; he couldn't; it was not that he *would* not, but that he *could* not.

If Satan is so powerful, like he seems to think; and desperately wants and incessantly tries to get us to believe he is; then why did he have to seek any permission from God in the first place?

For all of the foregoing reasons; whatever else one can say about Satan, this proves that he is not *omnipotent*; despite any attempts on his part to convince anyone otherwise.

There is a movement today that is attempting to portray Lucifer as a "son of light" because of his name. This is patent nonsense. As previously stated, this name was derived because of his appearance when he was cast out of heaven; an appearance likened to how Venus appears before sunrise, or a morning star; which of course Venus is not.

One of the most important things to understand about the enemy is that there is no common ground between he and He. Whatever God wants, he doesn't, and vice versa; so his goal is to defeat God, and thus his objectives are to oppose anything God does. Satan will oppose God even if it seems to make no sense whatsoever to do so. Satan is generally tactical and not strategic; strategic in the sense of *long* term planning. And he is the original loser. By design there was no such thing as losing, until *he* invented it.

It is also important to respect his capabilities, even if one has no real respect for him. Never fear him, never revere him, do not hate him; but always respect his capabilities. Even after being "spoiled" at Calvary; and this spoiling was huge; he remains yet a formidable adversary with the techniques that remain available to him. Satan can never claim victory, but victory can be handed to him; and he knows exactly what he is doing.

It is not wise to play with him, as this is not a game, this is a war. (Remember the definition of Host?) Satan is not out to just make life difficult for you. He is not out to insult you or hurt your feelings. He is out to destroy you. He wants you separated from God and off this earth as soon as possible; and this does not mean space travel. He wants that breath of life within all life forms that have the breath of life extinguished immediately. The level of abject hatred he has for all life is simply incomprehensible. This is a huge war that has been raging for an incalculable number of years.

Isaiah 14: 15-17 tells us:

> *"Nevertheless you will be thrust down to Sheol, To the recesses of the pit.*
> *"Those who see you will gaze at you, They will ponder over you, saying,*
> *'Is this the man who made the earth tremble, Who shook kingdoms, Who made the world like a wilderness And overthrew its cities, Who did not allow his prisoners to go home?'* [10.10]

Because of his spoiling at Calvary, there is a virtual absence of any *direct* physical manifestation that is easily and directly attributable to his activities. And because of this, many today do not believe this enemy exists. Even some who strongly believe in God do not believe the enemy exists. This presents a real problem because that necessarily means that God is a wicked God; else from where else could wickedness originate? Even worse than that, it then must also be the case that God can somehow be an evil God; which of course is impossible if evil is defined as acting against His will. God cannot engage in anything which is both consistent with His will, and at the same time is also against His will. Nevertheless some maintain this opinion, which of course pleases the enemy greatly.

Others attribute false characteristics to the enemy in order to avoid blame. "The devil made me do it," or the equivalent; this being something which of course is also impossible. Were this in fact possible, then we would not have free will; free will being something God went to an awful lot of trouble to be sure we had, and continue to have.

Probably the greatest source of beguilement is the conflation of what God is doing with what the enemy is doing until there is no longer any clarity. Laughing with sinners as opposed to crying with saints is one example. This is completely backwards.

The common misinterpretation of much of the book of Job is another problem. It is important to remember that it was Job who opened the door by practicing fear. It was Satan who came to God, in order to get Him to lower the hedge so that Job could be attacked. Contrary to the common misinterpretation that it was God who offered Job to the devil, this is not accurate. Had Satan not been paying attention, it is likely none of that mess would have ever happened. God did not offer up Job; instead God warned the devil.

What are the major weapons currently available to him today? The answer seems ridiculously simple. With respect to any direct action he has these: thoughts, ideas and suggestions. Barring any special considerations or dispensations from God, this is essentially his entire armamentarium. And when he does get those dispensations, the situation is carefully designed by God; because God is not a fool. Despite any claims by the enemy, this is not cheating. If Satan wants special permission, then he does whatever he is granted God's way, or not at all. It is his choice. This war takes place in or on the battlefield of the mind. Unfortunately, this is much more complex and represents much more power than may be initially evident.

Even at the risk of "herewegoagainisms," it is nevertheless fair to again bring up the **F=MA**'s. Up to this point, the value of "**F**" and even the value of "**f**" has been "positive;" positive in the sense of polarity; **F** here representing some type of force and **f** representing fear.

In actuality, the concept of $F_T$ being equal to the product of $F_A$ x $F_R$ is really another way of stating an **MA**. (mass x acceleration) One might say that of course this is so, after all it *is* an equation. But the point, is that the $F_A$, referring to the component of the $F_T$ which refers to the quantity or the amount contributing to the $F_T$ or total, can be considered really like an **M**, in many ways; but here in the sense that it is always positive in its nature.

Generally, a mass is never considered negative. It may have a perceived negative type impact on a situation, but it itself exists as a "positive quantity" on the material plane. If one receives a large sum of money, or loses a large sum of money, the money is the same; in that it exists in a "positive" sense. It may change hands, making one person happy and one person sad, but it has genuine positive existence, and thus "it" itself cannot be negative. (anti-matter reserved for another time and universe.)

If this is so stipulated, then the only way that $F_T$ can be negative is if $F_R$ is negative. What is the overall or net reason one is doing what he or she is doing; with whatever the amount of $F_A$ is being utilized? If the reason is negative, such as because of wickedness, then the polarity of the actual value of the product or $F_T$, is necessarily going to be negative.

For example: A waitress knowingly and on a regular basis leaves a portion of her tips in a jar, where her alcoholic significant other can find them; and he then goes out upon rising, and buys two 1.75 liters of cheap vodka while she is at work; and this is happening every day. She does this because she can then be sure exactly where he is and what he is doing (or not doing) at all times. In reality, what she really wants is a pet in a cage, and not a spouse. She knows he is an alcoholic, and yet she purposely enables this. There is no attempt here to single out waitresses or vodka drinkers, but this is actually from a true story.

The correct course of action being to make sure that does not happen, rather than contributing to the problem for selfish and sordid reasons. Treatment and not enabling should be the appropriate response. Thus, if the reasons or $F_R$ for the action undertaken is negative in nature, rendering the $F_T$ negative, then the resultant (equal but opposite in direction) compensation can be also expected to be negative. Remembering here that it is the *product* of the amount and the reasons which determine the quantity of this "equal and opposite" compensation, and also that opposite means back *to* you.

Had she genuinely not known of this disease, but rather left the money out for what she truly believed was good cause, then although the direct result may have been identical, the $F_R$ would have been positive, and the resultant compensation to her would necessarily be positive as well.

Whether $F_R$ is positive or negative is strictly a subjective matter. Phrased differently, the *actuality* of the positivity or negativity of this quantity is based upon; or in fact determined by one's *reality*; an seemingly unusual phenomenon. This reality consisting of the perception of the circumstances and the actual reasons for which one is acting, or utilizing the $F_A$. Based upon what one actually knows or believes, or should reasonably know or believe; whatever is or are the actual reasons or impetus for the action; will determine the value and polarity of the quantity.

This statement does not in any way imply however that the active party is capable of actually calculating the value of $F_R$ and thus the subsequent value of $F_T$. The *determination of polarity*, and the *calculation* of these values are entirely different matters. Why one does what one does, is a major factor in determining the polarity and thus the total value, but said quantities are something which only God can accurately calculate.

Comparing the actions of the waitress with the actions of Job, two entirely different situations become evident. What the waitress was doing was wicked. The polarity of $F_R$ was clearly negative. She wanted a situation that not only was she not deserving of, (nor he) but one that was also contrary to God's law. She actually did simultaneously reach out for people to help with the problem; at the same time she was knowingly and willfully facilitating the same. She liked the cage, but did not like the other concomitant results of the alcoholism.

With respect to Job, the polarity of $f_R$, or the reason (fear) for the burnt offerings, this is not so easily determined. There was nothing wrong with what Job wanted. Job just wanted his children to be safe, and undertook measures to try and insure that his children would remain immune from the ramifications from any potential sinful actions.

It is unclear if presumptive intercessory offerings are in any way as effective as presumptive intercessory prayer, or even have any substantial efficacy at all. In Job 42:8 God had said to Job's friends: "Now therefore, take for yourselves seven bulls and seven rams, and go to My servant Job, and offer up a burnt offering for yourselves, and My servant Job will pray for you." Here God had told Job's *friends* to offer up burnt offerings and that it was

*Job* who would do the intercessory praying. Nevertheless, prior to all of the calamity, presumptive intercessory offerings were precisely what Job had done.

Thus, although arising from different areas, it is reasonable to state that when **F$_R$** has a negative polarity because the reasons for the actions are wicked or evil; or in the case of **f$_R$** the reason being fear or lack of faith; the results can be quite similar.

This is important, because these are the main areas in which the enemy works.

Ephesians 6:12 tells us:

> *"For our struggle is not against flesh and blood, but against the rulers, against the powers, against the world forces of this darkness, against the spiritual forces of wickedness in the heavenly places."*[10.11]

This passage first tells us what our struggles are not. They are not against flesh and blood. It then goes on to tell us what our struggles actually are against:

1. Rulers. The Greek word is "2888 kosmokrator, from 2889 and 2902; A *world - ruler*, and epithet of Satan: - ruler."[10.12]
2. Powers.
3. World forces of this darkness.
4. Spiritual forces of wickedness.

From a Scriptural perspective, although some may argue that it was not always this way, today *all* of these battles take place in the mind. The use of the term "flesh and blood" likely means material battles or struggles waged against warm bodies; rather than a completely literal interpretation. Meaning, that had it said *with* flesh and blood, this does not mean a food fight. There remains an important distinction to be made.

If **A** hates **B**, it would be unreasonable for **A** to hate **B**, unless **B** is believed to have done something for which **A** could hate them. (Hatred itself is wrong, but that is another matter.) **B** is both material and immaterial in nature. Not liking the physical appearance of someone such as **B** is one thing, but hatred cannot not *reasonably* exist based upon this alone. Any hatred of **B** by **A** would generally have to be based upon something **B** is genuinely believed to have done or not done. Thus it would necessarily be the direct or indirect result of some portion of the immaterial part of **B** which resulted in the hatred of **B** by **A**.

This immaterial portion of **B** for which **B** is hated by **A**, is or was the resultant or a combination of that immaterial portion of **B** which was, shall we say, "breathed into his nostrils" by God; as well as the influences upon, or additions to this immaterial portion by the enemy. Unless God is in the habit of willfully "breathing" natures into people for which hatred is an understandable or appropriate emotion; then it is not that portion (the God part) of the immaterial side that is providing the alleged reason or justification for the hatred. By Hobson's choice it then can only be the influence by the enemy on the Godly immaterial portion, or additional immaterial portions provided by the enemy, which are the sources for this hatred.

So it was not really the "great big Hawaiian punch" in the nose that was the main problem, but rather, it was the decision that was made to throw the punch; and the punch merely followed. Was that decision which was made by some person to throw the punch at you something of God? If it was, then you probably deserved it and would not hate them for it.

Thus, it is not actually "flesh and blood" which represents the adversary, opponent, or enemy in this struggle or battle, but rather something that is immaterial in nature. There really should be a comma in Ephesians 6: 12 between the "wickedness" and "in." This meaning that it is the struggle or battle that takes place in "heavenly places," rather than the "forces of wickedness" being in "heavenly places."

As stated earlier, Proverbs 29:27 tells us that "An unjust man is abominable to the righteous, And he who is upright in the way is abominable to the wicked."[10.13]

In the first part, the unjust man causes repulsiveness to the righteous, because the nature of unjust man creates dissonance with the nature or immaterial side of the righteous man.

But when wickedness is the ruling characteristic, then an upright nature creates dissonance with the nature or immaterial portion of even the wicked man himself. You can often tell much about a person by what they object to, and also by what they find humorous.

As previously stated, today it is thoughts, ideas, and suggestions that are the means by which the enemy wages these struggles or battles, most of which occur in the mind; and he is amazingly adept at using these to his advantage. His ultimate goal being to get us "hosts" to take some sort of action on his ramblings, in order to cause manifestation of his will in the material realm.

His objectives are to cause either physical action or speaking; to convince us to do something or sow something. The aforementioned punch in the nose being an example of the resultant physical action from the loss of a mental or "heavenly places" battle.

His skills and abilities in "importuning" us into the bringing of his desires into the material realm by sowing something by speaking something can often be his most devious. This is the devil's counterfeit version of *"bara,"* (see Chapter 1) via a surrogate. The use of the term "you" or "I" in the following, refers to someone who is well known, perhaps even uniquely and very intimately well known.

Some common examples are:

1. I'm never gonna be rich.
2. I know I'm getting sick.
3. Everything stinks and then you die.
4. I'm getting senile.
5. I can't do it.

Probably the best one; usually proffered as a response to someone taking the time and effort to help another; is the "I know."

This one is also a hybrid. Here the enemy gets you to mix in a little pride with some degree of gratitude and there you have it.

When someone receives a bit of wisdom, what are considered the generally acceptable responses? Perhaps "thank you," or "that makes sense," or even an absolute truth such as "Thanks, I didn't know that." But the enemy gives just a little push, a small thought or idea, which sticks; because you really do not like having been ignorant of the wisdom with which you were just provided; and also because saying "I know" *feels* good.

Intellectually you needed the wisdom, which you now have, but you resent the fact that someone else had it and not you. You want to be polite and say something, so you combine that desire with the pride and it just kind of pops out— largely because of emotions and not intellect.

Then here come the justifications: "Well, it is true because when I said I knew it, I did know it because you had just told me." But of course that is not what you actually meant. (*She is my sister?*) Or, "I meant I agree." Then why did you not say "I agree?" The fact is that you just sowed a lie, as well as subsequent lies, and many more will likely to continue to be sown, until you stop talking.

You also just advised the "wisdomer," that you, the "wisdomee," did not really need the wisdom anyway(s). After a while, by your own choosing you get the reputation of a "know it all" and people will stop trying to help you; and the devil prefers the "hosts" as ignorant as possible. This is particularly true with spiritual matters; especially when the wisdom concerns defeating him. He generally does not really care how much you go to church, as long as going to church does not include going to school.

Now not did you only just lie, but you stole the wisdom; because you did not compensate the source of the wisdom in any appropriate manner. And worse, you imparted negativity, a kind of penalty, to the source of the wisdom; who just took time and effort to try and help you. You also made it less likely that the source of the wisdom will impart wisdom; not just to you; but to anyone else in the future. You just sowed at least three sins into the material plane. Each with its own negative $F_T$ which will "roll around" until they (the $MA$s) ultimately return to you. All of this was done simply because of pride; and because you did not like the truth; and because it temporarily *felt* good.

This is like the farmer coming into the house complaining that his garden is full of peppers.

His wife asks: "Why that is a problem?"
Farmer says: "I wanted tomatoes."
Wife: "What did you plant?"
Farmer: "Peppers."
Wife: "Why did you plant peppers when you wanted tomatoes?" (best case scenario→)
Farmer: "……"
Wife: "Why in the world did you think you were ever going to reap tomatoes, when you sowed peppers?" Farmer: "……"

Because it "feels good," garbage is sown; and then when we end up with a life surrounded with garbage; it is somehow a mystery as to where it all came from. Then the devil reminds you what God just did to you, and how you cannot trust Him.

In all fairness, "I know" is not always used in this way: even when proffered as a response. Sometimes, but rarely, it is used as an admission of the accuracy of a rebuke. (head down: "I knooowwwe, I'll try to do better." ) And sometimes it is offered as a rebuke for someone telling you something absurdly obvious. The "I know" may actually have more possible meanings than the "fuggetaboudit."

As a general rule, the faster one responds, the more likely the devil is involved in the answer. And also: the *degree* of his involvement is at least directly proportional to the rapidity with which it is said. The faster it comes out, the greater the percentage which is likely to be from him, and this may not even be linear; but it does create a mess.

And what about the Nephilim? This gives some insight into the capabilities of the enemy prior to his being "spoiled" at Calvary.

Genesis 6:4 tells us:

> *"The Nephilim were on the earth in those days, and also afterward, when the sons of God came in to the daughters of men, and they bore children to them. Those were the mighty men who were of old, men of renown."*[10.14]

This is a very interesting, but easily misread passage. Nephilim is the word: "5303 nephiyl, or nephil, from 5307; prop., a *feller*, i.e. a *bully* or *tyrant*: - giant. 5307 naphal, a prim. root; to *fall*, in a great variety of applications (intrans. or causat., lit. or fig.)..."[10.15]

The way this verse is normally interpreted, demons (fallen angels) had sexual relations with human women, and giants were the offspring of this union. These giants thus representing beings which were half human and half demon. This is the passage that is generally used to substantiate this theory.

The problem with this theory; is that this passage in no way reasonably substantiates any such thing. It states that the Nephilim were on the earth already and afterwards, when the sons of God had sexual relations with daughters of men. It does not state when *they* (the Nephilum) had relations, but rather when the *Sons of God* had relations; thus making a distinction between the two. The *"them"* then referring to the Sons of God, to whom the children were born; and not the Nephilim.

This demon theory also must presuppose that demons are to be considered "Sons of God." An argument would then logically follow that Messiah was the only begotten demon; which of course makes no sense. It also then follows that these Nephilim, half human half-demon beings are the ones who were of old and renown.

An alternate read would be that the mention of the Nephilim is merely to state the relative time when the events of the rest of the verse occurred. Thus in this reading, the Nephilim were on the earth, but are otherwise unrelated to the remainder of the passage. It would then actually be those from the other side (the Hebrews) who were these Sons of God; who then had sexual relations with the gentile daughters, or daughters of the (gentile) men, and bore children to them; the children then being half gentile and half Hebrew.

Based on this reading, the "those" refers to the men of old and renown, which then must either be the fathers, (Sons of God) of these same children, the children themselves, or the gentile "men" whose daughters it was who had relations with the Hebrew men.

But again, what about these Nephilim?

*The Interlinear Bible* version of Genesis 6:4 provides as translations: "Nephilim were in the earth" as well as "Nephilim were on the earth." Thus one translation is: "The giants were *in* the earth in those days, and even afterwards, when the sons of God...."[10.16] The use of the phrase "in the earth" much more closely describes a demonic entity, than "on the earth."

Exodus 20:4 tells us:

> "*You shall not make for yourself an idol, or any likeness of what is in heaven above or on the earth beneath or in the water under the earth.*"[10.17]

The actual word for "under" is "8478 tachath, from the same as 8430; the *bottom* (as *depressed*); only adv. *below* (often with prep. pref. *underneath*), in *lieu of*, etc.: - as, beneath..."[10.18] So it is certain that "under" (or bottom or below) is a fair translation; and this time water means water, or at least a liquid.

One might reasonably ask: "Precisely what is it that is or was in the water or liquid under the earth that one is not permitted to make a likeness of?" The answer of course presupposes that one knows what the water or liquid under the earth referred to actually is, or was, to begin with. This clearly does not refer to seas, lakes or other bodies of water that are on the surface of the earth, as they have earth beneath them and not above them. Thus these bodies of water or liquid are actually above the "earth," and not beneath.

There do exist, of course, bodies of water beneath the earth. However, it can also be stated that far under solid ground, other types of liquids exist; and exist in much greater quantity. Actually, these liquids are such that they have a freezing point above the surface temperature of the earth. So, depending on ones perspective, it could be said that the earth is actually really a liquid, with a thick frozen crust "floating" on this liquid; with this crust or land being the surface upon which we live. The nature and temperature of these liquids can be seen with a volcanic eruption. The science of plate tectonics is based upon this.

If God was referring to this liquid in Exodus 20:4, it clearly bears close resemblance to the common perception of hell.

Giardiasis is a parasitic infection often caused by drinking water that is contaminated with the intestinal parasite giardia lamblia. If one were to want to make an idol of G. Lamblia, how would one go about that? Since it cannot be seen with the naked eye, one would have to find some way to determine what it looked like, in order to make; say; a paper mache model. This image would have to be experienced and studied closely in order to make a physical likeness of it; requiring either a microscope, or the records of someone who had viewed it under a microscope.

If God was referring to the liquid under the earth as what we consider hell or the "underworld" to be, the question then arises as to how anyone knew what was in this "water" or liquid under the earth; much less what it looked like. And merely knowing what was in there, as in the case of G. Lamblia, would be of no help in making an idol or likeness unless its appearance was also known.

Yet God made a strict prohibition of making any idols or likeness of these that were under the water or liquid of the earth. It also seems likely that the recipients of this commandment would know what God was referring to, rather than thinking He was crazy. Ergo, many must have seen them.

A gargoyle is a rather hideous sight to most people, and doesn't resemble anything that is generally known to have existed on earth. It is likely more than merely coincidence that the word gargoyle, is named such from the same root as the word gargle, because water comes out of their mouths. "Old French gargole, gargouille throat, water spout; see GARGLE."[10.19]

Whether these Nephilim or gargoyles were physical concoctions of the enemy or his assistants via transformation of existing matter via spirit manipulations, or the enemy or his "assistants," manifesting physically themselves; it is likely that their origin, at least from the standpoint of their manifestation on the earth, was from these very waters or liquids under the earth.

It is important to understand the capabilities that the enemy possessed at that time. Whether it was these giants; or whatever other creatures the Hebrews were commanded to not make idols of; or the serpent that was transformed from a stick in Aaron's presence, the enemy at that time likely had these substantial capabilities of at least altering physical manifestation.

Goliath was likely a named Nephilim or giant.

In 1 Samuel 17:4 we are told:

> *"Then a champion came out from the armies of the Philistines named Goliath, from Gath, whose height was six cubits and a span"*[10.20]

A cubit is generally considered as eighteen inches, so Goliath was over nine feet tall. Even a cursory search on the internet will find known but inexplicable remains of giants such as these buried in graves as far away as Ohio. In some mass graves, for reasons unknown, they are buried all facing the same way.

But Satan was "spoiled" at Calvary; and thus most of his powers were lost at that time. Because of this, rarely if ever are theses types of powers ever witnessed today. As a result, many do not believe that Satan ever had these powers; and thus they also believe that any Scriptural evidence to the contrary of this current belief must necessarily be bunk. The reason for this is because the circumstances surrounding Calvary are often not well understood. As previously mentioned, this belief then often is extended to include denial that Satan currently exists, or ever existed.

The same can be said of so called "black magic" and other similar practices. Because we have lived for about 2000 years without the enemy having this kind of power; and thus because black magic no longer can function; it is often assumed, erroneously; that black magic never did function, and thus never existed.

It is amazing to witness how much influence the enemy has today, given what little is left for him to work with. The messes he can and does precipitate with only thoughts, ideas, and suggestions seem impossible. The good news is that if we just tell him to shut up, ignore him, and test anything against the word and the will of God, we can defeat his efforts.

Just something else for thought:

The following takes place shortly after Jesus calms the storm, while on His way to Gerasenes. When these verses are broken up into sections, as many Bibles do, it is easy to lose the continuity of the story. It is reasonable to assume that the famous storm He and the disciples encountered on the way, was designed to prevent, or at least delay, His arrival to this particular place.

Most know the story of this demon possessed crazy person who even shackles could not bind. The verse numbers are again removed for clearer understanding.

Luke 8:26-33 tells us:

> "Then they sailed to the country of the Gerasenes, which is opposite Galilee.
> And when He came out onto the land, He was met by a man from the city who was possessed with demons; and who had not put on any clothing for a long time, and was not living in a house, but in the tombs.
> Seeing Jesus, he cried out and fell before Him, and said in a loud voice, "What business do we have with each other, Jesus, Son of the Most High God? I beg You, do not torment me."
> For He had commanded the unclean spirit to come out of the man. For it had seized him many times; and he was bound with chains and shackles and kept under guard, and yet he would break his bonds and be driven by the demon into the desert.
> And Jesus asked him, "What is your name?" And he

> *said, "Legion"; for many demons had entered him. They were imploring Him not to command them to go away into the abyss.*
> *Now there was a herd of many swine feeding there on the mountain; and the demons implored Him to permit them to enter the swine.*
> *And He gave them permission.*
> *And the demons came out of the man and entered the swine; and the herd rushed down the steep bank into the lake and was drowned."*[10.21]

This multiple demon possessed man did two very interesting and unusual things: First he recognized Jesus for who He was, and fell before Him. Second, he or they asked Jesus for mercy. And Jesus did grant the demons' request, permitting precisely what the demons had asked him to.

The demons greatly preferred entering the swine to being sent to the abyss. Did they know that the swine were to commit suicide? It is not only likely that they knew this, but also that they in fact caused it. Had the demons been sent to the abyss, it is likely that either their existence or at least their ability to act would have ceased. By entering the swine, their destiny changed.

It is interesting that they entered an "unclean" animal. Had they asked Jesus to permit them to enter a "clean" animal, the result may have been quite different. It is also interesting that the swine died by drowning.

Why is this interesting?

Because in Luke 11:24 Jesus tells us:

> *"When the unclean spirit goes out of a man, it passes through <u>waterless</u> places seeking rest, and not finding any, it says, 'I will return to my house from which I came.'"*[10.22] *(Emphasis supplied)*

In this particular case, they sought not a waterless place, but ran right down the hill into the water and were drowned.

It is a fair question to ask why Jesus would permit the possibility that these demons would be capable of returning to the man, instead of sending the demons to the abyss. Clearly *they* thought He was about to send them to the abyss.

This is only a theory; but the demons recognized who Jesus was and fell before him. They confessed with their mouth who He was. (He had not yet rose from the dead, so the believing in their heart that He was resurrected part was not an option. Thomas also was in a sort of similar position for a short time.) They called on Him for mercy. They asked him for His permission, arguably recognizing Him as Lord. These are the very same things one does in order to be saved.

Is this story a recollection of saved demons?

You make the call.

MEEKRAKER *Beginnings…*

# Chapter 11

## Pericalvaric Apocrypha

The period of time beginning with Gethsemane through the crucifixion is a relatively short one. Thousands of years of both planning and acting by God, largely culminating in a series of events; many of which occurred in this relatively short time frame. This is *not* in any way meant to diminish the importance of any events that occurred outside of this time. But rather, in a time relative sense; to note that the understanding of many of these events; as well as the significance of these events; all of which happened in this short duration of time; requires a bit of careful reading.

There is an interesting initial thing to consider: What do the "Star of David," the Masonic "Square and Compasses," and the cross have in common? The Masonic "Square and Compasses" are in reality a hidden or veiled version of the "Star of David;"

thus there are really only two symbols; the "Star" and the Cross. This "Star" is really not a star at all. It is a symbol of two interlaced triangles. Despite the fact that it is usually shown as two superimposed triangles; they are not supposed to be superimposed, but are in fact supposed to be interlaced. A triangle with the base down, is generally considered to be a symbol of the material realm; and when it is the point or apex that is pointed downward, this generally symbolizes the immaterial realm. Thus when they are interlaced, this symbolizes complete harmony between the material and the immaterial. This is a very ancient symbol.

The cross is very similar. The vertical part of the cross symbolizes the immaterial; and the horizontal portion symbolizes the material realm. Thus the intersection represents the intersection of these two realms, with Jesus right in the middle.

"Jesus took the punishment for our sins, He died for our sins because he loves us."

The first part of this statement is not exactly true. There are two main results of sin; one occurring in the natural or the material plane, the other occurring in the immaterial plane. The material results, although having immaterial (F and MA) components, we call the law of compensation or karma. We reap what we sow. Had Jesus actually taken this (our) material punishment, He then necessarily would have also repealed the law of compensation or karma; if and when said compensation was the result of sinful behavior; at least from Calvary going forward. In addition, if this had actually happened, then God's mercy would no longer be necessary for sinful behavior. Mercy meaning intervention by God so that we *do not* get what we *do* deserve; and grace meaning intervention by God *to* give us what we *do not* deserve. This of course is not so; we still require mercy.

Secondly, the law of compensation or karma is not punitive in nature by design. It is in a sense neutral. When we choose to sin, we choose the results of sin. Likewise, when we choose to engage in upright behavior, we choose the results of upright behavior. Where the real trouble occurs, is when we think that we can mix and match these to our own liking. We think we can sin; and yet somehow not only *not* receive the karmic results of sin; but instead, somehow receive the results of upright behavior; and often it may actually appear that way to us at first. This of course being the bait; bait which is often very effective when we choose to do it our way; (usually with significant help from the enemy) and not God's way. It is interesting that no one ever seems to expect the reverse; that is to engage in upright behavior, and yet somehow receive the wages of sin; as though that situation, and that situation alone would somehow uniquely be unfair.

Jesus did not die for our sins. In a sense, He died because of our sins. This is more than just a semantic exercise. Because of our sin, we were disqualified from being connected to God; and thus the physical death (disconnection) of Jesus was necessary. Not in order to make the material results of sin irrelevant, but to restore the possibility of a spiritual reconnection. If Jesus brought us eternal life, then why do people still die? Because; it is this potential eternal soul to God connection that He brought; and not an eternal physical, or soul to body connection. Thus, at least for now, we still must die physically; but there is no longer any need to remain spiritually dead by maintaining spiritual disconnection.

"Jesus loves us." Very few people can have any idea what this actually means, because most people are not personally familiar with this *agape* or unconditional love; except perhaps in rare short duration episodes. Agape *is* complete unconditional love; a love that is never diminished no matter what the object of this love may do to you. Some may experience this in times of crisis; but it soon diminishes when the crisis passes. This love or agape that Jesus has for each and every human being is 100% and runs 24/7. The word agape also can mean opening in a wide manner, as in one's mouth when one is in total amazement.

Luke 22:39-46 tells us:

> *"And He came out and proceeded as was His custom*
> *to the Mount of Olives;*
> *and the disciples also followed Him.*

> *When He arrived at the place, He said to them, "Pray that you may not enter into temptation."*
> *And He withdrew from them about a stone's throw, and He knelt down and began to pray, saying, "Father, if You are willing, remove this cup from Me; yet not My will, but Yours be done."*
> *Now an angel from heaven appeared to Him, strengthening Him. And being in agony He was praying very fervently; and His sweat became like drops of blood, falling down upon the ground.*
> *When He rose from prayer, He came to the disciples and found them sleeping from sorrow, and said to them, "Why are you sleeping? Get up and pray that you may not enter into temptation."*[11.1]

This was a pivotal moment. The first thing and the last thing Jesus said to his disciples in these passages referred to temptation. Clearly temptation was on His mind. This was the last real chance the devil may have had to change the course of events. What was about to happen was not and would not ever be a matter of brute force. The events that transpired after this encounter would be a matter of His choosing; and would not in any way be any type of victory by the devil. At some point, the enemy put together what was actually happening, and it was likely around this time when he did so.

When Mel Gibson's *"The Passion of the Christ"* was released, he was of course criticized by many of the secular movie reviewers. Some of this criticism was because he had placed Satan in Gethsemane. There were claims that this inclusion of Satan in Gethsemane was Scripturally inaccurate, because it does not actually state such. Clearly this was a time of temptation for Jesus; as Satan realized what was about to transpire, and was not pleased with the circumstances. And if not from Satan, then whence came this temptation?

It was just a very short time before this, at the supper, when the devil had actually entered Judas.

John 13:25-27 tells us:

> *"He, (John) leaning back thus on Jesus' bosom, said to Him, "Lord, who is it?"*
> *Jesus then answered, "That is the one for whom I shall dip the morsel and give it to him."*
> *So when He had dipped the morsel, He took and gave it to Judas, the son of Simon Iscariot.*
> *After the morsel, Satan then entered into him.*
> *Therefore Jesus said to him, "What you do, do quickly."*[11.2]

At that juncture, Satan was going full speed ahead. His plan of course, was to have Judas betray Jesus to the authorities. There is no evidence that Satan was having any second thoughts at this time; else why would he have entered Judas at that time? And we know that Jesus knew this, because of the inclusion of the word "therefore."

But here in Gethsemane, Jesus is asking the Father (arguably three times) if He would (not could) change the course of events to follow; but if not, then Jesus would be willing go through with it. And just at that very time, an angel appeared from heaven; it states to "strengthen him." It is difficult to imagine what must have actually happened when this angel appeared. The story seems a bit underreported. It does not state that this angel and Satan had a few beers and talked about old times, as this could probably not be farther from the truth.

The Scriptures do not state who the angel was, but since it was Gabriel that God had sent to Mary; when any angel might have arguably worked just as well; it is likely that this particular angel, if not Gabe himself, clearly would have been a member of the "A Team." It does not state what Satan did at that time, but it does not seem likely that he was around very long after that. Had he in fact remained, there would likely have been the recounting of a rather spectacular battle included in the story. Likely, he fled; hoping to return at a more "opportune time."

Here in Gethsemane, the only begotten Son of God is now being attacked by Satan in order to try and stop Him from going through with this. It was just a short time ago that Satan entered Judas in furtherance of his plan; likely quite pleased with himself. Now he is suddenly trying his best to get Jesus to *not* go through with it.

One reasonable explanation being that here Satan was attempting (a tempting?) to get Jesus to sin. Had Jesus refused to go through with it, then He arguably would no longer be "without sin;" and thus all else would have become irrelevant. Satan likely believing (erroneously) that any such refusal would not change the course of events, but drastically altered the significance of said events. This meaning that Satan believed that Jesus would still be killed, but without providing redemption, salvation, or anything else.

Another explanation would be that this represented what probably would best be termed as an *"evilation;"* (authors' terminology) meaning a combination of the words evil and revelation; but revelation from deductive reasoning and not divine guidance. Satan is not so much concerned with always being wicked; but he is very concerned; some would say obsessed, with always being evil; evil again being defined as anything that is contrary to God's will. If God were wicked, which of course He is not; then Satan would probably be very nice; because then wickedness would be God's will.

No Scriptural evidence can be easily found with respect to the nature of this "evilation." At some point between entering Judas, and Jesus' decision to go to Gethsemane, Satan must have realized that all of his evil was playing right into God's hand. He likely did not know this at the time of the "Last Supper" or perhaps termed the "Last Seder," else he likely would have done things differently.

Satan may have sensed an interesting relationship between what was transpiring at this time, and something that had transpired in the past. The reason for the common confusion about the day of the crucifixion; and thus the subsequent "three days and three nights" discrepancy; is related to the fact that this Sabbath was to be The Passover, and not the usual Saturday Sabbath.

Up until this time, Passover related to the blood of a lamb being placed over the door posts and lintel in order to have the "angel" of death pass over, and save the first born children from physical death. This lamb had to live among the family for a week; and the lamb had to be killed at twilight, and had to be eaten.

This particular Passover it was the Lamb of God who was to give his blood, (more about this later) to save all those who believe from spiritual death, or spiritual disconnection from God. Jesus had lived among the people, and thus was killed sometime around twilight; this being the time in that culture when the new day began.

The word "save" can also mean except, or the making of an exception. It is easy to confuse the words "savior" and "salvation." Savior relates to the exception being made, salvation refers here to the salvaging or restoration of a previous relationship. Acceptance of this exception results in salvation; and both of these have specific meanings that are different than redemption.

It was likely because of this relationship that Jesus addressed the issues of His body and blood; as well as the remembrance; this being the new Passover to be remembered in lieu of the old.

Shortly after these events, they came to arrest Him, and John 18:4-6 tells us:

> *"So Jesus, knowing all the things that were coming upon Him, went forth and said to them,*
> *"Whom do you seek?"*
> *They answered Him, "Jesus the Nazarene."*
> *He said to them, "I am He." And Judas also, who was betraying Him, was standing with them.*
> *So when He said to them, "I am He," they drew back and fell to the ground."*[11.3]

This is a very important event. A crowd comes to arrest Jesus with torches, lanterns and swords, and Jesus merely speaks "I am He" and they all fall to the ground. They did not just fall, but drew back first, likely because of the magnitude of the force. There is no evidence to suggest any limits with respect to how many times this would have worked. When they arose, if Jesus had again said the same thing it seems likely that they would have all fallen to the ground again. This could have continued until each and every member of the crowd either starved to death, or died of old age. The importance being that Jesus could not have been arrested against His will, but He in fact chose to go with those who were sent to arrest Him.

It is always a spectacular scene in a movie when the bad guy gets shot by the good guy, and the force of the 44 magnum handgun projectile is so great, that the force of impact alone knocks the bad guy to the ground. The problem with this is that this is generally impossible in real life. The reason for this is again the law of "equal and opposite reactions." If the bad guy gets knocked to the ground; then since an equal but opposite force is imparted to the shooter, the good guy would also necessarily have to be knocked to the ground, unless there was a tremendous disparity in their masses, or a means of deflecting the force and preventing it from being imparted to the shooter. This is why large caliber weapons are often bolted down. In a way, it is something like trying to move a refrigerator in stocking feet. The person slides backwards and the refrigerator does not move.

But here, simply by saying "I am He," an entire crowd draws back and falls to the ground. There is no evidence that Jesus in any way moved. This by definition was a miracle, as it defied natural law. Likely this force came from the Father, and through Jesus.

Jesus knew "all the *things* (plural) that were coming upon him."

There are two relevant concepts which merit some attention: The first is that of substitution. We saw this earlier in the Old Testament with the use of the scapegoat. The idea of placing sin on the goat as a substitute for the actual sinner, represents a shadow of the mechanism that was to come; with Jesus as the vehicle for salvation.[11.4]

The other is very much like the Homeopathic "Law of Similars." In Homeopathy "Like cures like." A substance which is known to produce certain symptoms in a healthy individual, is used to cure an individual with those same symptoms. Although in actual practice this is not quite as simple as it sounds, because actual diagnosis is quite complex and appropriate methods of dilution and succussion are also employed.

This Homeopathic law is immaterial in nature. The lower the concentration by dilution and succession; the more potent the remedy. At some point in the dilution process the likelihood of even one molecule of the original substance being present approaches zero; thus, an inverse relationship existing between concentration and potency. It is the vibrational essence, and not the chemical characteristics that provide the efficacy.

There are actually at least three separate processes involved with events surrounding Calvary. There is the general process of saving, or making an exception of those who believe; as well as salvation, and also redemption. If a store clerk is asked for assistance in salvaging a coupon, they would likely offer adhesive tape. If asked for assistance in redeeming a coupon, they would likely be concerned with some type of a discount; or exchanging the coupon for some benefit to the consumer. Although an argument could be made that salvation is a type of redemption, they are not the same.

The salvation aspects of the events of Calvary are generally understood in terms of results, even if they are not completely understood in terms of the actual process. Basically, God did something so that He could stand to be connected to us.

The *redemptive* events, although similar in this regard, generally are another matter.

Firstly, there is the redemption of or from sickness or disease. The last line of Isaiah 53:5 tells us: "And by His scourging we are healed."[11.5] *The Interlinear Bible* version is: "and with His wounds we ourselves are healed."[11.6]

The actual word used for wounds is: "2250 chabbuwrah, or chabburah, or chaburah, from 2266; prop. *bound* (with stripes), i.e. a *weal* (or black - and - blue mark itself): - blueness, bruise, hurt, stripe, wound."[11.7]

The following word (2266) is the same root relating to the actual word for "waters," appearing back in early Genesis. "2266 chabar, a prim. root; to *join* (lit. or fig.); spec. (by means of spells) to fascinate: - charm (-er), be compact, couple (together), have fellowship with, heap up, join (self, together), league."[11.8]

It is interesting to note the relationship between these two words: *chabbuwrah* and *chabar*; one meaning injuries of various sorts; the other relating to joining, fellowship, fascination etc. As in Genesis, fascination necessarily implies the existence of some type of entity capable of successfully engaging in fascinating or charming. The idea of fellowship also requires another entity with which to have fellowship, and in this context does likely not mean God; else what was God doing in early Genesis while he was hovering over the surface of this seam. Hence this further supports the fact of the relationship between the existence of maladies and the involvement of the enemy.

The actual word used for healed is: "7495 rapha, or raphah, a prim. root; prop. to *mend* (by stitching), i.e. (fig.) to *cure*: - cure, (cause to) heal, physician, repair, x thoroughly, make whole."[11.9]

Proverbs 20:30 tells us:

> *"Stripes that wound scour away evil, And strokes reach the innermost parts."*[11.10]

The Interlinear Bible's "English" version of Proverbs 20:30 is "The stripes of a wound cleanse away evil; and strokes the inward parts of the heart.[11.11]

The "stripes" used in Proverbs 20:30, is the same word as "wounds" (2250 chaburah) in the *Interlinear Bible* version of Isaiah 53:5.

The "Hebrew" version in the Interlinear Bible of Proverbs 20:30 is: "Stripes of a wound cleanse away against evil and strokes the chambers of the heart."[11.12] Here again this same word is used for stripes.

The word for cleanse is "8562 tamruwq, or tamruq, or tamriyq, from 4838; prop. a *scouring*, i.e. *soap* or *perfumery* for the bath; fig. a *detergent*: - x cleanse, (thing for) purification (- fying)."[11.13]

In Malachi 3:2 God is speaking about Jesus, and He tells us "For He is like a refiner's fire and like fullers' soap."[11.14] Fullers' is

"3526 kabac, a prim. root; to *trample*; hence to *wash* (prop. by stamping with the feet), whether lit. (including the *fulling* process) or fig.: - fuller, wash (-ing)."[11,15]

There is no need to go into the details of the beatings and the scourging of Jesus prior to the crucifixion, as this is well known. Based upon the above, a fair conclusion being that it is these stripes; the ones inflicted upon Jesus; which are the very stripes referred to in the aforementioned passages. "His scourging" in Isaiah, and "He is like" in Malachi; both being capitalized; it is clear that this refers to deity; this deity being Messiah or The Christ. The one main problem is that Messiah or The Christ, by definition, uniquely had no evil to clean up. Were this not so, He could not have been Messiah.

Back to the "Law of Similars." It is by the infliction of these wounds on Messiah, who up until that time has no recorded history of ever being sick or ill; being made ill by the same; that would provide curing healing, or a remedy for those of us who were, are, or ever would be ill; hence "we are healed." This a kind of intercessory healing by the principles of the "Law of Similars;" perhaps better termed "Law of Intercessory Similars;" but likely only works with Jesus. But this is only a part of it. This is one result, albeit a very important one, of the cleansing away of the evil.

At this juncture Satan lost his right, but not his ability to inflict sickness upon us. There is sickness in the world today not because Satan has any "right" to inflict it upon us, but because he still has the power to inflict the same upon us; however he cannot any longer do so unilaterally.

But by the above definition of the word that is translated as healed, the word *raphah* also means "…repair, x thoroughly, make whole." Thus, there are other areas associated with this event other than physical illness. The "evil" which is "cleansed" also has to do with any other state of man's circumstances which are against God's will for us.

Usually God's will is only considered from a rather Narcissistic viewpoint: "What am I going to get in trouble for doing or not doing?" But God's will for us is not just about laws and rules. The 23rd Psalm is usually reserved for funerals and the like, but a reading of this outside of the funerary context can provide some insight into God's will for us.

In addition to redemption from sickness, there are some other clues in the events surrounding Calvary, which are consistent with this intercessory "Law of Similars" process:

1. They stole from Him, hence we are healed from poverty.
2. When faced with false accusations, he remained silent. Jesus' silence then, gives him the just authority now, to be the mediator that was cried out for in Job. When the devil goes to God regarding to what he is "entitled" to because we sinned; just as he did with Job; for believers, Jesus now can just say; "case dismissed."
3. The crown of thorns restored our kingship; the kingship which was lost as result of sin. It is important to remember that thorns and thistles were not originally enemies of the food supply, back when the mist "used to rise." The presence of these "weeds" in agriculture is the direct result of the transfer of some earthly authority to the enemy because of sin. Certainly we still have thorns; but this is about the kingship lost, and then restored by the King of kings; the use of the crown of thorns being a clue to this area of redemption.

Probably the most spectacular redemptive event was His blood contacting the ground. When God breathes into our nostrils the breath of life and we become living beings, this essence resides in the blood. In the case of Jesus, this essence was the Father Himself. When that blood containing the essence of the Father hit the ground over which Satan had been given (delivered) a large amount of authority because of sin, literally "all hell broke loose."

Generally, the movies depict the sky becoming darkened at the time of Jesus' physical death; arguably as a direct result of his death. This is generally perceived as the wrath of the Father, because of the murder of His Son. Most believe this darkening was the result of a perfectly timed solar eclipse.

According to Matthew, this darkening or "solar eclipse," as many believe, actually occurred from the sixth hour to the ninth hour.[11.16] Other accounts agree with this. The earliest time that can be determined for His physical death would be sometime during the "ninth hour;" the same generally assumed to be 3:00 PM. This of course would then necessarily be at the time of the ending of this darkness, and not the beginning.

With regard to the eclipse theory, this is quite problematic. According to *Wikipedia*: "The longest total solar eclipse during the 8,000-year period from 3000 BC to 5000 AD will occur on July 16, 2186, when totality will last 7 min 29 s"[11.17]

Solar eclipses are a phenomenon of short duration, and even this record eclipse in 2186, is clearly much shorter than the three hour duration of the darkness implied in the Bible. The sun travels 360 degrees in 24 hours. This amounts to 15 degrees per hour. Thus 45 degrees of solar motion would have had to occur in this three hour period. This (45 degrees) of solar motion would represent one fourth of the total motion of the sun (approximately 180 degrees) during daylight hours. This would have then have been an eclipse, the duration of which is far beyond the duration of any known eclipses.

In addition, according to *mreclipse.com* "An eclipse of the Sun (or solar eclipse) can *only* occur at New Moon when the Moon passes between Earth and Sun;"[11.18] and other sources agree with this requirement. The date of Passover is determined by the date of the first full moon after the vernal equinox; and Easter is determined by the first Sunday after the first full moon after the vernal equinox. This makes perfect sense, as it seems reasonable that the Exodus would occur when the moon was full. However, since one cannot simultaneously have a full moon and a new moon, the possibility of this darkness being the result of an eclipse appears to be zero.

Ergo, it can be conclusively proved that whatever caused this darkness, was not and could not have been a solar eclipse. The actual word used here for darkness is "4655 skotos, from the base of 4639; *shadiness*, i.e. *obscurity* (lit. or fig.): - darkness." "4639 skia, appar. A prim. word; "*shade*" or a shadow (lit. or fig. [darkness of *error* or an *adumbration*] ): - shadow."[11.19]

This word skotos seems to be a member of the previously referenced "skoteinos" family of words, meaning tent or covering. The word adumbration contains the same root of umbra; from which we derive the word umbrella. Thus, just as in the darkness referenced in Genesis, again we see this concept of not just darkness as merely the absence of light; but rather the darkness existing because of shading or a cover. The concept of a shade implies there is light, but it is blocked; with the resulting area of less light described as shade. Even today, we refer to the victim of a dishonest scheme as being kept "in the dark," by a "shady" character.

Some secular sources try to place place the birth of Jesus somewhere in the range of approximately 3BC to 3AD. This error may very well be due to referencing when the known solar eclipses occurred, and then counting backwards approximately 33 years.

This 3:00 PM time of His death is uncertain for several reasons. There is the matter of removal of the bodies from the crosses because of the approaching Sabbath. The Jewish time for the beginning of the day is sundown, and not midnight or sunrise. The sixth hour is generally assumed to be six hours after sunrise, or approximately at noon. The ninth assumed to be nine hours later, or at 3:00 PM. If this were all so, then He died at 3:00 PM; and then the body must have been on the cross for approximately three hours from the time of death; this being from 3:00 until sundown; the time when this Sabbath was to begin.

But in that culture, the 24 hour day was broken up into three hour segments. The night segments were called watches and the day segments were called hours. These were named by the times they began; either after sunrise or sunset. The first *watch* began at sunset or about 6:00 PM until about 8:59PM, followed by the second watch. The first *hour* began at sunrise or about 6:00 AM, and lasted until 8:59 AM; but unlike the night watches, was actually followed by the *third* (not second) hour beginning at 9:00 AM.[11.20]

Thus, when the Bible speaks of the "sixth hour" or the "ninth hour," it is not necessarily referring to the time that would appear on a clock; or the hours counted from sunrise; which is presumed to be at 6:00 AM. Rather it is referring to a *period* of time of three hours, which merely *begins* at that time. The "sixth hour" would then be a period of time lasting from approximately 12:00 noon until approximately 2:59 PM; and the "ninth hour" would then be a period of time lasting from approximately 3:00 PM until approximately 5:59 PM.

According to Mark, the crucifixion of Jesus actually began at the "third hour." Mark 15:25 tells us: "It was the third hour when they crucified Him."[11.21] Thus, according to Mark, this would be between 9:00 AM and noon.

According to John, the crucifixion of Jesus actually began at the "sixth hour."

John 19:14-15 tells us:

> "Now it was the day of preparation for the Passover; it was about the sixth hour. And he said to the Jews, "Behold, your King!"
> So they cried out, "Away with Him, away with Him, crucify Him!"
> Pilate said to them, "Shall I crucify your King?"
> The chief priests answered, "We have no king but Caesar."[11.22]

Thus, according to John, this would be between noon and 3:00 PM.

Ergo, this darkness cannot definitively be placed at the beginning of the crucifixion or in the middle of it; but what can be said, is that it did not begin *after* His death.

John was an eyewitness to these events. We know this because Jesus spoke to him from the cross as stated in John

19:26.[11.23]

Here in John 19:31-34 he tells us:

> "Then the Jews, because it was the day of preparation, so that the bodies would not remain on the cross on the Sabbath (for that Sabbath was a high day), asked Pilate that their legs might be broken, and that they might be taken away.
> So the soldiers came, and broke the legs of the first man and of the other who was crucified with Him; but coming to Jesus, when they saw that He was already dead, they did not break His legs.
> But one of the soldiers pierced His side with a spear, and immediately blood and water came out."[11.24]

Here the Jews are asking that the legs of all three be broken so that *they,* not *He* could be taken down and/or away, because of the "high day." One theory for this request is that this would accelerate death. Another would be that this was to insure that none of them would be able to escape once taken down from the cross; and they did not want them hanging on the cross on this "high day." Generally, crucifixion is believed to have been invented by the Romans; however—

Deuteronomy 21:22-23 may be related to both their desire for crucifixion and their request for the leg breaking, because of concerns about them being taken away:

> *"If a man has committed a sin worthy of death and he is put to death, and you hang him on a tree, his corpse shall not hang all night on the tree, but you shall surely bury him on the same day (for he who is hanged is accursed of God), so that you do not defile your land which the* LORD *your God gives you as an inheritance."*[11.25]

When it was seen by the soldiers that Jesus was already dead, His legs were not broken; so either theory would support this. He was "pierced" likely to make certain that He was in fact dead then, as a kind of insurance had He not actually been dead before this. This is also likely the reason why they "looked at whom they pierced" to make certain that He had exsanguinated; the soldiers not realizing that their acts fulfilled two Messianic prophesies. (Actually three if *not* breaking His bones is considered.)

It is not stated if the Jews took away the bodies of the other two; it is possible they did; and they may or may not have still been alive. It seems likely that Golgotha was named such because of the collection of skulls from those who were crucified and whose bodies were merely left there. The more modern explanation of the origin of name being that this hill resembles a skull, hence its name.

Nevertheless, and despite the additional requirements of Deuteronomy 21:22-23, they did not take away the body of Jesus for burial; obviously unconcerned with any aspect of proper treatment of the dead; they being concerned only with the fact that he was dead.

This "high day" Sabbath is also a source of confusion regarding the Resurrection. It is generally assumed that this Sabbath is the normal Saturday Sabbath, which would begin Friday at sundown. Thus it is believed that the death must have occurred on Friday, at or sometime prior to sundown. But this was not the normal Sabbath. Rather, it was the case that "that Sabbath was a high day." It was Passover, not the normal Friday at sundown until Saturday at sundown Sabbath.

In Matthew 12:40, Jesus is speaking and tells us:

> *"for just as JONAH WAS THREE DAYS AND THREE NIGHTS IN THE BELLY OF THE SEA MONSTER, so will the Son of Man be three days and three nights in the heart of the earth."*[11.26]

Thus if you back out from Sunday at dawn three days and nights, Friday around sundown being the time of His death simply will not work. Neither will this work if the resurrection occurred at dawn; no matter what day is used as a starting point.

If the death occurred at or near sundown, which seems a certainty; then the resurrection must have occurred three days and three nights later; at or near sundown.

John 20:1 tells us:

> "Now on the first day of the week Mary Magdalene came early to the tomb, while it was still dark, and saw the stone already taken away from the tomb."[11.27]

The first day of the week being Sunday in that culture, and it was still dark when she discovered that He was gone. Ergo, the Resurrection had already occurred while it was still dark, and not at dawn, early or otherwise.

Thus it had to be on Wednesday, sometime between 3:00PM and sundown that was the actual time of His death. The Resurrection must have occurred three days and three nights later, on Saturday sometime between 3:00 PM and sundown.

Mark 15:42-44 tells us:

> "When evening had already come, because it was the preparation day, that is, the day before the Sabbath, Joseph of Arimathea came, a prominent member of the Council, who himself was waiting for the kingdom of God; and he gathered up courage and went in before Pilate, and asked for the body of Jesus.
> Pilate wondered if He was dead by this time, and summoning the centurion, he questioned him as to whether He was already dead. And ascertaining this from the centurion, he granted the body to Joseph."[11.28]

It seems likely that at this juncture Pilate did not really know what was going on; including whether or not Jesus was taken away alive, left there alive with His legs broken, or if he was dead. He had previously agreed to permit having all their legs broken, so that they could be "taken away." But he did not seem to know that Jesus was already dead, and subsequently pierced to make certain.

The *King James* version of Mark 15:42-44 substitutes the words "any while dead" for "already dead."[11.29] This translation makes it appear that Pilate was also concerned with how long Jesus was dead, as though beyond a certain period of time Pilate would be safe. Perhaps a more contemporary phraseology would be "Is he dead enough?" Alternately, since death from crucifixion generally required several days, perhaps it was merely that Pilate was surprised that Jesus was dead. This could be contradicted however, because the breaking of the legs was also a death accelerant.

There is an issue with the conversation between Jesus and one of the thieves on the cross; which as commonly believed, makes little sense if taken literally as it appears. The citation for this appears in Luke.

Luke 23:42-43 tells us:

> "And he was saying, "Jesus, remember me when You come in Your kingdom!" And He said to him, "Truly I say to you, today you shall be with Me in Paradise."[11.30]

As it appears, it seems quite easy to understand. Here the thief believed Jesus was the Christ, and was asking to be saved. It is interesting that two men were crucified alongside Jesus, and their names are not even mentioned. Clearly this thief was not referring to any physical kingdom. But the problem with this citation is that the answer given by Jesus, as written, cannot possibly be true.

The word paradise comes from para-deity, which means next to God. Obviously, Jesus had said this to the thief while He was still alive. If it is true, that as in the case of the Passover lamb, Jesus actually died at sundown; then this would have technically been the next day. Thus, Jesus would still have been alive the entire day He made this statement, and could not have gone to paradise on that day.

If it is believed that he died before sundown; clearly before the beginning of the next day; then He did not go to "paradise" on that next day either.

This is known because in John 20:17 it states:

> "Jesus said to her, "Stop clinging to Me, for I have not yet ascended to the Father; but go to My brethren and say to them, 'I ascend to My Father and your Father, and My God and your God.'"[11.31]

This statement was made by Jesus *after* the resurrection.

The problem with this citation, Luke (23:42-43), lies with the placement of the comma. The comma belongs after the "today" and not after the "you." Thus it should read: "Truly I say to you *today*, you shall be with Me in Paradise." The today referring to when the statement was being made, and not when the thief would be with Jesus; as Jesus would not be in paradise until 40 days had passed.[11.32] It is believed that the original Biblical writings were written in continuous form and contained no punctuation. This misplaced comma was added later.

There is scant information about the earthquake contained in the four Gospels. It seems that Matthew is the only one of the four who provides any substantial amount of information.

Matthew 27: 50-54 tells us:

> "And Jesus cried out again with a loud voice, and yielded up His spirit.
> And behold, the veil of the temple was torn in two from top to bottom; and the earth shook and the rocks were split.
> The tombs were opened, and many bodies of the saints who had fallen asleep were raised;
> and coming out of the tombs after His resurrection they entered the holy city and appeared to many."
> Now the centurion, and those who were with him keeping guard over Jesus, when they saw the earthquake and the things that were happening, became very frightened and said,
> "Truly this was the Son of God!"[11.33]

These five verses arguably span at least forty days; that being approximately the duration of time from the crucifixion to the resurrection. But if verse 53 is temporarily removed, the chronology seems reasonably consistent.

In verse 51 three things are happening. They seem to be related in terms of cause and effect, but this may not necessarily be so.

"The veil of the temple was torn in two."

It is easy for the mind to create an image of what this veil was; like a larger version of what a bride wears. Tearing it in half seems like no great effort. But this veil in no way resembled such a veil.

It is not clear from this passage alone, if this "veil" is the "screen" which was the entrance to the tent; or if it was the veil that separated the holy room from the inner room, or the Holy of Holies.

The original Greek word used for veil is: "2665 katapetasma, from a comp.of 2596 and a congener of 4072; something *spread thoroughly*, i.e. (spec.) the door screen (to the Most Holy Place) in the Jewish Temple: - vail."[11.34] Thus it appears that this veil was the inner veil, separating the Holy room from the Most Holy Place.

Exodus 26: 31-33 describes this veil:

> "You shall make a veil of blue and purple and scarlet material and fine twisted linen; it shall be made with cherubim, the work of a skillful workman.
> "You shall hang it on four pillars of acacia overlaid with gold, their hooks also being of gold, on four sockets of silver.
> "You shall hang up the veil under the clasps, and shall bring in the ark of the testimony there within the veil; and the veil shall serve for you as a partition between the holy place and the holy of holies."[11.35]

This veil was large, and substantial enough to require four pillars on which it was to hang. In the case of an earthquake, it seems more likely that the pillars would have fallen, rather than the veil being torn in two from top to bottom. Yet, this is not what happened.

*The Interlinear Bible* version of Matthew 27:51 states "was torn into two, from above *until* below."[11.36] The original Greek word translated as "until" is: "2193 heos, of uncert. affin.; a conj., prep. and adv. of continuance, until (of time and place): - even (until, unto), (as) far (as), how long, (un-) til (-l), (hither-, un-, up) to, while (-s).[11.37]

Thus, there is an implication that this tearing was not instantaneous. The use of the phrase *"from top to bottom,"* strictly indicates the location of the tear. The term *"from above until below,"* suggests that both time and location were factors. Perhaps this was a slow motion tearing, beginning at the top and continuing downward; a rather unusual sight unless one is familiar with Doberman Pinchers and upholstered furniture. It is difficult to imagine what it must have been like to watch this veil tear itself in half, from the top to the bottom. The human mind likely imagining this tearing, as though a pair of invisible hands were tearing this substantial fabric in half.

God had resided on the other side of this veil. "This most sacred enclosure had only one item of furniture, the ark of the Covenant."[11.38] Only once a year, on the day of atonement, was a human even permitted to enter this Holy of Holies. Yet, upon the death of Jesus, this veil was completely torn. Was this so that God could get out?

The answer is no. God could have easily gotten out without the tearing of this veil. The veil was torn in this manner so that all would *know* he had gotten out. Upon the death of Jesus, a substantial portion of the world was "un-handed-over" to Satan. Prior to this, God only had license to be present on the earth under certain circumstances, the ark being one. But all of this had just changed.

In the following passage from Luke 4:5-7, the "he" is Satan, the 'Him" is Jesus.

> *"And he led Him up and showed Him all the kingdoms of the world in a moment of time. And the devil said to Him, "I will give You all this domain and its glory; for it has been handed over to me, and I give it to whomever I wish.*

*"Therefore if You worship before me, it shall all be Yours."*[11.39]

Given the circumstances, it is likely that it was only because of the nature of Jesus, that his answer to the devil was not: "Why should I do that? I am going to get it all back anyway?"

It would probably make the most sense to take another look at Mathew 27:54 and the centurion, in order to get some insight into the verses that precede it.

This can fairly be treated as a type of conclusive statement based upon the real time observation of events: "Now the centurion, and those who were with him keeping guard over Jesus, when they saw the earthquake and the things that were happening, became very frightened and said, "Truly this was the Son of God!"

A centurion is not just a Roman soldier. He is the leader of a large group of foot soldiers; possibly as many as one hundred; hence the name. A centurion was likely quite used to "killing people and breaking things;" which is generally the main task of any military organization; as well as countless times being an eyewitness the same. It was a centurion who was going to "examine" (by scourging) Paul, until he found out that Paul was a Roman citizen.

This was a man who had seen much. He was entrusted to "guard" Jesus; keeping in mind that of course there are two types of guards. One type of guard, such as a bodyguard, is there to insure that the person he is guarding *is* able to do what he wants to do. The other type of guard, such as a prison guard, is there to insure that the person he is guarding *is not* able to do what he wants to do. The same can be said of "chaperones," but that is another matter.

What would or could it take to not merely frighten such a man, but to make him "very frightened?"

In verse 54, Matthew had told us that they "saw the earthquake and the things that were happening" The actual Greek word used which is translated as earthquake is: "4578 seismos, from 4579; a *commotion*, i.e. (of the air) a *gale*, (of the ground) an *earthquake*: - earthquake, tempest.[11.40]

Thus this word "seismos" is a general term denoting commotion; which can be applied to the air, the ground or a storm, or anything else. The decision to mistranslate a word denoting general commotion into earthquake, leads the reader to an unwarranted conclusion; likely translated as such because of the English word seismic usually relating to earthquakes. There is a difference however, between an earthquake and the earth quaking.

The former is a specific event, usually tectonic in origin, which often causes the crust of the earth to "quake." The latter is a condition of the mere quaking of the earth, which could be caused by many other phenomena as well. As written this "seismos" does not necessarily relate to the ground, but likely is also assumed to be so because of the following statement, which actually precedes the "earthquake" translation.

"And the earth shook and the rocks were split."

This would have been another opportunity for the translator to have translated the word as earthquake; yet at least in this verse, he, she or they did not.

The original Greek word used here for earth is: "1093 *ge,* contr. From a prim. word; *soil*; by extens. a *region*, or the solid part or the whole of the *terrene* globe (includ. the occupants in each application): - country, earth (-ly), ground, land, world."[11.41] The original Greek work for shook is "4579 seio, appar. a prim. verb; to *rock* (*vibrate*, prop. sideways or to and fro), i.e. (gen.) to *agitate* (in a any direction; cause to *tremble*); fig. to throw into a *tremor* (of fear or concern): - move, quake, shake."[11.42]

Neither "seio" nor "seismos" specifically relate to an earthquake, but rather motion or commotion respectively. However, the use of the "ge" indicates that "seio" in this passage was related to the ground. Thus it seems that a fair interpretation that it was both the soil or ground; *as well as the occupants* which were rocking or vibrating either sideways or to and fro. It does not state that anyone fell down during this time.

Back in Matthew 12:40, when Jesus told us "the Son of Man be three days and three nights in the heart of the earth," many people believe this refers to His time in the tomb. But His tomb was not actually in the heart of the earth, either literally or figuratively, thus He was not even in the ground, but was in what essentially was a cave.

Ephesians 4:9-10 tells us:

> *"(Now this expression, "He ascended," what does it mean except that He also had descended into the lower parts of the earth?*
> *He who descended is Himself also He who ascended far above all the heavens, so that He might fill all things.)"*[11.43]

So we have some confirmation that the "heart of the earth" as likely meaning "the lower parts of the earth." It seems that when Jesus descended into the heart or lower parts of the earth, the ground above and the occupants began to move. (As an aside, was this the same area previously discussed; relating to the prohibited likenesses or images?) To suggest that this was in any way an earthquake in the normal sense, takes away from the significance of the events going on between the forces of light and the forces of darkness. It would be unfair to characterize this as an underground battle, as the battle had already been fought and won. It is likely this was more an enforcement issue.

It is also interesting that the rocks were split. The word "split" is "4977 schizo, appar. a prim. verb; to *split* or *sever* (lit. or fig.): - break, divide, open, rend, make a rent"[11.44] It does not say crushed.

"The tombs were opened, and many bodies of the saints who had fallen asleep were raised"

Tombs: "3419 mnemeion, from 3420; a *remembrance*, i.e. *cenotaph* (*place of interment*): - grave, sepulchre, tomb."[11.45]

Bodies: "4983 soma, from 4982; the *body* (as a *sound* whole), used in a very wide application, lit. or fig.: - bodily, body, slave.[11.46]

Saints: "40 hagios, from hagos (an *awful* thing) [comp. 53, 2282]; *sacred* (phys. *pure*, mor. *blameless* or *religious*, cer. *consecrated*): - (most) holy (one, thing), saint."[11.47]

Asleep: "2837 koimao, from 2749; to *put to sleep* i.e. (pass. or reflex.) to *slumber*; fig. to *decease*: - (be a -, fall a -, fall on) sleep, be dead."[11.48]

Raised: "1453 egeiro, prob. Akin to the base of 58 (through the idea of *collecting* one's faculties); to *waken* (trans. or intrans.), i.e. *rouse* (lit. from sleep, from sitting or lying, from disease, from death; or fig. from obscurity, inactivity, ruins, nonexistence): - awake, lift (up), raise (again, up), rear up, (a - ) rise (again, up), stand, take up."[11.49]

There seems to be no way around the fact that the only reasonable read on this passage is that this must have actually happened as described. The word "tomb," tends to make one think only of a mausoleum, but *mnemeion* seems to refer to *any* place of interment. It must be noted that there seems to be a time lag between when these were raised, (at the crucifixion), and when they actually entered the city, (at the resurrection).

Here is what appears to be the likely situation: The centurion guard is on the hill close to the crosses, likely facing Jesus. (Mark 15:39) It is unnaturally dark. Nearby him is the crowd that is mocking Jesus. (Mark 15:29) Farther away are the followers of Jesus. (Luke 23:49) As previously stated, this hill is named Calvary or Golgotha, meaning skull, allegedly called such because the hill resembled a skull; but more than likely named so because of the remaining skulls of most of those who were crucified there.

This centurion is making sure that no one, especially Jesus, gets off the crosses and escapes; either in case His reputed powers actually existed, or in case He had obtained assistance. Those around him are taunting and mocking Jesus. Then at some point the darkness lifts and Jesus in a loud voice gives up his spirit. This likely surprises them because the actual cause of death by crucifixion at that time was prolonged, and believed to be by either suffocation or exhaustion.[11.50]

Then this veil gets slowly ripped in half, from top to bottom, with no one appearing to be tearing it. Then the ground shakes as though an earthquake, but the crosses do not fall. Then graves and tombs open up and those previously interred get up and start walking around. At this point, the centurion came to the conclusion that the Jews had been wrong.

Luke 23:48 tells us:

> *"And all the crowds who came together for this spectacle, when they observed what had happened, began to return, beating their breasts."*[11.51]

It seems that once the crowd saw that Jesus was dead; and since the "fun" was all over, they had begun to leave. But when they observed what had then subsequently happened, something was not "right," or at least not what they had expected, or had come to usually expect; so they began to return to the area. At this point they, like the centurion, had become very frightened.

This beating of the breasts is important. This Greek word for beating is "5180 tupto, a prim. verb (in a strength. form); to "*thump*", i.e. *cudgel* or *pummel* (prop. with a stick or *bastinado*), but in any case by *repeated* blows; thus differing from 3817 and 3960, which denote a [usually single] blow with the hand or any instrument, or 4141 with the *fist* [or a *hammer*], or 4474 with the *palm*; as well as from 5177, an *accidental* collision); by impl. to *punish*; fig. to *offend* (the conscience): - beat, smite, strike, wound. [11.52]

According to "*Illustrated Dictionary of the Bible*," beating one's breast was a sign of intense sorrow.[11.53]

As a reference; earlier in Luke 18:13 Jesus is speaking and it states therein:

"But the tax collector, standing some distance away, was even unwilling to lift up his eyes to heaven, but was beating his breast, saying, 'God, be merciful to me, the sinner!" [11.54]

MEEKRAKER *Beginnings…*

# Chapter 12

## Reprise

This represents the final chapter in this work. Some of the contents herein or therein may result in a tremendous amount of misery inflicted upon those who expect the Word to confess to them; rather than it being they who confess the Word. Confessing in this usage again meaning one's agreeing with what was already said; in this case already said by God. This would be unfortunate and certainly is not intentional. Absolute truth and wisdom, and not misery, have consistently been the authors' objectives.

Nevertheless, speaking metaphorically, some of the authors' efforts may produce a large amount of "fireworks" in the minds of those who consistently believe that if the Word disagrees with what they believe, then of course it is the Word that must be in error. This "discrepancy" between what one wants to believe and what the Word actually states; naturally and quite predictably;

is almost exclusively blamed on "translational errors." The removal of the possibility of any such errors, being a major factor for which it was herein endeavored to reasonably alleviate.

But one thing is for certain; and is something upon which almost all would agree. No matter how good any "fireworks" display may be, we all know that it is incomplete without that last loud one in the grand finale. Thus, despite any wishes to the contrary, it is quite possible that the following may very well suffice in that regard....

Malachi 3:1 tells us:

> *"Behold, I am going to send My messenger, and he will clear the way before Me. And the Lord, whom you seek, will suddenly come to His temple; and the messenger of the covenant, in whom you delight, behold, He is coming," says the LORD of hosts."*[12.1]

God is speaking here about what was to happen before the first coming of Jesus. This is entirely different than Malachi 4:5 which refers to the "great and terrible day of the Lord;"[12.2] that passage being concerned with His second coming; a matter which is further detailed in the Book of Revelation. There is often conflation of these two separate events into one. But the first coming of Jesus, as a laundryman's soap, although certainly great; was only terrible for two; those two being Jesus and the devil.

God is telling us here that He will be sending a forerunner; a messenger sent before Jesus who was to clear the way. But who is or was this messenger to be? Some believe that it was to be an angel. Perhaps this refers to Gabriel, as when he visited Mary. But that really doesn't make very much sense; as Gabriel visited Mary because he needed her permission for the "immaculate conception." That hardly represented clearing the way for anything; arguably not even the conception, as there was nothing to clear. Perhaps it was the time when Gabriel visited Joseph. But that also makes little sense, as he only wanted to let "Joe" know that Mary wasn't "cheating on him." After all, they did stone "adulteresses" back then; even though they (Mary and Joseph) were not yet; (and perhaps never actually were), married.

The Jewish people today believe that this messenger is to be (future tense used purposely), Elijah. They very much want Elijah to come; because they believe that this is necessary before the Messiah arrives, just as Malachi states; and they desperately want the Messiah. In fact; generally at the Passover Seder; a place and a glass of wine is set for Elijah; and the front door is symbolically opened and closed to admit him; welcoming him and facilitating his entry; should he choose to arrive at their home.

But for Christians, the arrival of this messenger is not a matter of the future, but of the past. Since Jesus has already come the first time; and since God told us there would be a forerunner; then of course to Christians, the circumstances surrounding the arrival of this forerunner must necessarily be a historical fact, and not a future matter.

The disciples of Jesus knew that He must have been preceded by a forerunner, but did not believe that they had any knowledge of the arrival of the forerunner. So they asked Him about this very issue.

Matthew 17:10-13 tells us:

> "And His disciples asked Him, "Why then do the scribes say that Elijah must come first?"
> And He answered and said, "Elijah is coming and will restore all things; but I say to you that Elijah already came, and they did not recognize him, but did to him whatever they wished.
> So also the Son of Man is going to suffer at their hands." Then the disciples understood that He had spoken to them about John the Baptist."[12.3]

Here the disciples and the scribes knew that this forerunner was not to be an angel; and they knew then, just as Jews believe today, that this forerunner was to be Elijah.

Matthew 11:7-14 tells us:

> *"As these men were going away, Jesus began to speak to the crowds about John,*
> *"What did you go out into the wilderness to see? A reed shaken by the wind?*
> *"But what did you go out to see? A man dressed in soft clothing? Those who wear soft clothing are in kings' palaces! "But what did you go out to see? A prophet? Yes, I tell you, and one who is more than a prophet*
> *"This is the one about whom it is written,*
> *'BEHOLD, I SEND MY MESSENGER AHEAD OF YOU, WHO WILL PREPARE YOUR WAY BEFORE YOU.'*
> *"Truly I say to you, among those born of women there has not arisen anyone greater than John the Baptist! Yet the one who is least in the kingdom of heaven is greater than he.*
> *"From the days of John the Baptist until now the kingdom of heaven suffers violence, and violent men take it by force.*
> *"For all the prophets and the Law prophesied until John."And if you are willing to accept it, John himself is Elijah who was to come."*[12.4]

Now this seems to work out well, because as far as we know, Elijah was taken into heaven "in corpus," as 2 Kings 2:11 tell us:

> *"As they were going along and talking, behold, there appeared a chariot of fire and horses of fire which separated the two of them. And Elijah went up by a whirlwind to heaven."*[12.5]

Thus, all that God had to do was send the chariot of fire back and drop off Elijah, and all would be fine. This is not in any way an attempt to be flippant, as it just seems that the logical purpose for bringing Elijah into heaven in that manner, was to be able to return him as the forerunner. God knew He had additional plans for Elijah, and this would be a reasonable explanation. But the Bible clearly shows us that this is *not* in any way what He did.

This is a bit long, but Luke 1:5-20 tell us what God actually *did* do:

> "In the days of Herod, king of Judea, there was a priest here was a priest named Zacharias, of the division of Abijah and he had a wife from the daughters of Aaron, and her name was Elizabeth. They were both righteous in the sight of God, walking blamelessly in all the commandments and requirements of the Lord. But they had no child, because Elizabeth was barren, and they were both advanced in years.
> Now it happened that while he was performing his priestly service before God in the appointed order of his division, according to the custom of the priestly office, he was chosen by lot to enter the temple of the Lord and burn incense. And the whole multitude of the people were in prayer outside at the hour of the incense offering.
> And an angel of the Lord appeared to him, standing to the right of the altar of incense. Zacharias was troubled when he saw the angel, and fear gripped him.
> But the angel said to him, "Do not be afraid, Zacharias, for your petition has been heard, and your wife Elizabeth will bear you a son,
> and you will give him the name John.
> "You will have joy and gladness, and many will rejoice at his birth. "For he will be great in the sight of the Lord; and he will drink no wine or liquor, and he will be filled with the Holy Spirit while yet in his mother's womb.
> "And he will turn many of the sons of Israel back to the Lord their God.
> "It is he who will go as a forerunner before Him in the spirit and power of Elijah, TO TURN THE HEARTS OF THE FATHERS BACK TO THE CHILDREN, and the disobedient to the attitude of the righteous, so as to make ready a people prepared for the Lord."
> Zacharias said to the angel, "How will I know this for certain? For I am an old man and my wife is advanced in years."

> *The angel answered and said to him, "I am Gabriel, who stands in the presence of God, and I have been sent to speak to you and to bring you this good news. "And behold, you shall be silent and unable to speak until the day when these things take place, because you did not believe my words, which will be fulfilled in their proper time."*[12.6]

Zacharias was a holy man. He and Elizabeth were righteous in the sight of God; walking blamelessly in all commandments and requirements. The use of the term "walking" in the Scriptures generally means lifestyle, rather than ambulation. They were blameless, but it does not state innocent. Although these words are often used interchangeably, they are not synonyms. Blameless meaning cannot be blamed for wrongs; innocent at a minimum meaning you didn't do anything wrong or mean to cause any harm. The word innocence is derived from the Latin "nocere;" as in the Latin "Primum non nocere." This is roughly translated as "first do no harm; and is provided as a guide for physicians. Guilty and not guilty, in the legal usage, have nothing whatsoever to do with what one did or did not do, but rather what can or cannot be proved. It would probably be fair to say that this couple endeavored to live a holy lifestyle, made some mistakes, but their hearts were in the right place. Elizabeth was now barren, likely had always been barren, as they had no children; and now they were both getting older. It does not seem that Zacharias would have been the type who would ever have introduced Elizabeth as his sister.

So now one day, Zacharias is performing priestly service according to all the customs, and he is chosen by lot to enter and burn incense. This is not actually stated, but there must have been more men wanting to enter and burn incense as a lottery was used to determine who would enter that day. So then it was by "random" that he happened to be in the temple that day. But of course there is no such thing as random.

While he is in this temple, an angel appears and tells Zacharias (who is terrified) that his petition has been heard. Up to this point, it is not stated that they had been praying for a child, but they must have been. The angel tells Zacharias that this son will be named John, and tells Zacharias a few other things as well.

John "will drink no wine or liquor." A Nazarite or Nazarene was one who took special vows which could be for life, or for a fixed period of time. These vows usually included not drinking alcohol, and not cutting one's hair. Jesus was also a Nazarite or Nazarene. That is why when someone suggests that it is not known whether or not Jesus had long hair; this is false. We know that he did, because he had also taken these vows, which include the vow to not cut His hair.

John will be filled with the Holy Spirit (Ghost) in the womb. This is important because when Mary is pregnant and meets Elizabeth, (who was Mary's relative), when Elizabeth was six months pregnant, there is a reaction from John within Elizabeth's womb. It is also important because it is when Jesus is later baptized by John, it is at that time that the Holy Ghost descends upon Him.

Zacharias is then advised that it is his son John, who is to be the forerunner for Jesus in the "spirit and power of Elijah."

This word "spirit" used in this passage can be a subject of much confusion. Many profess that this simply means that John would be like or similar to Elijah; but that John was not in fact Elijah; as in the "spirit of the law" as opposed to the "letter of the law." But the word "spirit" comes from the word "spiritus" which means breath. Since we know that man becomes a living soul when God breathes the breath of life into his nostrils, then the literal "spirit of Elijah" would then necessarily be the same breath that God originally breathed into Elijah's nostrils; by definition.

Furthermore, the actual Greek word used for spirit in this passage is: "4151 pneuma, from 4154; a *current* of air, i.e. *breath* (*blast*) or a *breeze*; by anal. or fig. a *spirit*, i.e. (human) the rational *soul*, (by impl.) *vital principle*, mental *disposition*, etc., or (superhuman) an *angel, demon*, or (divine) *God*, Christ's *spirit*, the Holy *Spirit*: - ghost, life, spirit (-ual - ually), mind."[12.7]

The word used for power is: "1411 dunamis, from 1410; *force* (lit. or fig.); spec. miraculous *power* (usually by impl. a *miracle* itself): - ability, abundance, meaning, might (-ily, - y, -y deed), (worker of) miracle (-s), power, strength, violence, mighty (wonderful) work."[12.8]

This is difficult to envision. An angel comes to Zacharias (obviously after he or they had been praying for a son), scaring the dickens out of him; tells him that his petition has been heard and that he will be given a son; including what to name him, and that he will be the prophesied forerunner. And what is Zack's response? "How will I know this for certain? For I am an old man and my wife is advanced in years." The angel then tells Zacharias that he (the angel) is Gabriel, and warns him: "And behold, you shall be silent and unable to speak until the day when these things take place, because you did not believe my words, which will be fulfilled in their proper time."

Zacharias was described as a priest. He knew full well the significance of the forerunner; this same forerunner for whom Jewish people today set a place, pour wine, and open the door.

The way this reads, it sounded like he did not actually say that he did not believe it; but rather that he wanted insurance. But the *Interlinear Bible* version is: "By what shall I know this?"[12.9] Thus, a fair read is that Zacharias was actually asking for a sign. Since he commented on his age, it is likely he wanted a sign soon; or at least before his son reached adulthood.

It would seem otherwise fair to ask the question as to why Gabriel not only insisted on Zacharias silence; but also made him physically unable to speak until after John was born and named. After all, when Sarah was told she would bear a son, and when they laughed because they did not believe God; neither God nor any angel on His behalf silenced them. Instead, He just named the child Isaac, which means "laughter" or "he laughs." So the question becomes: that if Zacharias was asking for a sign; why then did Gabriel choose silence as this sign instead of something else?

There is a reason why Gabriel caused Zacharias to be physically unable to speak. This reason is because even long before Newton, whose name was also to be Isaac; Gabriel understood **F=MA**. At this juncture, Zacharias simply could not be permitted to create or sow a negative $F_T$ by speaking out loud $F_A$, with his doubt creating a negative $F_R$, rendering the total force negative. Remember Job?

This was a "tight" time. There was no time for error correction. Back when Abram/Abraham took matters into his own hands by the comedy with Hagar, there was ample time for course correction. But here timing was critical; for among other reasons; Jesus and John were only to be about six months apart gestationally.

Gabriel had advised Zacharias that his son John was to be "in the spirit and power of Elijah." The scribes of that time, as Jews today, believed the forerunner was to be Elijah. The disciples believed Elijah was to come first and had asked Jesus about it. Jesus had told them in Matthew 17:10-13, that "Elijah is coming and will restore all things; but I say to you that Elijah already came, and they did not recognize him, but did to him whatever they wished;" which resulted in the disciples understanding "that He had spoken to them about John the Baptist." Jesus also stated in Matthew 11:14; "And if you are willing to accept *it,* John himself is Elijah who was to come." And one additional fact is that John's mother's name was Elizabeth, which means house of Elijah.

Thus there is little possible doubt that John the Baptist was Elijah. If that were not so, then all of these people, including Jesus twice, are or were wrong. And if they are or were wrong, then there is a missing forerunner. But the problem is that Elijah did not return to earth as the adult male who had left in the whirlwind. (This event possibly being reserved for the "witnesses" before the great and terrible day in the end times.) Instead, he was born in as the result of a "normal" pregnancy. Thus, there is no possible reasonable conclusion other than that John the Baptist was Elijah reincarnated.

But this tells us only that Elijah was reincarnated as John. This could have been a one-time event; as was the "immaculate conception;" because there is no reference or suggestion in the passages referenced thus far; that it had ever happened at any other time; or with or to anyone else.

John 9:1-5 tells us:

> *"As He passed by, He saw a man blind from birth. And His disciples asked Him,*
> *"Rabbi, who sinned, this man or his parents, that he would be born blind?"*
> *Jesus answered, "It was neither that this man sinned, nor his parents; but it was so that the works of God might be displayed in him.*
> *"We must work the works of Him who sent Me as long as it is day; night is coming when no one can work.*
> *"While I am in the world, I am the Light of the world."*[12.10]

This passage is part of the story about Jesus performing a miracle in restoring sight to a blind man. As it reads, it shows the power Jesus had from the Father, and that it was the works of Him be displayed in this person.

But there is additional revelation contained here that is very easy to miss. The disciples asked Jesus who sinned that he should be born blind. Now it might be easy to make the case that the parents had sinned, and the result was that the child was born blind. This argument could be raised today when children are born addicted to drugs or when they are born with AIDS. Whether or not one agrees that using crack cocaine or sexual promiscuity constitute sinful behaviors, could arguably be argued. Nevertheless, a child *can* be born with a malady as a result of a parent's or the parents' behavior.

The actual Greek word translated as sinned is: "264 hamartano, perh. from *1* (as a neg. particle) and the base of 3313; prop. to *miss the mark* (and so *not share* in the prize), i.e. (fig.) to *err*, esp. (mor.) to *sin*; - for your faults, offend, sin, trespass."[12.11]

But it is the other possibility that the disciples raised, which contains the revelation. Most societies and religions acknowledge the fact that there are threshold ages with respect to knowing right from wrong; as well as threshold ages for responsibility for one's actions. This is seen in the ages for the Catholic First Communion and Confirmation. It is also evident with the ages required for barmitzvahs and bas-mitzvahs. There are also legal age requirements with respect to knowing right from wrong, or whether one should be tried as an adult. The actual ages are not important here; but rather the concept that before a certain age, sin is not possible because the child is incapable of knowing right from wrong. So as a child, before reaching a certain age, this person or any person simply was incapable of sinning.

But the fact is that the disciples did not ask Jesus if it was a sin of this person as a child that resulted in his blindness. Nor did they ask Jesus if it was possible that this man could have sinned, and that this resulted in him being born blind. What they actually asked was if it was *because* he sinned that he was (would be) born blind. There is a major difference. The only possible supposition for this question, of course being that it was their position that this man could have first sinned, and then been born.

Since it is not possible for an unborn child to know right from wrong, there is no possible way this child could have sinned while in the womb. And even if he somehow could have known right from wrong, it is difficult to imagine what that sinful behavior could have possibly been. Furthermore, according to Genesis 2:7 man does not become a living soul until God breathes into his nostrils, which happens at the first breath; something which simply cannot physically happen while in the womb.

Thus, what the disciples were actually asking Jesus, was if it was a sin from a time when this man could have sinned; which necessarily had to be prior to his birth. This means that the man would have had to have been old enough to know right from wrong, at some time prior to his birth. This also necessarily means knowing right from wrong prior to becoming a fetus, an embryo, a morula or a fertilized egg. There is no conclusion possible; other than they meant sinning in a prior life.

Jesus did not respond by inquiring as to whether or not they had had hidden pocket flasks originally filled with water at the wedding; flasks which were very recently emptied. He did not inquire as to whether they had been having headaches lately. Instead he answered them, and the answer was neither. Thus, although today making an inquiry as to whether sin in a previous life could result in a malady in the next life would be considered as blasphemy; it most certainly was not such to Jesus at that time. Had this been so; His response would have been "as their folly deserved," as Jesus was known for "telling it like it is." Instead He considered it a legitimate question, and He answered "according to" it.

There is no other reasonable conclusion other than Jesus and His disciples did not believe that reincarnation was a singular event; meaning one which had only ever occurred with the reincarnation of Elijah as John the Baptist.

Matthew 16: 13-16 tells us:

> *"Now when Jesus came into the district of Caesarea Philippi, He was asking His disciples, "Who do people say that the Son of Man is?"*
> *And they said, "Some say John the Baptist; and others, Elijah; but still others, Jeremiah, or one of the prophets." He said to them, "But who do you say that I am?"*
> *Simon Peter answered, "You are the Christ, the Son of the living God."*[12.12]

Here Jesus is asking his disciples who it was that common people believed He was. The four answers that the disciples received from the people regarding who "He is" all had one thing in common. All of these individuals were deceased at that time; noting that the phrase: "one of the prophets," represents an unspecified number of possibilities.

Thus, this idea of reincarnation was not limited to Jesus and His disciples, but also believed by the common people at that time. It was not arcane knowledge, but rather common knowledge; irrespective of the fact that it is generally considered at best heresy; more likely blasphemy, in today's "religious" circles.

As with most subjects; distinctions must be made; and very specific terminology used, in order to adequately understand any phenomenon.

The general term "reincarnation" can be broken down into three parts. The "re;" the "in;" and the "carnation." The "re" generally means to do something again. The "in" of course means in, or within; and the "carnation" refers to a process concerning flesh. The words carnage, carnal, and even the flower "carnation" all related to "flesh." Thus reincarnation refers to the process of the reintroduction of something into the flesh.

There are believed to be three possible categories of reincarnation:

The first category of reincarnation is termed *metempsychosis*. This word can be broken down literally as metem-psych-osis. The "Metem" or "met" meaning a change in, or in the middle. The psych referring to the soul, and osis being a suffix usually meaning an "abnormal condition of." *Merriam-Webster.com* provides the following: "Definition of *METEMPSYCHOSIS*: the passing of the soul at death into another body either human or animal… from meta- + empsychos animate, from en- + psychē soul"[12,13] This definition provides a little additional insight, but may be a bit misleading; depending upon precisely what is meant by the use of the term "animal" in the definition.

Metempsychosis is the term generally recognized to represent that category of reincarnation which maintains the view that reincarnation is kind of a one way street; meaning that there is no possibility of regression. The term "regression" as used here does not mean the "regression" process that involves an individual attempting to find out about past lives, but rather reincarnating to a "lesser state."

The tenets of this view include that whatever the status of a life form in a given incarnation; this represents the highest level of existence ever yet attained by that being. One cannot go backwards, as say a human being reincarnated as a cow or a snake. Thus when someone at a cocktail party claims that he or she was once the King of some country; or that they were some famous, wealthy, or extremely talented person in another life; this is highly unlikely or even impossible according to the tenets of metempsychosis. Whatever they currently are represents the highest level at which they have ever been, according to this view. Of course, it is often difficult to objectively determine precisely what constitutes "highest."

*"Transmigration of Souls"* is another category of reincarnation. The term is not migration but rather transmigration. Here the "soul path" if you will, is considered to be two way. In this category, the direction of the soul is generally believed to be related to Karma, and with this view; one can return as either higher or lower status, including the type of life form. Depending on Karmic factors, one is believed to be able to return as a "reward" or "punishment" for their behavior in his or her past life or lives.

The question that the disciples asked Jesus about the blind man; "was it he or his parents who sinned," tends to lead one to believe that this question relates to the Transmigration of Souls view. When Jesus answered "neither," this could be construed either as an outright negation or rejection of this view; or, that it just did not apply to this particular situation. When Jesus gave the reason "*it was* so that the works of God might be displayed in him," this could be construed as support of the metempsychosis; as it does not seem likely that this man had ever been involved in such a great event as to be recorded as a party to a miracle of Jesus. On the other hand, it could also be that this man was never reincarnated, indicating that the question was irrelevant with respect to this man.

Both Metempsychosis and Transmigration of Souls require that the soul returns and resides in a different, generally a new body, and generally at the time of birth. When the soul returns to the same body, this arguably represents is the third type of reincarnation called *resurrection*.

This word resurrection contains the suffix "rection" which refers to being erect. This is seen in the term "insurrection," and essentially means to rise up. So the word can reasonably be defined as to rise up again. Thus, there is an implied requirement that this person or body must have been erect at one time; else how could they become re-erect or resurrected?

Jesus was resurrected, as it seems were all those who came out of the graves after the crucifixion. There is a belief that the original reason for embalming a corpse, is because many years ago certain cultures believed that they would ultimately be resurrected, and took measures to preserve the body for that day. This is to be distinguished from the mere application of makeup for a viewing. It is also likely that this could also be the reason for the elaborate burial procedures for kings in ancient cultures. It is not revealed what, if any, body preparation may have been done to those in the graves who were resurrected at the time of the crucifixion. Neither is it revealed how long these bodies had been interred.

This subject is a matter of grave (sorry) controversy. Most religious leaders will reject and avoid any discussion of reincarnation, even to the point of absurdity. In fact, in referencing *Strong's Exhaustive Concordance*, the word reincarnation does not even appear anywhere in the King James version of the Bible. This cannot be cited as a quote here, because Strong's does not actually make that statement; but rather, the word simply does not appear in their concordance. Nevertheless, the passages previously cited in this chapter are what they are, and state what they state.

Following are a few actual real life common attempts to "dismiss" the concept of reincarnation via Scriptural, or quasi-Scriptural references:

> 1) The insertion of the word "*the*" or the phrase "*as an*" before "Elijah" in Luke 1:17, so that it reads differently; the latter an attempt to make the phrase a simile, which it clearly is not.

> 2) An attempt to reinterpret the passages, so that it was "the ministry of John the Baptist which was carried out "in the spirit and power of Elijah."

> 3) John 1:21 tells us. "They asked him, "What then? Are you Elijah?" And he said, "I am not." "Are you the Prophet?" And he answered, "No."[12.14] In order to have this prove that John was not Elijah, the setting up of a sort of syllogism is required.

> Major Premise: All reincarnated people must know who they were in a previous life.  Minor Premise: John the Baptist denied (did not know) that he was Elijah.
> Conclusion: Therefore; John the Baptist could not possibly have been Elijah in a former life.
> ***Bonus Conclusion*** the doctrine of reincarnation is totally disproved.

Arguments are generally considered as valid or invalid. Statements are considered true or false. In order for this conclusion to be true, the Major Premise and Minor Premise must be true. There is no factual basis to even suggest, much less require, that any reincarnated person would or must know their identity or name from a former life. Thus the major Premise is not true. In fact, there is an entire industry that claims to engage in "regression" so that people can find out who they were in a former life. And of course, the "Bonus Conclusion" would be totally invalid and untrue even if all else were true. As an aside, it is also possible that John was telling "a truth" for protection, as his name in his current life actually was John.

> 4) Hebrews 9:27-28 tells us "And inasmuch as it is appointed for men to die once and after this *comes* judgment, so Christ also, having been offered once to bear the sins of many, will appear a second time for salvation without *reference to* sin, to those who eagerly await Him."[12.15]

The actual word for appointed is "606 apokeimai, from 575 and 2749; to *be reserved*; fig. to *await*: - be appointed, (be) laid up.[12.16]

Taken in context, the subject under explanation has to do with why Jesus did not have to offer himself more than once. It has nothing whatsoever to do with reincarnation. It is stated merely to support the conclusion; which is what follows the word "so;" or one could substitute "therefore." A better translation for appointed would be reserved or laid up. Laid up generally means stored or non-functional.

This likely refers to spiritual death from sin, which means separation from God. No longer do men spiritually die or be separated from God because of sin, as salvation justifies those who accept this salvation. All of the Old Testament prophets and holy men did not have this option. These Jesus rescued at or after Calvary; depending upon ones perspective. As previously discussed, there is no real spiritual "death;" death meaning non-existence; as we continue to exist somewhere forever, either heaven or hell. Physical death is merely a separation from the body, with neither ceasing to exist. In addition, if this is taken to mean that it is Divine will that men die only once physically, then it is arguable that Jesus sinned when He raised or resurrected Lazarus as well as others.

*The Interlinear Bible* translation translates "appointed" as "reserved."[12.17]

It is not clear as to precisely what it is that the "once" refers. It could refer to the "laid up/reserved," or it could refer to the "die." For the purposes of argument, if it is the die, and the die refers to "physical death" then it may very well mean that men dying once has been laid up; and now men physically die more than once. If it is the reserved/laid up to which the word "once" refers, and would be more consistent with the context; which is concerned with explaining why it is that Jesus only had to suffer once. If one takes the position that "Each human being lives once as a mortal on earth, dies once," is what is meant; and it is that concept or rule which was laid up; then either no one lives anymore, or it clearly proves physical rebirth.

MEEKRAKER *Beginnings...*

# About the Title

What on earth is a MeekRaker?

This word can be broken down into two parts "Meek" and "Raker." Capital letters were used in order to minimize any mispronunciations such as Mee- kraker; but the "etymology" is actually the fusion of these two words.

What is meek? And who in their right mind would ever want to be meek? Courage, strength, and bravery are characteristics that are generally considered desirable; but meek? No thanks. Unfortunately, the meaning of this word has been distorted over time to include things such as timidity, or shyness; weakness, or cowardice, but this is not; or rather should not be so.

*Chambers* states: "meek adj. Probably before 1200 meok gentle, humble, in Ancrene Riwle; later mec (probably about 1200, in the *The Ormlum* ); borrowed from a Scandanavian source (Compare Old Icelandic mjukr soft pliant gentle...."[AT-1]

These origins seem to be adjectival in nature, and describe a condition of humility or softness. Thus a meek person, by these definitions would indicate a humble or soft person. The opposite of this would then be a person who is prideful or hard.

Humble vs. prideful is an easy one. Who would want to be prideful? The Bible is replete with warnings about pride; and it was pride that started all of the messes to begin with. Pride may make one "feel good" for a short period of time, but as previously referenced; the Bible is quite clear that on that path there lies destruction.

But what does the Bible actually have to say about being a meek person? It tells us that the meek shall (*not will or might*) inherit the earth.[AT-2] It further tells us that the meek will be guided in judgment will be taught His way.[AT-3] The meek will be lifted up by the Lord, and He will cast the wicked down to the ground.[AT-4] He will save all the meek of the earth.[AT-5]

And what about the Bible's statements regarding being "hard?" "For their heart was hardened."[AT-6] "Have ye your heart yet hardened?"[AT-7] "… their eyes and hardened their heart."[AT-8] "But they and our fathers dealt proudly, and hardened their necks, and hearkened not to thy commandments, and refused to obey, neither were mindful of thy wonders that thou didst among them; but hardened their necks, and in their rebellion…"[AT-9] "Happy is the man that feareth always: But he that hardeneth his heart shall fall into mischief."[AT-10] "He that being often reproved hardeneth his neck, shall suddenly be destroyed, and that without remedy."[AT-11]

The actual word in all of these citations which is translated as hard is: "4456 poroo (a kind of stone); to *petrify*, i.e. (fig.) to *indurate* (*render stupid* or *callous*): - blind, harden.[AT-12]

With respect to hard, there is a clear Scriptural relationship between the same and disobedience; not being mindful of God performing wonders in one's life, rebellious, falling into mischief, and being destroyed without remedy. In addition, by the very definition of the original word, one who is "hard" is also stupid callous and blind. (If a physical heart were actually to turn into stone, you are just dead; so surely that definition does not apply in this context or usage.)

Thus, meek or soft; that being the opposite of hard; would tend to be obedient, be mindful of God performing wonders, not rebellious, not falling into mischief, and not destroyed. Furthermore, one would not be stupid, callous or blind.

The use of the term meek as soft, also implies teachable.

Hardhead: will not change mind. Hardhearted: will not change heart. Hard necked: junction between head and heart is hard, and will not permit mental change to be transmitted to change the heart.

If it is firmly established that the term "revelation" has the prerequisite of being *the* truth; when confronted with potential revelation; it has been the authors' experiences that hard persons; specifically those of the head, neck, and heart variety; will generally behave according to the "Three A's:"

> $A_1$ is *anger*. This is the first response. This anger is not so much because there is a remote chance that they may be wrong, but rather when it is somewhat clear that they *are* wrong. This would be best illustrated as a line on a graph rising from left to right; with the level of anger represented by the vertical axis, and time represented by the horizontal axis.

> $A_2$ is *argument.* This generally begins with emotionally (anger) driven arguments. As the arguments begin to fail, the level and usually the slope of $A_1$ will increase. When all possible arguments, logical, relevant or otherwise have been proffered, the original arguments will then return. This would be best illustrated as a circle under the rising anger line referenced above. Often, what is just under the skin, (which is generally the reason for the pride and subsequent anger) will pop its "head" out; revealing things previously unknown about this individual.

> $A_3$ is *absconding*. When all of the arguments and the repetition thereof have unquestionably failed, the hard person will generally abscond; or run away. This may be represented by actual physical separation, changing the subject or in some other manner. This could be perceived as the disappearance of the anger line, but is only subjective; as the true level of anger then

becomes somewhat hidden.

Contrarily, the meek will weigh the value of any purported revelation; and then decide precisely what it is that merits their belief. Sincere questioning and even some arguments will be presented; but here not with the primary purpose of proving that they, the inquirer, is correct; but rather to understand precisely what it is that this revelation represents; knowing that if it in fact does represent revelation, then this will be to their benefit. A logical decision will then be made with respect to what constitutes the truth.

The primary basis for the actions of a "hard-head," is emotional in nature. The primary basis for the actions of the meek; although perhaps including some emotional factors; (i.e. passion), is largely intellectual.

In a sense, the purpose of a rake is to separate the soft from the hard. The Bible refers to separating the wheat from the chaff, the silver from the dross; hence the title.

The authors neither ask nor expect readers to believe everything contained herein. Meek or hard is not so much determined by what one believes; but rather by the *process* involved in making these determinations.

# Glossary

**'âbad** (H) "5647 'âbad a prim. Root; to *work* (in any sense); by impl. To *serve, till,* (caus.) *enslave,* etc.: - x be, keep in bondage…"[3.43]

**'âdâm** (H) "120 'âdâm, from 119; *ruddy,* i.e. a *human being* (an individual or the species, *mankind*, etc.): - x another, + hypocrite, + common sort, x low, man (mean, of low degree), person."[4.13]

**Adam** (G) 76 Adam, of Heb. or. [121]; *Adam*, the first man; typ. (of Jesus) *man* (as his representative): - Adam."[4.14]

**'âphâr** (H) "6083 'âphâr from 6080; *dust* (as *powdered* or *gray*); hence *clay, earth, mud*: - ashes, dust, earth, ground, morter, powder, rubbish." "6080 aphar a prim. root; mean. either to *be gray* or perh. rather to *pulverize*; used only as denom. from 6083, to *be dust*: - cast [dust])." [4.5]

**apŏkĕimai** (G) "606 apŏkĕimai, from 575 and 2749; to *be reserved*; fig. to *await*: - be appointed, (be) laid up. [12.16]

**'âsâh** (H) "6213 'âsâh, …accomplish, advance, appoint…"[2.21]

**bâchan** (H) 974 bâchan, a prim. root; to *test*…" [12.2]

**bânâh** (H) "1129 bânâh, a prim. root; to *build* (lit. and fig.): - (begin to) build (-er), obtain children, make, repair, set (up), x surely." [4.28]

**bârâ'** "1254 bârâ', a prim. root; (absol.) to create; (qualified) to cut down (a wood), select, feed (as formative processes): - choose, create (creator), cut down, dispatch, do, make (fat)." [1.12] "The verb expresses creation out of nothing…" [1.12A]

**bên** (H) "1121 bên, from 1129; a *son*…" [5.26]

**betser** (H) "1220 betser, from 1219, "strictly a *clipping*, i.e. *gold* (as *dug* out): - gold defence." [9.22]

**c⁵gôwr** (H) "5458 c⁵gôwr, from 5462; prop. *shut up*, i.e. the *breast* (as inclosing the heart); also *gold* (as generally *shut* up safely): - caul, gold." [9.24]

**châbar** (H) "2266 châbar, a prim. root; to *join* (lit. or fig.); spec. (by means of spells) to fascinate: - charm (-er), be compact, couple (together), have fellowship with, heap up, join (self, together), league."[11.7]

**chabbûwrâh** (H) "2250 chabbûwrâh, or chabburah, or chaburah, from 2266; prop. *bound* (with stripes), i.e. a *weal* (or black - and - blue mark itself): - blueness, bruise, hurt, stripe, wound." [11.6]

**chôshek** (H) "chôshek, (2822) from 2821; the *dark;* hence (lit.) *darkness;* fig. *misery, destruction, death, ignorance, sorrow, wickedness:* - dark (-ness), night, obscurity. [2.2]

**chûwl** (H) "2342 chûwl or chiyla, a prim. root; prop; to *twist* or *whirl* (in a circular or spiral manner), i.e. (spec.) to *dance*, to *writhe* in pain (espec. of parturition) or fear;…" [3.32]

**dâshâ** (H) "1876 dâshâ, a prim. root; to *sprout*- bring forth, spring," [2.26]

**d⁵mûwth** (H) "1823 d⁵mûwth, from 1819; *resemblance;* coner, *model, shape;* adv. *like:* - fashion, like (-ness, as), manner, similitude." "1819 damah a prim. root; to compare; by impl. to resemble, liken, consider: - compare, devise, (be) like (-n), mean, think, use similitudes." Strong's also indicates that Genesis 1:26 is the first time the word *likeness* appears in the Bible. [3.20]

**dunamis** (G) "1411 dunamis, from 1410; *force* (lit. or fig.); spec. miraculous *power* (usually by impl. a *miracle* itself): - ability, abundance, meaning, might (-ily, - y, -y deed), (worker of) miracle (-s), power, strength, violence, mighty (wonderful) work."[12.8]

**ĕgĕirō** (G) "1453 ĕgĕirō, prob. Akin to the base of 58 (through the idea of *collecting* one's faculties); to *waken* (trans. or intrans.), i.e. *rouse* (lit. from sleep, from sitting or lying, from disease, from death; or fig. from obscurity, inactivity, ruins, nonexistence): - awake, lift (up), raise (again, up), rear up, (a - ) rise (again, up), stand, take up." [11.47]

**ĕpithumĕō** (G) "1937 ĕpithumĕō, to set the heart *upon*, i.e. *long* for (rightfully or otherwise): - covet, desire, would fain, lust (after)." [8.10]

**ĕpithumia** (G) "1939 ĕpithumia, from 1937; a *longing* (espec. for what is forbidden)…" [8.11]

**ĕschatŏs** (G) "2078 ĕschatŏs, a superl. prob. from 2192 (in the sense of *contiguity*); *farthest, final,* (of place or time): - ends of, last, latter end, lowest, uttermost." [4.16]

**'etseb** (H) "6089 'etseb, from 6087; an earthen *vessel*; usually (painful) *toil*; also a *pang* (whether of body or mind): - grievous, idol, labor, sorrow." [5.24]

**'êzer** (H) "5828 'êzer, from 5826; *aid*: - help." " 5826 azar, a prim. root; to *surround*, i.e. *protect* or *aid*: - help, succour." [4.26]

**gan** (H) "1588 gan from 1598; a *garden* (as *fenced*): - garden. 1598 ganan a prim. root; to *hedge* about, i.e. (gen.) *protect*: - defend" [4.7]

**gē** (G) "1093 gē, contr. From a prim. word; *soil*; by extens. a *region*, or the solid part or the whole of the *terrene* globe (includ. the occupants in each application): - country, earth (- ly), ground, land, world."[11.39]

**hagiŏs** (G) "40 hagiŏs, from hagos (an *awful* thing) [comp. 53, 2282]; *sacred* (phys. *pure*, mor. *blameless* or *religious*, cer. *consecrated*): - (most) holy (one, thing), saint." [11.45]

**hamartanō** (G) "264 hamartanō, perh. from *1* (as a neg. particle) and the base of 3313; prop. to *miss* the mark (and so *not share* in the prize), i.e. (fig.) to *err*, esp. (mor.) to *sin*; - for your faults, offend, sin, trespass." [12.11]

**hĕōs** (G) "2193 hĕōs, of uncert. affin.; a conj., prep. and adv. of continuance, until (of time and place): - even (until, unto), (as) far (as), how long, (un-) til (-l), (hither-, un-, up) to, while (-s). [11.35]

**hêrôwn** (H) "2032 hêrôwn or herayown; from 2029; *pregnancy*: - conception." "2029 harah, a prim. root; to *be* (or *become*) *pregnant*, *conceive* (lit. or fig.); - been, be with child, conceive, progenitor." [5.25]

**'itstsâbôwn** (H) "6093 'itstsâbôwn, from 6087; *worrisomeness*, i.e. *labor* or *pain*: - sorrow, toil." "6087 is atsab, a prim. root; prop. to *carve*, i.e. *fabricate* or *fashion*; hence, (in a bad sense) to *worry*, *pain* or *anger*; - displease, grieve, hurt, make, be sorry, vex, worship, wrest." [5.22]

**Job 'Iyôwb** (H) "347 'Iyôwb, from 340; *hated* (i.e. *persecuted*); *Ijob*, the patriarch famous for his patience: - Job." [9.1]

**kâbac** (H) "3526 kâbac, a prim. root; to *trample*; hence to *wash* (prop. by stamping with the feet), whether lit. (including the *fulling* process) or fig.: - fuller, wash (-ing)." [11.14]

**kâlâh** (H) "3615 kâlâh a prim. root; to *end*, whether intrans. (to *cease*, *be finished*, *perish*) or trans. (to *complete*, *prepare*, *consume*)..." [4.3]

**Kasday** (H) "3779 Kasday (Chald.), corresp. to 3778; a *Chaldean* or inhab. of Chaldea; by impl. a *Magian* or professional astrologer: - Chaldean." [9.36]

**Kasdîy** (H) 3778 "Kasdîy, (occasionally with enclitic) Kasdiymah *towards* the *Kasdites*: - into Chaldea), patron. from 3777 (only in the plur.); a *Kasdite*, or desc. of Kesed; by impl. A *Chaldean* (as if so descended); also an *astrologer* (as if proverbial of that people: - Chaldeans, Chaldees, inhabitants of Chaldea." [9.35]

**kâshaph** (H) "3784 kâshaph, a prim. root; prop. To *whisper* a spell, i.e. to *inchant* or practise magic: - sorcerer, (use) witch (-craft)." [9.38]

**katapĕtasma** (G) "2665 katapĕtasma, from a comp.of 2596 and a congener of 4072; something *spread thoroughly*, i.e. (spec.) the door screen (to the Most Holy Place) in the Jewish Temple: - vail."[11.32]

**kŏimaō** (G) "2837 kŏimaō, from 2749; to *put to sleep* i.e. (pass. or reflex.) to *slumber*; fig. to *decease:* - (be a -, fall a -, fall on) sleep, be dead." [11.46]

**keceph** (H) 3701 keceph, from 3700; *silver* (from its *pale* color); by impl. *money*; - money, price, silver (-ling). [7.14]

**kîy** (H) "3588 kîy, a prim. particle [the full form of the prepositional prefix] indicating causal relations of all kinds..." [5.10]

**kŏsmŏkratōr** (G) "2888 kŏsmŏkratōr, from 2889 and 2902; A *world - ruler*, and epithet of Satan: - ruler." [10.5]

**machbereth** (H) "4225 machbereth, from 2266; a *junction*, ie. seam or sewed piece; - coupling." 2266 "chabar a prim. root; to *join* (lit. or fig.); spec. (by means of spells) to *fascinate:* - charm-(er), be compact, couple (together), have fellowship with, heap up, join (self, together), league." [2.9]

**mayim** (H) "4325 mayim dual of a prim. noun (but used in a sing. sense); *water...* " [2.20]

**m$^{e}$'ôd** (H) "3966 m$^{e}$'ôd... prop. *vehemence*, i.e. (with or without prep.) *vehemently;* by impl. w*holly, speedily*, etc...." [3.25]

**mîyn** (H) "4327 mîyn,, from an unused root mean. to *portion* out; a *sort*, i.e. *species*: - kind. Comp. 4480." [3.9] "4480 min or minniy, or minney, prop. a part of; hence (prep.), from or out of in many senses (as follows): - above, after, among, at, because of by (reason of), from (among), in, x

neither, x nor, x (out) of, over, since, x then, through, x whether, with."
[3.10] In the "Strongest Strong's;" the definition of 4480 includes: "marker of a source or extension from a source." [3.11]

**mnēmĕiŏn** (G) "3419 mnēmĕiŏn, from 3420; a *remembrance*, i.e. *cenotaph* (*place of interment*): - grave, sepulchre, tomb." [11.43]

**nâchâsh** (H) "5175 nâchâsh, from 5172; a *snake* (from its *hiss*); - serpent." 5172 nachash a prim. root; prop. to *hiss*, i.e. *whisper* a (magic) spell; gen. to *prognosticate*: - x certainly, divine, enchanter, (use) x enchantment, learn by experience, x indeed, diligently observe." [3.33]

**nâta'** (H) "5193 nâta', a prim. root; prop. to *strike* in, i.e. *fix*; spec. to *plant* (lit. or fig.): - fastened, plant (-er)." [4.9]

**nâthan** (H) "5414 nâthan a prim. root; to *give*, used with greatest latitude of application (*put, make*, etc.)" [2.30]

**nephesh** (H) "5315 nephesh from 5314; prop. a *breathing* creature" "5314 Naphash a prim. root; to *breathe*; pass., to *be breathed* upon, i.e. (fig.) *refreshed* (as if by a current of air): - (be) refresh selves (-ed)." [3.16]

**Nephilim** (H) "5303 nᵉphîyl, or nᵉphîl, from 5307; prop., a *feller*, i.e. a *bully* or *tyrant*: - giant. 5307 naphal, a prim. root; to *fall*, in a great variety of applications (intrans. or causat., lit. or fig.)…" [10.8]

**'ôwlâm** (H) "5769 'ôwlâm or 'ôlâm, from 5956; prop. *concealed*, i.e. the *vanishing* point; gen. time *out of mind* (past or fut.), i.e. (practically) *eternity*; …." "5956 alam, a prim. root; to *veil* from sight, i.e. *conceal* (lit. or fig.): - x any ways, blind, dissembler, hide (self), secret (thing)." [5.29]

**'ôwth** (H) "226 'ôwth, prob. from 225 (in the sense of *appearing*); a *signal* (lit. or fig.), as a *flag, beacon, monument, omen, prodigy, evidence*, etc.: - mark, miracle, (en-) sign, token." [2.31]

**pnĕuma** (G) "4151 pnĕuma, from 4154; a *current* of air, i.e. *breath* (*blast*) or a *breeze*; by anal. or fig. a *spirit*, i.e. (human) the rational *soul*, (by impl.) *vital principle*, mental *disposition*, etc., or (superhuman) an *angel, demon,* or (divine) *God,* Christ's *spirit,* the Holy *Spirit:* - ghost, life, spirit (-ual - ually), mind." [12.7]

**prōtŏs** (G) "4413 prōtŏs, contr. superl. of 4253; *foremost* (in time, place, order or importance): - before, beginning, best, chief (-est), first (of all), former." [4.15]

**rahab** (H) "7293 rahab from 7292, *bluster (-er):* - proud, strength. [3.31]

**râphâ** (H) "7495 râphâ, or raphah, a prim. root; prop. to *mend* (by stitching), i.e. (fig.) to *cure:* - cure, (cause to ) heal, physician, repair, x thoroughly, make whole." [11.8]

**râqîyaʻ** (H) "7549 râqîyaʻ, from 7554; prop. an *expanse,* i.e. the *firmament* or (apparently) visible arch of the sky:- firmament." 7554 "raqa; a prim. root; to *pound* the earth (as a sign of passion); by analogy to *expand* (by hammering); by impl. to *overlay* (with thin sheets of metal);- beat, make broad, spread abroad (forth, over, out, into plates), stamp, stretch." [2.18]

**sōma** (G) "4983 sōma, from 4982; the *body* (as a *sound* whole), used in a very wide application, lit. or fig.: - bodily, body, slave. [11.44]

**schizō** (G) "4977 schizō, appar. a prim. verb; to *split* or *sever* (lit. or fig.): - break, divide, open, rend, make a rent" [11.42]

**sĕiō** (G) "4579 sĕiō, appar. a prim. verb; to *rock* (*vibrate,* prop. sideways or to and fro), i.e. (gen.) to *agitate* (in a any direction; cause to *tremble*); fig. to throw into a *tremor* (of fear or concern): - move, quake, shake." [11.40]

**sĕismŏs** (G) "4578 sĕismŏs, from 4579; a *commotion,* i.e. (of the air) a *gale,* (of the ground) an *earthquake:* - earthquake, tempest. [11.38]

**shâgâh** (H) "7686 shâgâh, a prim. root; to *stray* (caus. *mislead*), usually (fig.) to *mistake*, espec. (mor.) to *transgress*; by extens. (through the idea of intoxication) to *reel*, (fig.) *be enraptured:* - (cause to) go astray, deceive, err, be ravished, sin through ignorance, (let, make to) wander." [5.2]

**shûwph** (H) "7779 shûwph, a prim. root; prop. to *gape*, i.e. *snap* at; fig. to *overwhelm*: - break, bruise, cover." [5.18]

**skŏtĕinŏs** (G) "4652 skŏtĕinŏs, from 4655 opaque, i.e. (fig.) benighted; - dar, full of darkness." [2.5] The root of this word also is utilized in the formation of other words describing a cover, such as skene; which means a tent. [2.6]

**tachath** (H) "8478 tachath, from the same as 8430; the *bottom* (as *depressed*); only adv. *below* (often with prep. pref. *underneath*), in *lieu of*, etc.: - as, beneath…"[10.11]

**tamrûwq** (H) "8562 tamrûwq, or tamruq, or tamriyq, from 4838; prop. a *scouring*, i.e. *soap* or *perfumery* for the bath; fig. a *detergent*: - x cleanse, (thing for) purification (- fying)." [11.12]

**tâvek** (H) "8432 tâvek from an unused root mean. to *sever;* a *bisection*, …" [2.19]

**tᵉhôwm** (H) "8415 tᵉhôwm, or tehom from 1949; an *abyss* (as a *surging* mass of water), espec. the *deep* (the *main* sea or the subterranean *wate-supply*): - deep (place), depth." "1949 huwm a prim. root {comp. 2000}; to *make an uproar*, or *agitate* greatly: - destroy, move, make a noise, put, ring again." [2.8]

**tĕlŏs** (G) "5056 tĕlŏs from a prim. tello (to *set out* for a definite point or goal); prop. the point aimed at as a *limit*, i.e. (by impl.) the *conclusion* of an act or state…" [4.17]

**tôwlᵉdâh** (H) "8435 tôwlᵉdâh or toledah from 3205; (plur. only) *descent*, i.e. *family*; (fig.) *history*: - birth, generations." [3.40]

**tsâbâ'** (H) "6635 tsâbâ' or tsᵉba'ah, from 6633; a *mass* of persons (or fig. things), espec. reg. organized for war (an *army*); by impl. a *campaign,* lit. or fig. (spec. *hardship, worship):* - appointed time, (+) army, (+) battle, company, host, service, soldiers, waiting upon, war (-fare). 6633 tsaba a prim. root; to *mass* (an army or servants): - assemble, fight, perform, muster, wait upon, war." [3.28]

**tuptō** (G) "5180 tuptō, a prim. verb (in a strength. form); to *"thump"*, i.e. *cudgel* or *pummel* (prop. with a stick or *bastinado*), but in any case by *repeated* blows; thus differing from 3817 and 3960, which denote a [usually single] blow with the hand or any instrument, or 4141 with the *fist* [or a *hammer*], or 4474 with the *palm*; as well as from 5177, an *accidental* collision); by impl. to *punish*; fig. to *offend* (the conscience): - beat, smite, strike, wound. [11.50]

**Ur** (H)
1. "218 'Uwr, the same as 217; Ur, a place in Chaldea; also an Isr.: - Ur."
2. "217 'ûwr, from 215; *flame*, hence (in the plur.) the *East* (as being the region of light): - fire, light. See also 224."
3. "215 'ôwr, a prim. root; to *be* (caus. *make*) *luminous* (lit. and metaph.): - x break of day, glorious, kindle, (be, en-, give, show) light (-en, - ened), set on fire, shine."
4. "224 'Uwriym, plur. of 217; *lights*; *Urim*, the oracular brilliancy of the figures in the high-priest's breastplate: - Urim." [9.39]

**yâm** (H) "3220 yâm, from an unused root mean. to *roar; a sea* (as breaking in *noisy* surf)" [2.24]

**yir'ah** (H) "3374 yir'ah, fem. of 3373; *fear* (also used as infin.); mor. *reverence*..."[7.4]

**yâtsâ'** (H) "3318 yâtsâ', a prim. root; to *go* (causat. *bring) out,* in a great variety of applications, lit. and fig., direct and proxim.: - x after, appear x assuredly, bear out..." [3.14]

**yâtsar** (H) "3335 yâtsar, prob. identical with 3334 (through the *squeezing* into shape); ([comp. 3331]); to     *mould* into a form; espec. as a *potter;* ... 3334 yatsar a prim. root; to *press* (intrans.) ... 3331 yatsa a prim. root; to *strew* as a surface..."[4.4]

**yom or yôwm** (H) "3117 yôwm, from an unused root mean. To be hot: a day (as the warm hours) whether lit. (from sunrise to sunset, or from one sunset to the next), or fig. (a space of time defined by an associated term) -age,... season..."[2.14]

**zâhâb** (H) "2091 zâhâb, from an unused root mean. to *shimmer*; *gold*; fig. something *gold – colored* (i.e. *yellow*)..."[7.17]

*(H denotes Hebrew; G denotes Greek)*

# Bibliography

## Chapter 1

1.1 *New American Standard Bible*: 1995 update. 1995 (Gen. 1:1-2) The Lockman Foundation: Lahabra, CA

1.2 *Holy Bible, The New Open Bible™ Study Edition NASB*. copyright © 1990 Thomas Nelson, Inc., Nashville, TN "The Six Days of Creation" p. 5

1.3 *NASB / The Message Parallel Study Bible*. copyright © 2004 Zondervan, Grand Rapids, MI p.1

1.4 *New American Standard Bible*: 1995 update. 1995 (Is. 40:8) The Lockman Foundation: Lahabra, CA

1.5 *Scripture4all.org* (Genesis 1:2) Online Interlinear Bible

1.6 Strong, James. *Strong's Exhaustive Concordance of the Bible*. © 1890 James Strong, Madison, NJ pp. 47, 107 (Hebrew)

1.7 *New American Standard Bible*: 1995 update. 1995 (Jer.4:23-28) The Lockman Foundation: Lahabra, CA

1.8 *New American Standard Bible*: 1995 update. 1995 (Rev. 8:12) The Lockman Foundation: Lahabra, CA

1.9 *New American Standard Bible*: 1995 update. 1995 (Rev.19:19) The Lockman Foundation: Lahabra, CA

1.10 *New American Standard Bible*: 1995 update. 1995 (Jer.

4:29) The Lockman Foundation: Lahabra, CA
1.11 *Holy Bible, Saint Joseph New Catholic Edition.* copyright 1962, copyright 1957-1949 Catholic Book Publishing Co., N.Y. p15
1.12 Strong, James. *Strong's Exhaustive Concordance of the Bible.* © 1890 James Strong, Madison, NJ p. 23 (Hebrew)
1.13 *Vine's Complete Expository Dictionary of Old and New Testament Words.* W. E. Vine, Merill F. Unger, William White, Jr. © 1984, 1996 Thomas Nelson, Inc., Nashville, TN p. 51

# Chapter 2

2.1 *New American Standard Bible*: 1995 update. 1995 (Gen. 1:2-5) The Lockman Foundation: Lahabra, CA
2.2 Strong, James. *Strong's Exhaustive Concordance of the Bible.* © 1890 James Strong, Madison, NJ p. 44 (Hebrew)
2.3 *New American Standard Bible*: 1995 update. 1995 (John 1:3-5) The Lockman Foundation: Lahabra, CA
2.4 *Interlinear Bible Hebrew Greek English, 1 Volume edition.* © 1976, 1977, 1978, 1979, 1980, 1981, 1984. Second Edition, © 1986 Jay P. Green, Sr., Hendrickson Publishers (John 1:3-5) p. 818
2.5 Strong, James. *Strong's Exhaustive Concordance of the Bible.* © 1890 James Strong, Madison, NJ p. 65 (Hebrew)
2.6 *Vine's Complete Expository Dictionary of Old and New Testament Words.* W. E. Vine, Merill F. Unger, William White, Jr. © 1984, 1996 Thomas Nelson, Inc., Nashville, TN p. 259
2.7 Strong, James. *Strong's Exhaustive Concordance of the Bible.* © 1890 James Strong, Madison, NJ p. 95 (Hebrew)
2.8 Strong, James. *Strong's Exhaustive Concordance of the Bible.* © 1890 James Strong, Madison, NJ pp. 123, 32 (Hebrew)
2.9 Strong, James. *Strong's Exhaustive Concordance of the Bible.* © 1890 James Strong, Madison, NJ pp. 64, 36 (Hebrew)

2.10 *New American Standard Bible*: 1995 update. 1995 (Gen. 1:3) The Lockman Foundation: Lahabra, CA

2.11 *New American Standard Bible*: 1995 update. 1995 (Ps. 33:9) The Lockman Foundation: Lahabra, CA

2.12 *Interlinear Bible Hebrew Greek English, 1 Volume edition.* © 1976, 1977, 1978, 1979, 1980, 1981, 1984. Second Edition, © 1986 Jay P. Green, Sr., Hendrickson Publishers (Gen. 1: 3) p. 1

2.13 *New American Standard Bible*: 1995 update. 1995 (Gen. 1:4-5) The Lockman Foundation: Lahabra, CA

2.14 Strong, James. *Strong's Exhaustive Concordance of the Bible.* © 1890 James Strong, Madison, NJ p. 48 (Hebrew)

2.15 *New American Standard Bible*: 1995 update. 1995 (2 Peter 3:8) The Lockman Foundation: Lahabra, CA

2.16 *New American Standard Bible*: 1995 update. 1995 (Ps.90:4) The Lockman Foundation: Lahabra, CA

2.17 *New American Standard Bible*: 1995 update. 1995 (Gen.1:6-8) The Lockman Foundation: Lahabra, CA

2.18 Strong, James. *Strong's Exhaustive Concordance of the Bible.* © 1890 James Strong, Madison, NJ p.110 (Hebrew)

2.19 Strong, James. *Strong's Exhaustive Concordance of the Bible.* © 1890 James Strong, Madison, NJ p.123 (Hebrew)

2.20 Strong, James. *Strong's Exhaustive Concordance of the Bible.* © 1890 James Strong, Madison, NJ p. 65 (Hebrew)

2.21 Strong, James. *Strong's Exhaustive Concordance of the Bible.* © 1890 James Strong, Madison, NJ p. 92 (Hebrew)

2.22 *New American Standard Bible*: 1995 update. 1995 (Gen. 1:9-10) The Lockman Foundation: Lahabra, CA

2.23 *New American Standard Bible*: 1995 update. 1995 (Ps. 33:7). The Lockman Foundation: Lahabra, CA

2.24 Strong, James. *Strong's Exhaustive Concordance of the Bible.* © 1890 James Strong, Madison, NJ p. 50 (Hebrew)

2.25 *New American Standard Bible*: 1995 update. 1995 (Gen. 1:11-13) The Lockman Foundation: Lahabra, CA

2.26 Strong, James. *Strong's Exhaustive Concordance of the Bible.* © 1890 James Strong, Madison, NJ p. 31 (Hebrew)

2.27 *New American Standard Bible*: 1995 update. 1995 (Gen.

1:14-19) The Lockman Foundation: Lahabra, CA
2.28 Strong, James. *Strong's Exhaustive Concordance of the Bible.* © 1890 James Strong, Madison, NJ p. 92 (Hebrew)
2.29 *Interlinear Bible Hebrew Greek English, 1 Volume edition.* © 1976, 1977, 1978, 1979, 1980, 1981, 1984. Second Edition, © 1986 Jay P. Green, Sr., Hendrickson Publishers (Gen. 1:14) p. 1
2.30 Strong, James. *Strong's Exhaustive Concordance of the Bible.* © 1890 James Strong, Madison, NJ p. 81 (Hebrew)
2.31 Strong, James. *Strong's Exhaustive Concordance of the Bible.* © 1890 James Strong, Madison, NJ p. 10 (Hebrew)
2.32 *Chambers Dictionary of Etymology.* Copyright © 1988 The H. W. Wilson Company, New York, NY p. 844

# Chapter 3

3.1 *http://www.literature.org/authors/twain-mark/huckleberry* (Huckleberry Finn Introduction)
3.2 Strong, James. *Strong's Exhaustive Concordance of the Bible.* © 1890 James Strong, Madison, NJ p. 65 (Hebrew)
3.3 *New American Standard Bible*: 1995 update. 1995 (Gen. 1:20) The Lockman Foundation: Lahabra, CA
3.4 *Interlinear Bible Hebrew Greek English, 1 Volume edition.* © 1976, 1977, 1978, 1979, 1980, 1981, 1984. Second Edition, © 1986 Jay P. Green, Sr., Hendrickson Publishers (Gen. 1:20) p.1
3.5 *New American Standard Bible*: 1995 update. 1995 (Gen. 1:21) The Lockman Foundation: Lahabra, CA
3.6 *Interlinear Bible Hebrew Greek English, 1 Volume edition.* © 1976, 1977, 1978, 1979, 1980, 1981, 1984. Second Edition, © 1986 Jay P. Green, Sr., Hendrickson Publishers (Gen. 1:21) p. 1
3.7 *New American Standard Bible*: 1995 update. 1995 (Gen. 1:22) The Lockman Foundation: Lahabra, CA
3.8 Strong, James. *Strong's Exhaustive Concordance of the Bible.*© 1890 James Strong, Madison, NJ p. 14

3.9 Strong, James. *Strong's Exhaustive Concordance of the Bible.* © 1890 James Strong, Madison, NJ p. 65 (Hebrew)

3.10 Strong, James. *Strong's Exhaustive Concordance of the Bible.* © 1890 James Strong, Madison, NJ p. 67 (Hebrew)

3.11 *The Strongest Strong's Exhaustive Concordance of the Bible.* James Strong, revised and corrected by John R. Kohlenberger III and James A. Swanson, copyright © 2001 by Zondervan, Grand Rapids, MI p.1527

3.12 *New American Standard Bible*: 1995 update. 1995 (Gen. 1:23) The Lockman Foundation: Lahabra, CA

3.13 *New American Standard Bible*: 1995 update. 1995 (Gen. 1:24-25) The Lockman Foundation: Lahabra, CA

3.14 Strong, James. *Strong's Exhaustive Concordance of the Bible.* © 1890 James Strong, Madison, NJ p. 51 (Hebrew)

3.15 Strong, James. *Strong's Exhaustive Concordance of the Bible.* © 1890 James Strong, Madison, NJ p. 92 (Hebrew)

3.16 Strong, James. *Strong's Exhaustive Concordance of the Bible.* © 1890 James Strong, Madison, NJ p. 80 (Hebrew)

3.17 *New American Standard Bible*: 1995 update. 1995 (Gen. 1:26-27) The Lockman Foundation: Lahabra, CA

3.18 *Chambers Dictionary of Etymology.* Copyright © 1988 The H. W. Wilson Company, New York, NY p. 508

3.19 *Chambers Dictionary of Etymology.* Copyright © 1988 The H. W. Wilson Company, New York, NY p. 596

3.20 Strong, James. *Strong's Exhaustive Concordance of the Bible.* © 1890 James Strong, Madison, NJ p. 31 (Hebrew)

3.21 *New American Standard Bible*: 1995 update. 1995 (John 4:24) The Lockman Foundation: Lahabra, CA

3.22 *New American Standard Bible*: 1995 update. 1995 (Gen. 1:28) The Lockman Foundation: Lahabra, CA

3.23 *New American Standard Bible*: 1995 update. 1995 (Gen. 1:29-31) The Lockman Foundation: Lahabra, CA

3.24 *http://www.ccel.org/e/easton* (Manna) Easton's Online Bible Dictionary

3.25 Strong, James. *Strong's Exhaustive Concordance of the Bible.* © 1890 James Strong, Madison, NJ p. 60 (Hebrew)

3.26 *New American Standard Bible*: 1995 update. 1995 (Gen. 2:1) The Lockman Foundation: Lahabra, CA

3.27 *Chambers Dictionary of Etymology*. Copyright © 1988 The H. W. Wilson Company, New York, NY p. 492

3.28 Strong, James. *Strong's Exhaustive Concordance of the Bible*. © 1890 James Strong, Madison, NJ p. 98 (Hebrew)

3.29 Asimov, Isaac. *The Complete Stories Vol. 2*, Isaac Asimov. © 1992 by Isaac Asimov, A Foundation Book published by Doubleday, a division of Bantam, Doubleday, Dell Publishing Group, Inc. New York, NY *"The Monkey's Finger"*, Isaac Asimov, © 1952 by Better Publications Inc. P. 196

3.30 *New American Standard Bible*: 1995 update. 1995 (Job 26:10-14) The Lockman Foundation: Lahabra, CA

3.31 Strong, James. *Strong's Exhaustive Concordance of the Bible*. © 1890 James Strong, Madison, NJ p. 107 (Hebrew)

3.32 Strong, James. *Strong's Exhaustive Concordance of the Bible*. © 1890 James Strong, Madison, NJ p. 37 (Hebrew)

3.33 Strong, James. *Strong's Exhaustive Concordance of the Bible*. © 1890 James Strong, Madison, NJ p. 78 (Hebrew)

3.34 *Interlinear Bible Hebrew Greek English, 1 Volume edition*. © 1976, 1977, 1978, 1979, 1980, 1981, 1984. Second Edition, © 1986 Jay P. Green, Sr., Hendrickson Publishers (Job 26:12) p. 454

3.35 *New American Standard Bible*: 1995 update. 1995 (Ez. 28:16-17) The Lockman Foundation: Lahabra, CA

3.36 *New American Standard Bible*: 1995 update. 1995 (Prov. 16:18) The Lockman Foundation: Lahabra, CA

3.37 *New American Standard Bible*: 1995 update. 1995 (Gen. 2:2-3) The Lockman Foundation: Lahabra, CA

3.38 Strong, James. *Strong's Exhaustive Concordance of the Bible*. © 1890 James Strong, Madison, NJ pp. 11, 640

3.39 *New American Standard Bible*: 1995 update. 1995 (Gen. 2:4) The Lockman Foundation: Lahabra, CA

3.40 Strong, James. *Strong's Exhaustive Concordance of the Bible*. © 1890 James Strong, Madison, NJ p. 123 (Hebrew)

3.41 Strong, James. *Strong's Exhaustive Concordance of the Bible.* © 1890 James Strong, Madison, NJ pp. 11, 640
3.42 *New American Standard Bible*: 1995 update. 1995 (Gen. 2:5) The Lockman Foundation: Lahabra, CA
3.43 Strong, James. *Strong's Exhaustive Concordance of the Bible.* © 1890 James Strong, Madison, NJ p. 84 (Hebrew)
3.44 *New American Standard Bible*: 1995 update. 1995 (Gen. 2:6) The Lockman Foundation: Lahabra, CA

# Chapter 4

4.1 *New American Standard Bible*: 1995 update. 1995 (Gen. 2:7) The Lockman Foundation: Lahabra, CA
4.2 *New American Standard Bible*: 1995 update. 1995 (Gen. 2:1-4) The Lockman Foundation: Lahabra, CA
4.3 Strong, James. *Strong's Exhaustive Concordance of the Bible.* © 1890 James Strong, Madison, NJ p. 55 (Hebrew)
4.4 Strong, James. *Strong's Exhaustive Concordance of the Bible.* © 1890 James Strong, Madison, NJ p. 51 (Hebrew)
4.5 Strong, James. *Strong's Exhaustive Concordance of the Bible.* © 1890 James Strong, Madison, NJ p. 90 (Hebrew)
4.6 *New American Standard Bible*: 1995 update. 1995 (Gen. 2:8) The Lockman Foundation: Lahabra, CA
4.7 Strong, James. *Strong's Exhaustive Concordance of the Bible.* © 1890 James Strong, Madison, NJ p. 28 (Hebrew)
4.8 *Chambers Dictionary of Etymology.* Copyright © 1988 The H. W. Wilson Company, New York, NY p. 442
4.9 Strong, James. *Strong's Exhaustive Concordance of the Bible.* © 1890 James Strong, Madison, NJ p. 78 (Hebrew)
4.10 *New American Standard Bible*: 1995 update. 1995 (Gen. 3:17-19) The Lockman Foundation: Lahabra, CA
4.11 *New American Standard Bible*: 1995 update. 1995 (1 Cor. 15:45) The Lockman Foundation: Lahabra, CA
4.12 *Interlinear Bible Hebrew Greek English, 1 Volume*

*edition.* © 1976, 1977, 1978, 1979, 1980, 1981, 1984. Second Edition, © 1986 Jay P. Green, Sr., Hendrickson Publishers

4.13 Strong, James. *Strong's Exhaustive Concordance of the Bible.* © 1890 James Strong, Madison, NJ p. 8 (Hebrew)

4.14 Strong, James. *Strong's Exhaustive Concordance of the Bible.* © 1890 James Strong, Madison, NJ p. 8 (Greek)

4.15 Strong, James. *Strong's Exhaustive Concordance of the Bible.* © 1890 James Strong, Madison, NJ p. 63 (Greek)

4.16 Strong, James. *Strong's Exhaustive Concordance of the Bible.* © 1890 James Strong, Madison, NJ p. 33 (Greek)

4.17 Strong, James. *Strong's Exhaustive Concordance of the Bible.* © 1890 James Strong, Madison, NJ p. 71 (Greek)

4.18 *New American Standard Bible*: 1995 update. 1995 (Heb. 7:3) The Lockman Foundation: Lahabra, CA

4.19 *New American Standard Bible*: 1995 update. 1995 (Gen. 2:9) The Lockman Foundation: Lahabra, CA

4.20 *New American Standard Bible*: 1995 update. 1995 (Gen. 2:19-20) The Lockman Foundation: Lahabra, CA

4.21 *New American Standard Bible*: 1995 update. 1995 (Gen. 3:12) The Lockman Foundation: Lahabra, CA

4.22 *New American Standard Bible*: 1995 update. 1995 (Gen. 2:10-14) The Lockman Foundation: Lahabra, CA

4.23 *New American Standard Bible*: 1995 update. 1995 (Gen. 2:15) The Lockman Foundation: Lahabra, CA

4.24 *New American Standard Bible*: 1995 update. 1995 (Gen. 2:16-17) The Lockman Foundation: Lahabra, CA

4.25 Strong, James. *Strong's Exhaustive Concordance of the Bible.* © 1890 James Strong, Madison, NJ p. 238

4.26 *New American Standard Bible*: 1995 update. 1995 (Gen. 2:18-20) The Lockman Foundation: Lahabra, CA

4.27 Strong, James. *Strong's Exhaustive Concordance of the Bible.* © 1890 James Strong, Madison, NJ p. 87 (Hebrew)

4.28 *New American Standard Bible*: 1995 update. 1995 (Gen. 2:21-25) The Lockman Foundation: Lahabra, CA

4.29 Strong, James. *Strong's Exhaustive Concordance of the Bible.* © 1890 James Strong, Madison, NJ p. 22 (Hebrew)

# Chapter 5

5.1 *New American Standard Bible*: 1995 update. 1995 (Prov. 20:1) The Lockman Foundation: Lahabra, CA
5.2 Strong, James. *Strong's Exhaustive Concordance of the Bible*. © 1890 James Strong, Madison, NJ p. 112 (Hebrew)
5.3 *New American Standard Bible*: 1995 update. 1995 (Gen. 3:1-3) The Lockman Foundation: Lahabra, CA
5.4 Strong, James. *Strong's Exhaustive Concordance of the Bible*. © 1890 James Strong, Madison, NJ p. 78 (Hebrew)
5.5 *New American Standard Bible*: 1995 update. 1995 (Gen. 3:4-5) The Lockman Foundation: Lahabra, CA
5.6 *New American Standard Bible*: 1995 update. 1995 (Gen. 3:6-7) The Lockman Foundation: Lahabra, CA
5.7 *New American Standard Bible*: 1995 update. 1995 (Gen. 3:8-13) The Lockman Foundation: Lahabra, CA
5.8 *New American Standard Bible*: 1995 update. 1995 (Gen. 3:14) The Lockman Foundation: Lahabra, CA
5.9 Strong, James. *Strong's Exhaustive Concordance of the Bible*. © 1890 James Strong, Madison, NJ p. 103
5.10 Strong, James. *Strong's Exhaustive Concordance of the Bible*. © 1890 James Strong, Madison, NJ p. 55 (Hebrew)
5.11 *New American Standard Bible*: 1995 update. 1995 (Gen. 1:24) The Lockman Foundation: Lahabra, CA
5.12 *New American Standard Bible*: 1995 update. 1995 (Gen. 2:19) The Lockman Foundation: Lahabra, CA
5.13 *New American Standard Bible*: 1995 update. 1995 (Luke 4:5) The Lockman Foundation: Lahabra, CA
5.14 *New American Standard Bible*: 1995 update. 1995 (Ex. 3:4-5) The Lockman Foundation: Lahabra, CA
5.15 *New American Standard Bible*: 1995 update. 1995 (Gen. 3:17-23) The Lockman Foundation: Lahabra, CA
5.16 *New American Standard Bible*: 1995 update. 1995 (Gen.

3:17) The Lockman Foundation: Lahabra, CA

5.17 *New American Standard Bible*: 1995 update. 1995 (Gen. 3:15) The Lockman Foundation: Lahabra, CA

5.18 Strong, James. *Strong's Exhaustive Concordance of the Bible*. © 1890 James Strong, Madison, NJ p. 114 (Hebrew)

5.19 Strong, James. *Strong's Exhaustive Concordance of the Bible*. © 1890 James Strong, Madison, NJ p. 152

5.20 *New American Standard Bible*: 1995 update. 1995 (Gen. 3:16) The Lockman Foundation: Lahabra, CA

5.21 *Interlinear Bible Hebrew Greek English, 1 Volume edition.* © 1976, 1977, 1978, 1979, 1980, 1981, 1984. Second Edition, © 1986 Jay P. Green, Sr., Hendrickson Publishers (Gen. 3:16) p. 3

5.22 Strong, James. *Strong's Exhaustive Concordance of the Bible*. © 1890 James Strong, Madison, NJ p. 90 (Hebrew)

5.23 *Interlinear Bible Hebrew Greek English, 1 Volume edition.* © 1976, 1977, 1978, 1979, 1980, 1981, 1984. Second Edition, © 1986 Jay P. Green, Sr., Hendrickson Publishers (Gen. 3:16) p. 3

5.24 Strong, James. *Strong's Exhaustive Concordance of the Bible*. © 1890 James Strong, Madison, NJ p. 90 (Hebrew)

5.25 Strong, James. *Strong's Exhaustive Concordance of the Bible*. © 1890 James Strong, Madison, NJ p. 33 (Hebrew)

5.26 Strong, James. *Strong's Exhaustive Concordance of the Bible*. © 1890 James Strong, Madison, NJ p. 21 (Hebrew)

5.27 *New American Standard Bible*: 1995 update. 1995 (Gen. 3:18-19) The Lockman Foundation: Lahabra, CA

5.28 *New American Standard Bible*: 1995 update. 1995 (Gen. 3:20-24) The Lockman Foundation: Lahabra, CA

5.29 Strong, James. *Strong's Exhaustive Concordance of the Bible*. © 1890 James Strong, Madison, NJ pp. 86, 89 (Hebrew)

# Chapter 6

6.1 *Holy Bible, The New Open Bible® Large Print Edition New King James Version*. copyright © 1990, 1985, 1983 Thomas Nelson, Inc., Nashville, TN p.139

6.2 *New American Standard Bible*: 1995 update. 1995 (Heb. 11:6) The Lockman Foundation: Lahabra, CA

6.3 *Holy Bible, The New Open Bible™ Study Edition NASB.* copyright © 1990 Thomas Nelson, Inc., Nashville, TN p. 282

6.4 *Comparative Study Bible, Revised Edition KJV*. Copyright © 1999 The Zondervan Corporation, Grand Rapids MI (2 Tim. 1:7)

6.5 *Illustrated Dictionary of the Bible*. Herbert Lockyer, SR., Editor, with F. F. Bruce and R. K. Harrison, Copyright © 1986 Thomas Nelson Publishers, Nashville, TN p. 219

6.6 *New American Standard Bible*: 1995 update. 1995 (Gen. 14:13) The Lockman Foundation: Lahabra, CA

6.7 *New American Standard Bible*: 1995 update. 1995 (Gen. 5:5) The Lockman Foundation: Lahabra, CA

6.8 *New American Standard Bible*: 1995 update. 1995 (Gen. 5:3) The Lockman Foundation: Lahabra, CA

6.9 *New American Standard Bible*: 1995 update. 1995 (Gen. 4:17-22) The Lockman Foundation: Lahabra, CA

6.10 *New American Standard Bible*: 1995 update. 1995 (Gen. 4:16) The Lockman Foundation: Lahabra, CA

6.11 *Chambers Dictionary of Etymology*. Copyright © 1988 The H. W. Wilson Company, New York, NY p. 428

# 2nd Second Intermission

I2.1 *New American Standard Bible*: 1995 update. 1995

(Mal.3:10) The Lockman Foundation: Lahabra, CA
I2.2 Strong, James. *Strong's Exhaustive Concordance of the Bible.* © 1890 James Strong, Madison, NJ p. 86, 19 (Hebrew)
I2.3 *Physicsclassroom .com*
I2.4 *New American Standard Bible*: 1995 update. 1995 (Prov. 16:2) The Lockman Foundation: Lahabra, CA
I2.5 *Physicsclassroom .com*
I2.6 *Physicsclassroom .com*
I2.7 *New American Standard Bible*: 1995 update. 1995 (2Cor. 9:7) The Lockman Foundation: Lahabra, CA
I2.8 *New American Standard Bible*: 1995 update. 1995 (Prov 18:20-21) The Lockman Foundation: Lahabra, CA
I2.9 *New American Standard Bible*: 1995 update. 1995 (Matt.15:11) The Lockman Foundation: Lahabra, CA
I2.10 *Physicsclassroom .com*

# Chapter 7

7.1 *New American Standard Bible*: 1995 update. 1995 (Prov. 21:31) The Lockman Foundation: Lahabra, CA
7.2 *Holy Bible, The New Open Bible® Large Print Edition New King James Version.* copyright © 1990, 1985, 1983 Thomas Nelson, Inc., Nashville, TN (Heb. 11:1)
7.3 *New American Standard Bible*: 1995 update. 1995 (Gen. 20:1-2) The Lockman Foundation: Lahabra, CA
7.4 Strong, James. *Strong's Exhaustive Concordance of the Bible.* © 1890 James Strong, Madison, NJ p. 52 (Hebrew)
7.5 *New American Standard Bible*: 1995 update. 1995 (Gen. 15:1) The Lockman Foundation: Lahabra, CA
7.6 *New American Standard Bible*: 1995 update. 1995 (Gen.15:4-5) The Lockman Foundation: Lahabra, CA
7.7 *New American Standard Bible*: 1995 update. 1995 (Gen. 20:3-7) The Lockman Foundation: Lahabra, CA

7.8 *New American Standard Bible*: 1995 update. 1995 (Gen. 16) The Lockman Foundation: Lahabra, CA

7.9 *New American Standard Bible*: 1995 update. 1995 (Gen. 20:8-11) The Lockman Foundation: Lahabra, CA

7.10 *New American Standard Bible*: 1995 update. 1995 (Gen. 20:12-13) The Lockman Foundation: Lahabra, CA

7.11 *New American Standard Bible*: 1995 update. 1995 (Gen. 20:14-18) The Lockman Foundation: Lahabra, CA

7.12 *New American Standard Bible*: 1995 update. 1995 (Gen. 26:6-11) The Lockman Foundation: Lahabra, CA

7.13 *New American Standard Bible*: 1995 update. 1995 (Gen. 13:2) The Lockman Foundation: Lahabra, CA

7.14 Strong, James. *Strong's Exhaustive Concordance of the Bible*. © 1890 James Strong, Madison, NJ p. 57 (Hebrew)

7.15 Strong, James. *Strong's Exhaustive Concordance of the Bible*. © 1890 James Strong, Madison, NJ p. 928

7.16 Strong, James. *Strong's Exhaustive Concordance of the Bible*. © 1890 James Strong, Madison, NJ p. 412

7.17 Strong, James. *Strong's Exhaustive Concordance of the Bible*. © 1890 James Strong, Madison, NJ p. 34 (Hebrew)

7.18 *New American Standard Bible*: 1995 update. 1995 (Gen. 23:15-16) The Lockman Foundation: Lahabra, CA

7.19 *Interlinear Bible Hebrew Greek English, 1 Volume edition*. © 1976, 1977, 1978, 1979, 1980, 1981, 1984. Second Edition, © 1986 Jay P. Green, Sr., Hendrickson Publishers (Job 3:25) p. 18

7.20 Strong, James. *Strong's Exhaustive Concordance of the Bible*. © 1890 James Strong, Madison, NJ p. 928

7.21 *New American Standard Bible*: 1995 update. 1995 (Gen. 12:16) The Lockman Foundation: Lahabra, CA

# Chapter 8

8.1 *New American Standard Bible*: 1995 update. 1995 (Ex. 20:14) The Lockman Foundation: Lahabra, CA

8.2 *New American Standard Bible*: 1995 update. 1995 (Matt. 5:27-28) The Lockman Foundation: Lahabra, CA
8.3 *Chambers Dictionary of Etymology*. Copyright © 1988 The H. W. Wilson Company, New York, NY p.15
8.4 *Chambers Dictionary of Etymology*. Copyright © 1988 The H. W. Wilson Company, New York, NY p.1181
8.5 *Chambers Dictionary of Etymology*. Copyright © 1988 The H. W. Wilson Company, New York, NY p.776
8.6 *New American Standard Bible*: 1995 update. 1995 (Matt. 5:48) The Lockman Foundation: Lahabra, CA
8.7 *New American Standard Bible*: 1995 update. 1995 (Prov. 6:32) The Lockman Foundation: Lahabra, CA
8.8 *New American Standard Bible*: 1995 update. 1995 (Jer. 3:9) The Lockman Foundation: Lahabra, CA
8.9 *New American Standard Bible*: 1995 update. 1995 (1Kings 11:13) The Lockman Foundation: Lahabra, CA
8.10 Strong, James. *Strong's Exhaustive Concordance of the Bible*. © 1890 James Strong, Madison, NJ p. 31 (Greek)
8.11 Strong, James. *Strong's Exhaustive Concordance of the Bible*. © 1890 James Strong, Madison, NJ p. 31 (Greek)
8.12 *New American Standard Bible*: 1995 update. 1995 (Matt. 19:6, 19:9) The Lockman Foundation: Lahabra, CA
8.13 *Encarta ® World English Dictionary*. copyright 1998-2004 Microsoft Corp.

# Chapter 9

9.1 Strong, James. *Strong's Exhaustive Concordance of the Bible*. © 1890 James Strong, Madison, NJ p. 11 (Hebrew)
9.2 *New American Standard Bible*: 1995 update. 1995 (Job 42:7-8) The Lockman Foundation: Lahabra, CA
9.3 *New American Standard Bible*: 1995 update. 1995 (Job 1:5) The Lockman Foundation: Lahabra, CA

9.4 *Interlinear Bible Hebrew Greek English, 1 Volume edition.* © 1976, 1977, 1978, 1979, 1980, 1981, 1984. Second Edition, © 1986 Jay P. Green, Sr., Hendrickson Publishers (Job 3:25) p. 444

9.5 *New American Standard Bible*: 1995 update. 1995 (Job 1:6-7) The Lockman Foundation: Lahabra, CA

9.6 *New American Standard Bible*: 1995 update. 1995 (Job 1:8) The Lockman Foundation: Lahabra, CA

9.7 *Interlinear Bible Hebrew Greek English, 1 Volume edition.* © 1976, 1977, 1978, 1979, 1980, 1981, 1984. Second Edition, © 1986 Jay P. Green, Sr., Hendrickson Publishers (Job 1:8) p.443

9.8 *New American Standard Bible*: 1995 update. 1995 (Job 2:3) The Lockman Foundation: Lahabra, CA

9.9 *New American Standard Bible*: 1995 update. 1995 (Job 1:9-12) The Lockman Foundation: Lahabra, CA

9.10 *Holy Bible, The New Open Bible™ Study Edition NASB.* copyright © 1990 Thomas Nelson, Inc., Nashville, TN "The Time of Job" p. 575

9.11 *Holy Bible, The New Open Bible® Large Print Edition New King James Version.* copyright © 1990, 1985, 1983 Thomas Nelson, Inc., Nashville, TN p.18

9.12 *Holy Bible, The New Open Bible™ Study Edition NASB.* copyright © 1990 Thomas Nelson, Inc. Nashville, TN p. 2

9.13 *Illustrated Dictionary of the Bible.* Herbert Lockyer, SR., Editor, with F. F. Bruce and R. K. Harrison, Copyright © 1986 Thomas Nelson Publishers, Nashville TN p. 512

9.14 *Illustrated Dictionary of the Bible.* Herbert Lockyer, SR., Editor, with F. F. Bruce and R. K. Harrison, Copyright © 1986 Thomas Nelson Publishers, Nashville TN p. 512

9.15 *New American Standard Bible*: 1995 update. 1995 (Gen. 48:28) The Lockman Foundation: Lahabra, CA

9.16 *New American Standard Bible*: 1995 update. 1995 (Gen. 50:26) The Lockman Foundation: Lahabra, CA

9.17 *New American Standard Bible*: 1995 update. 1995 (Gen. 12:4) The Lockman Foundation: Lahabra, CA

9.18 *Encarta ® World English Dictionary.* copyright 1998-

2004 Microsoft Corp.

9.19 Strong, James. *Strong's Exhaustive Concordance of the Bible*. © 1890 James Strong, Madison, NJ p. 412

9.20 *New American Standard Bible*: 1995 update. 1995 (Job 3:15) The Lockman Foundation: Lahabra, CA

9.21 *New American Standard Bible*: 1995 update. 1995 (Job 22:24-25) The Lockman Foundation: Lahabra, CA

9.22 Strong, James. *Strong's Exhaustive Concordance of the Bible*. © 1890 James Strong, Madison, NJ p. 23 (Hebrew)

9.23 *New American Standard Bible*: 1995 update. 1995 (Job 28:15) The Lockman Foundation: Lahabra, CA

9.24 Strong, James. *Strong's Exhaustive Concordance of the Bible*. © 1890 James Strong, Madison, NJ p. 82 (Hebrew)

9.25 *Holy Bible, The New Open Bible® Large Print Edition New King James Version.* copyright © 1990, 1985, 1983 Thomas Nelson, Inc., Nashville, TN p. 586

9.26 *New American Standard Bible*: 1995 update. 1995 (Gen. 11:28) The Lockman Foundation: Lahabra, CA

9.27 *Illustrated Dictionary of the Bible*. Herbert Lockyer, SR., Editor, with F. F. Bruce and R. K. Harrison, Copyright © 1986 Thomas Nelson Publishers, Nashville TN p. 215

9.28 *Illustrated Dictionary of the Bible*. Herbert Lockyer, SR., Editor, with F. F. Bruce and R. K. Harrison, Copyright © 1986 Thomas Nelson Publishers, Nashville TN p. 215

9.29 *New American Standard Bible*: 1995 update. 1995 (Neh. 9:7) The Lockman Foundation: Lahabra, CA

9.30 *New American Standard Bible*: 1995 update. 1995 (Gen. 11:31) The Lockman Foundation: Lahabra, CA

9.31 *Holy Bible, The New Open Bible™ Study Edition NASB.* copyright © 1990 Thomas Nelson, Inc., Nashville, TN Genesis Timeline p. 65

9.32 *Illustrated Dictionary of the Bible*. Herbert Lockyer, SR., Editor, with F. F. Bruce and R. K. Harrison, Copyright © 1986 Thomas Nelson Publishers, Nashville TN p. 1082

9.33 *Ancienthistoryencyclopedia.com*

9.34 *Holy Bible, The New Open Bible® Large Print Edition New King James Version.* copyright © 1990, 1985, 1983 Thomas Nelson, Inc., Nashville, TN "Date of Creation" p. 2

9.35 *New American Standard Bible*: 1995 update. 1995 (Gen. 5:5) The Lockman Foundation: Lahabra, CA

9.36 Strong, James. *Strong's Exhaustive Concordance of the Bible.* © 1890 James Strong, Madison, NJ p. 57 (Hebrew)

9.37 Strong, James. *Strong's Exhaustive Concordance of the Bible.* © 1890 James Strong, Madison, NJ p. 57 (Hebrew)

9.38 *Encarta ® World English Dictionary.* copyright 1998-2004 Microsoft Corp.

9.39 Strong, James. *Strong's Exhaustive Concordance of the Bible.* © 1890 James Strong, Madison, NJ p. 58 (Hebrew)

9.40 *New American Standard Bible*: 1995 update. 1995 (Job 4:12-16) The Lockman Foundation: Lahabra, CA

9.41 *Holy Bible, The New Open Bible® Large Print Edition New King James Version.* copyright © 1990, 1985, 1983 Thomas Nelson, Inc., Nashville, TN Job p. 589-590

9.42 Strong, James. *Strong's Exhaustive Concordance of the Bible* © 1890 James Strong, Madison, NJ pp. 9, 10 (Hebrew)

# Third Intermission

I3.1 Martin Schwartz. *Amateur Radio Theory Course.* Copyright 1981 The AMECO Publishing Corp., Williston, NY pp. 28-29

I3.2 *Textbook of Medical Physiology.* Sixth Edition, Arthur C. Guyton, M.D. © 1981 W. B. Saunders Company, Philadelphia, PA p. 104

I3.3 *Textbook of Medical Physiology.* Sixth Edition, Arthur C. Guyton, M.D. © 1981 W. B. Saunders Company, Philadelphia, PA p. 106

I3.4 *Textbook of Medical Physiology.* Sixth Edition, Arthur C. Guyton, M.D. © 1981 W. B. Saunders Company,

Philadelphia, PA p. 568

13.5 Robert A. Heinlein. *Waldo*, copyright 1940, 1942, 1950, 1951, Robert A. Heinlein. Copyright 1951 World Additions Inc., Doubleday and Co., Garden City, NY pp. 268-269

# Chapter 10

10.1 *New American Standard Bible*: 1995 update. 1995 (Gen. 3:1) The Lockman Foundation: Lahabra, CA

10.2 *New American Standard Bible*: 1995 update. 1995 (Rev. 12:7-9) The Lockman Foundation: Lahabra, CA

10.3 Strong, James. *Strong's Exhaustive Concordance of the Bible*. © 1890 James Strong, Madison, NJ p. 53 (Greek)

10.4 *New American Standard Bible*: 1995 update. 1995 (Luke 10:18) The Lockman Foundation: Lahabra, CA

10.5 *New American Standard Bible*: 1995 update. 1995 (1Peter 5:8) The Lockman Foundation: Lahabra, CA

10.6 *New American Standard Bible*: 1995 update. 1995 (Luke 1:26) The Lockman Foundation: Lahabra, CA

10.7 *New American Standard Bible*: 1995 update. 1995 (Matt. 1:20) The Lockman Foundation: Lahabra, CA

10.8 *New American Standard Bible*: 1995 update. 1995 (Job 1:7) The Lockman Foundation: Lahabra, CA

10.9 *New American Standard Bible*: 1995 update. 1995 (Job 2:3) The Lockman Foundation: Lahabra, CA

10.10 *New American Standard Bible*: 1995 update. 1995 (Is. 14:15-17) The Lockman Foundation: Lahabra, CA

10.11 *New American Standard Bible*: 1995 update. 1995 (Eph. 6:12) The Lockman Foundation: Lahabra, CA

10.12 Strong, James. *Strong's Exhaustive Concordance of the Bible*. © 1890 James Strong, Madison, NJ p. 43 (Greek)

10.13 *New American Standard Bible*: 1995 update. 1995 (Prov. 29:27) The Lockman Foundation: Lahabra, CA

10.14 *New American Standard Bible*: 1995 update. 1995 (Gen. 6:4) The Lockman Foundation: Lahabra, CA

10.15 Strong, James. *Strong's Exhaustive Concordance of the Bible*. © 1890 James Strong, Madison, NJ p.79 (Hebrew)

10.16 *Interlinear Bible Hebrew Greek English, 1 Volume edition.* © 1976, 1977, 1978, 1979, 1980, 1981, 1984. Second Edition, © 1986 Jay P. Green, Sr., Hendrickson Publishers (Gen. 6:4) p.5

10.17 *New American Standard Bible*: 1995 update. 1995 (Ex. 20:4) The Lockman Foundation: Lahabra, CA

10.18 Strong, James. *Strong's Exhaustive Concordance of the Bible*. © 1890 James Strong, Madison, NJ p.124 (Hebrew)

10.19 *Chambers Dictionary of Etymology*. Copyright © 1988 The H. W. Wilson Company, New York, NY p.422

10.20 *New American Standard Bible*: 1995 update. 1995 (1Sam. 17:4) The Lockman Foundation: Lahabra, CA

10.21 *New American Standard Bible*: 1995 update. 1995 (Luke 26:33) The Lockman Foundation: Lahabra, CA

10.22 *New American Standard Bible*: 1995 update. 1995 (Luke 11:24) The Lockman Foundation: Lahabra, CA

# Chapter 11

11.1 *New American Standard Bible*: 1995 update. 1995 (Luke 22:39-46) The Lockman Foundation: Lahabra, CA

11.2 *New American Standard Bible*: 1995 update. 1995 (John 13:25-27) The Lockman Foundation: Lahabra, CA

11.3 *New American Standard Bible*: 1995 update. 1995 (John 18:4-6) The Lockman Foundation: Lahabra, CA

11.4 *New American Standard Bible*: 1995 update. 1995 (Lev. 16:20-27) The Lockman Foundation: Lahabra, CA

11.5 *New American Standard Bible*: 1995 update. 1995 (Is. 53:5) The Lockman Foundation:   Lahabra, CA

11.6 *Interlinear Bible Hebrew   Greek English, 1 Volume*

*edition*. © 1976, 1977, 1978, 1979, 1980, 1981, 1984. Second Edition, © 1986 Jay P. Green, Sr., Hendrickson Publishers (Is. 53:5) p.572

11.7 Strong, James. *Strong's Exhaustive Concordance of the Bible*. © 1890 James Strong, Madison, NJ p.36 (Hebrew)

11.8 Strong, James. *Strong's Exhaustive Concordance of the Bible*. © 1890 James Strong, Madison, NJ p.36 (Hebrew)

11.9 Strong, James. *Strong's Exhaustive Concordance of the Bible*. © 1890 James Strong, Madison, NJ p.110 (Hebrew)

11.10 *New American Standard Bible*: 1995 update. 1995 (Prov. 20:30) The Lockman Foundation: Lahabra, CA

11.11 *Interlinear Bible Hebrew Greek English, 1 Volume edition*. © 1976, 1977, 1978, 1979, 1980, 1981, 1984. Second Edition, © 1986 Jay P. Green, Sr., Hendrickson Publishers (Prov. 20:30) p.522

11.12 *Interlinear Bible Hebrew Greek English, 1 Volume edition*. © 1976, 1977, 1978, 1979, 1980, 1981, 1984. Second Edition, © 1986 Jay P. Green, Sr., Hendrickson Publishers p. 522

11.13 Strong, James. *Strong's Exhaustive Concordance of the Bible*. © 1890 James Strong, Madison, NJ p.125 (Hebrew)

11.14 *New American Standard Bible*: 1995 update. 1995 (Mal. 3:2) The Lockman Foundation: Lahabra, CA

11.15 Strong, James. *Strong's Exhaustive Concordance of the Bible*. © 1890 James Strong, Madison, NJ p.54 (Hebrew)

11.16 *New American Standard Bible*: 1995 update. 1995 (Matt 27:45) The Lockman Foundation: Lahabra, CA

11.17 *Wikipedia.com*

11.18 *Mreclipse.com*

11.19 Strong, James. *Strong's Exhaustive Concordance of the Bible*. © 1890 James Strong, Madison, NJ p. 65 (Greek)

11.20 *Holy Bible, The New Open Bible™ Study Edition NASB*. copyright © 1990 Thomas Nelson, Inc. Nashville, TN p.1545

11.21 *New American Standard Bible*: 1995 update. 1995 (Mark 15:25) The Lockman Foundation: Lahabra, CA

11.22 *New American Standard Bible*: 1995 update. 1995 (John 19:14-15) The Lockman Foundation: Lahabra, CA
11.23 *New American Standard Bible*: 1995 update. 1995 (John 19:26) The Lockman Foundation: Lahabra, CA
11.24 *New American Standard Bible*: 1995 update. 1995 (John 19:31-34) The Lockman Foundation: Lahabra, CA
11.25 *New American Standard Bible*: 1995 update. 1995 (Deut 21:22-23) The Lockman Foundation: Lahabra, CA
11.26 *New American Standard Bible*: 1995 update. 1995 (Matt. 12:40) The Lockman Foundation: Lahabra, CA
11.27 *New American Standard Bible*: 1995 update. 1995 (John 20:1) The Lockman Foundation: Lahabra, CA
11.28 *New American Standard Bible*: 1995 update. 1995 (Mark 15:42-44) The Lockman Foundation: Lahabra, CA
11.29 *Comparative Study Bible, Revised Edition*. Copyright © 1999 The Zondervan Corporation, Grand Rapids, MI (KJV) (Mark 15:42-44)
11.30 *New American Standard Bible*: 1995 update. 1995 (Luke 23:42-43) The Lockman Foundation: Lahabra, CA
11.31 *New American Standard Bible*: 1995 update. 1995 (John 20:17) The Lockman Foundation: Lahabra, CA
11.32 *New American Standard Bible*: 1995 update. 1995 (Acts 1:3) The Lockman Foundation: Lahabra, CA
11.33 *New American Standard Bible*: 1995 update. 1995 (Matt. 27:50-54) The Lockman Foundation: Lahabra, CA
11.34 Strong, James. *Strong's Exhaustive Concordance of the Bible*. © 1890 James Strong, Madison, NJ p.40 (Greek)
11.35 *New American Standard Bible*: 1995 update. 1995 (Ex. 26:31-33) The Lockman Foundation: Lahabra, CA
11.36 *Interlinear Bible Hebrew Greek English, 1 Volume edition*. © 1976, 1977, 1978, 1979, 1980, 1981, 1984. Second Edition, © 1986 Jay P. Green, Sr., Hendrickson Publishers (Matt. 27:51) p.765
11.37 Strong, James. *Strong's Exhaustive Concordance of the Bible*. © 1890 James Strong, Madison, NJ p. 34 (Greek)
11.38 *Holy Bible, The New Open Bible™ Study Edition NASB*.

copyright © 1990 Thomas Nelson, Inc., Nashville, TN p. 114

11.39 *New American Standard Bible*: 1995 update. 1995 (Luke 4:5-7) The Lockman Foundation: Lahabra, CA

11.40 Strong, James. *Strong's Exhaustive Concordance of the Bible*. © 1890 James Strong, Madison, NJ p. 64 (Greek)

11.41 Strong, James. *Strong's Exhaustive Concordance of the Bible*. © 1890 James Strong, Madison, NJ p. 20 (Greek)

11.42 Strong, James. *Strong's Exhaustive Concordance of the Bible*. © 1890 James Strong, Madison, NJ p. 64 (Greek)

11.43 *New American Standard Bible*: 1995 update. 1995 (Eph. 4:9-10) The Lockman Foundation: Lahabra, CA

11.44 Strong, James. *Strong's Exhaustive Concordance of the Bible*. © 1890 James Strong, Madison, NJ p. 70 (Greek)

11.45 Strong, James. *Strong's Exhaustive Concordance of the Bible*. © 1890 James Strong, Madison, NJ p. 48 (Greek)

11.46 Strong, James. *Strong's Exhaustive Concordance of the Bible*. © 1890 James Strong, Madison, NJ p. 70 (Greek)

11.47 Strong, James. *Strong's Exhaustive Concordance of the Bible*. © 1890 James Strong, Madison, NJ p. 7 (Greek)

11.48 Strong, James. *Strong's Exhaustive Concordance of the Bible*. © 1890 James Strong, Madison, NJ p. 42 (Greek)

11.49 Strong, James. *Strong's Exhaustive Concordance of the Bible*. © 1890 James Strong, Madison, NJ p. 25 (Greek)

11.50 *Illustrated Dictionary of the Bible*. Herbert Lockyer, SR., Editor, with F. F. Bruce and R. K. Harrison, Copyright © 1986 Thomas Nelson Publishers, Nashville TN, p. 267

11.51 *New American Standard Bible*: 1995 update. 1995 (Luke 23:48) The Lockman Foundation: Lahabra, CA

11.52 Strong, James. *Strong's Exhaustive Concordance of the Bible*. © 1890 James Strong, Madison, NJ p. 73 (Greek)

11.53 *Illustrated Dictionary of the Bible*. Herbert Lockyer, SR., Editor, with F. F. Bruce and R. K. Harrison, Copyright © 1986 by Thomas Nelson Publishers, Nashville TN, p. 191

11.54 *New American Standard Bible*: 1995 update. 1995 (Luke 18:13) The Lockman Foundation: Lahabra, CA

## Chapter 12

12.1 *New American Standard Bible*: 1995 update. 1995 (Mal. 3:1) The Lockman Foundation: Lahabra, CA
12.2 *New American Standard Bible*: 1995 update. 1995 (Mal. 4:5) The Lockman Foundation: Lahabra, CA
12.3 *New American Standard Bible*: 1995 update. 1995 (Matt. 17:10-13) The Lockman Foundation: Lahabra, CA
12.4 *New American Standard Bible*: 1995 update. 1995 (Matt. 11:7-14) The Lockman Foundation: Lahabra, CA
12.5 *New American Standard Bible*: 1995 update. 1995 (2Kings 2:11) The Lockman Foundation: Lahabra, CA
12.6 *New American Standard Bible*: 1995 update. 1995 (Luke 1:5-20) The Lockman Foundation: Lahabra, CA
12.7 Strong, James. *Strong's Exhaustive Concordance of the Bible*. © 1890 James Strong, Madison, NJ p. 58 (Greek)
12.8 Strong, James. *Strong's Exhaustive Concordance of the Bible*. © 1890 James Strong, Madison, NJ p. 24 (Greek)
12.9 *Interlinear Bible Hebrew Greek English, 1 Volume edition*. © 1976, 1977, 1978, 1979, 1980, 1981, 1984. Second Edition, © 1986 Jay P. Green, Sr., Hendrickson Publishers p. 786
12.10 *New American Standard Bible*: 1995 update. 1995 (John 9:1-5) The Lockman Foundation: Lahabra, CA
12.11 Strong, James. *Strong's Exhaustive Concordance of the Bible*. © 1890 James Strong, Madison, NJ p. 10 (Greek)
12.12 *New American Standard Bible*: 1995 update. 1995 (Matt. 16:13-16) The Lockman Foundation: Lahabra, CA
12.13 *Merriam-Webster.com*
12.14 *New American Standard Bible*: 1995 update. 1995 (John

1:21) The Lockman Foundation: Lahabra, CA
12.15 *New American Standard Bible*: 1995 update. 1995 (Heb. 9:27-28) The Lockman Foundation: Lahabra, CA
12.16 Strong, James. *Strong's Exhaustive Concordance of the Bible.* © 1890 James Strong, Madison, NJ p.14 (Greek)
12.17 *Interlinear Bible Hebrew Greek English, 1 Volume edition.* © 1976, 1977, 1978, 1979, 1980, 1981, 1984. Second Edition, © 1986 Jay P. Green, Sr., Hendrickson Publishers p. 933 (Heb. 9:27

# About the Title

AT1 *Chambers Dictionary of Etymology.* Copyright © 1988 The H. W. Wilson Company, New York, NY p.648
AT2 *www.kingjamesbibleonline.org* (KJV) (Matt.5:5) retrieved June 2011
AT3 *www.kingjamesbibleonline.org* (KJV) (Ps. 25:9) retrieved June 2011
AT4 *www.kingjamesbibleonline.org* (KJV) (Ps. 147:6) retrieved June 2011
AT5 *www.kingjamesbibleonline.org* (KJV) (Ps. 76:9) retrieved June 2011
AT6 *www.kingjamesbibleonline.org* (KJV) (Mark 6:52) retrieved June 2011
AT7 *www.kingjamesbibleonline.org* (KJV) (Mark 8:17) retrieved June 2011
AT8 *www.kingjamesbibleonline.org* (KJV) (John 12:40) retrieved June 2011
AT9 *www.kingjamesbibleonline.org* (KJV) (Neh. 9:16) retrieved June 2011
AT10 *www.kingjamesbibleonline.org* (KJV) (Prov. 28:14) retrieved June 2011
AT11 *www.kingjamesbibleonline.org* (KJV) (Prov. 29:1) retrieved June 2011

AT12 Strong, James. *Strong's Exhaustive Concordance of the Bible*. © 1890 James Strong, Madison, NJ p. 63 (Greek)

MEEKRAKER *Beginnings…*

www.ingramcontent.com/pod-product-compliance
Lightning Source LLC
Chambersburg PA
CBHW020056020526
44112CB00031B/192